Islamic Psychology - Integrative Dialogue

Islamic Psychology and Biopsychological Basics of Life in Education and Health

Dian Sari Utami, Emi Zulaifah, Marcus Stueck (eds.)

Volume 1

PETER LANG

Wanadya Ayu Krisna Dewi, Emi Zulaifah,
Dian Sari Utami, Marcus Stueck (eds.)

Islamic Psychology - Integrative Dialogue

Psychology, Spirituality, Science and Arts

PETER LANG

Bibliographic Information published by the Deutsche Nationalbibliothek
The Deutsche Nationalbibliothek lists this publication in the Deutsche Nationalbibliografie; detailed bibliographic data is available online at http://dnb.d-nb.de.

Library of Congress Cataloging-in-Publication Data
A CIP catalog record for this book has been applied for at the Library of Congress.

ISBN 978-3-631-87603-9 (Print)
E-ISBN 978-3-631-87658-9 (E-PDF)
E-ISBN 978-3-631-87659-6 (EPUB)
DOI 10.3726/b19627

Peter Lang – Berlin · Bern · Bruxelles · New York · Oxford · Warszawa · Wien

This publication has been peer reviewed.

www.peterlang.com

Emi Zulaifah

PREFACE
Islamic Psychology: An Overview of a Discipline and Its Current Development

Bismillahirrahmanirrahiim. In the name of God, the most beneficent, the most merciful.

This writing is intended to give an overview of Islamic Psychology, which, in the last decades receive an immense attention and interest from Muslim Psychologists around the world. To name a few of the developments is the successful event of Islamic Psychology conference, held in many parts of the world, especially in Indonesia, through its professional association. Furthermore, an international body called International Association of Muslim Psychologists was successful in conducting five conferences, held in different countries, with the last one held in 2016 in Yogyakarta Indonesia before the pandemic, and in 2022 through online meetings. Along with the major conference and congress of IAMP, a few smaller conferences were independently organized in India, Russia, Pakistan, and Indonesia, between the years 2018 to 2021.

This book is a collection of articles written and presented at one of the conferences organized by Universitas Islam Indonesia (UII), in 2018. The conference was held in collaboration with the Bionet Network, to foster dialog between Islamic Psychology and the various perspectives in Psychology. Prior to the collaboration with Bionet, with the direction of Prof. Dr. Marcus Stueck, three consecutive conferences were held in 2015, 2016 and 2017. UII has always been one of the institutions in the forefront in developing Islamic Psychology through research, community engagement and research dissemination. In its latest development, the conference is open for Psychologists especially Muslim Psychologists from around the world and are welcoming various collaboration for the purpose of bridging dialog between Islamic Psychology and other school of thoughts and different perspectives of psychology. This book is a collection of research articles from such a convention held in Yogyakarta. The conference became a unique forum that disseminated research from Biopsychology and Islamic Psychology, with speakers coming from Indonesia, Germany, Australia, and the UK.

It is my responsibility as one of the steering committees of the Islamic Psychology and Bionet conference, to provide a brief overview of Islamic

Psychology. In this opportunity I would try to touch on some subtopics on the main principles in Islamic Psychology, the method of inquiry, its applications and research studies that have been developed so far.

1. Islamic Psychology: Developing Human Beings, Building Society

In the discourse of modern psychology, Islamic Psychology is an endeavor that answers the concerns of many Muslim psychologists in the world (Badri, 1979) who feel that modern science could isolate them from their belief related to their core identity as God's creation. For people who believe in God, emphasizing that such belief is a taboo in the scientific understanding about a human being, will impact on the way people view themselves, their relationships with God (Badri, 2020), with others, and the natural surroundings. In Islam, the perspective on the self and the surrounding environment has clear theological foundations, can be traced in their holy book, and are described in the narrations about attitudes, actions and examples given by the Prophet Muhammad- peace be upon him. Alienating the Supreme Being from these relationships will eventually strip the essence of their faith. Furthermore, it has always been clear for every devout Muslim that scientific inquiry as an attempt to understand the law and work of nature and life does not have to put aside the Creator. The Quran explained in the following verses, as translated by Khattab (2018) and cited by Auda (2021) in the online lecture series of understanding Quran with Muslims Association of Canada:

> *Verily, in the creation of the skies and the earth, and the alternation of night and day, and the ships that run in the seas with what benefits people, and what Allah has sent down from the sky of water so He revived with it the earth after its death and spread within it from every treading creature, and the dispensation of winds and the enabling clouds between the sky and the earth, are signs for a people that reason (2:164).*
> *And of His signs that He created you from earth, then [be- hold] you are human beings proliferating (30:21).*
> *And of His signs is that He created for you mates of your beings [essence] that you may find tranquillity with them and placed between you friendship and mercy. Verily, in this are signs for a people who think (30:22).*
> *And of His signs is the creation of the skies and the earth and the difference of your tongues [languages] and your colours. Verily, in this are signs for the knowers (30:23).*

Bakhtiar (2002) stated that although Islamic Psychology and mainstream Psychology similarly focused on describing emotions, behavior and cognition, "*Islamic Psychology includes metaphysics, theology, cosmology and natural science as the basis of the underlying principle for what we feel, do or think.*" It becomes comprehensive and non-partial in understanding human beings. The material and metaphysical element of the human life now is known in the Maqasid approach (Purpose based approach) as those of the observed (shahada) or seen reality on which we can have access for direct observation and the unseen reality despite its existence, as some creations fall into this category. Included in this unseen reality is the hereafter, the angels, as stated in the pillars of faith of Islam, and of course the Real One, that is God.

The attempt to explain human Psychology had begun early for Muslims. If tracing of its history must be done, then some early works will appear to the forefront. Over one thousand years ago from the work of Al Balkhi (Sustenance of the Body and Soul) from the 9th century we can learn how mental balance may be achieved. This work has surprised many Psychologists and Psychiatrists today (Awaad and Ali, 2016) as Al Balkhi, a physician in profession, described in detail the type of prevention from and treatment of psychological diseases, which resemble todays much appraised cognitive behavioral therapy (Badri, 2013), or from the work of Abu Hamid Muhammad Al Ghazzali, the Alchemy of happiness from the 10th century. Again, in her explanation on the works of Al Ghazzali, one of the many Muslim scholars who wrote extensively on the issues of Psychology in the first millennium, Bakhtiar further noted that:

> *"The basis for the understanding of self is the Tawhid, Monotheism. A monotheist (hanif or following a straight path) like Al Ghazzali, sees the entire universe as a single entity… Everything comes from God and will return to Him. While a multitheist (mushrik) sees the world as a collection of diverse and full of divisions, contradictions, and heterogeneity, includes various poles that are free and contradictory, unconnected desires, habits, goals, desires, gender, sect, color, race, class and faith. "*

In Islam, humans like other creatures are clearly said to be the creation of God (Allah), subject to His laws that are laid out in nature and life, and that these divine statements are recorded in the holy book. There will be a time when humans will return to Allah, their Creator. The centrality of a Muslim's belief in Allah dictates an intellectual inquiry that does not distance him from God, on the contrary it becomes a way to understand the Creator.

As mentioned by Auda (2021) in one online lecture on the Maqasid methodology, if it must be defined in one word related to knowledge in Islam, then "it is a way to know Allah (Makrifatullah)." Based on this highest purpose, scientific endeavors are translated to the next noble purpose of revelation: such as spreading maslaha (good doings), justice, mercy, defending the poor/ the weak, protection of life to ensure a regeneration and so on. Further in his book he stated that the highest purpose of scientific and intellectual engagement is to worship God, whose knowledge is all encompassing. When the origin and destination of a Muslim is from and will return to Allah, then it becomes very important for him to know who the Being is, to whom all creatures will ultimately return. This sentence has also been stated by Bakhtiar (2002) in his introduction to the translation of Al Ghazzali's much known book of the Alchemy of Happiness. Religion is one of the points that in time will lead to our Center and origin. Religion-based psychology (in this case Islam) thus has the aim of "helping individuals and human societies to find that Center when we are preparing to return to our origins." A beautiful statement related to the premise of the centrality of God can be found in the Quran, in Surah Al Hasyr, verse 18. "O believers! Be mindful of Allah and let every soul look to what deeds' it has sent forth for tomorrow." This statement is then continued to verse 19: "And do not be like those who forgot Allah, so He made them forget themselves…"

The instructions for learning and gaining knowledge that is sign based ('ilm) are made very clear in the Qur'an. Prophet Muhammad, peace be upon him, stated that it is "obligatory for every Muslim to seek knowledge." Achieving knowledge, reflecting, and understanding the universe is a goal that must be seriously pursued, up to going through the process and making use of the results, for the wider societies. As a matter of fact, in Muneim's study of the semantic networks in the Quran, the term 'Ilm (knowledge) comes from the same root word of 'a, la, ma in Arabic and exist in connection with the words Al 'Alim (The All Knowing, source of knowledge – God), Al 'Alam (the universe, where the signs are laid for the human to learn and understand), 'Ilm (sign based knowledge), Muta'alim (human- as the learner of knowledge), and Mu'allim (the deliverer of knowledge). 'Ilm, or the sign-based knowledge are thus something that every Muslim are called for as they start to understand the holly book. In our understanding, when we think of the term knowledge, this is something that must be sign based, and there are statements in the Quran which emphasize this sign-based precondition for acceptance of knowledge, a subtopic that will be explained further.

This element of the purpose (Maqasid) of acquiring knowledge is highly emphasized, because it becomes our basis in evaluating the quality of the knowledge produced. The purpose of worshiping God has an ethical consequence in how we conduct our ikhtiar (endeavors) in knowledge searching and building. God is the place where all creation returns, and by Him they will be held accountable for their actions when they lived on earth, including learning, and producing knowledge. This basic belief makes Islamic Psychology develop principles which in certain respects have similarities with science in general but shows its comprehensive side because they include what Bakhtiar (2002) mentioned above. Furthermore, the centrality of God in this basic belief makes the Islamic definition of science unique and authentic. This belief is the basis for laying down the holy book as an inspiration to learn and develop endless knowledge from the exploration of nature and life. The Quran stated that:

> *And if all the trees on earth were pens and the ocean were ink, with seven oceans behind it to add to its (supply) yet would not the words of Allah be exhausted (in the writing): For Allah is Exalted in Power, full of wisdom.* (Surah Luqman, verses 27).

In the view of Islam, the holy book is not something that hinder Muslim from pondering and contemplating. The Quran clearly glorifies intelligence, observation of nature, as well as the life of society and human beings in general. For many believing Muslims, knowledge that will alienate them from God will not provide complete enlightenment and complete benefit. Based on such beliefs, Islamic Psychology was developed as a unique science (sign-based knowledge). From several tracings of Islamic scholarship (Iqbal, 2009; Koenig and Shohaib, 2014; Saliba, 2007), Muneim (2018) proposed the scientific endeavor concept through the Maqasid (arabic word meaning purpose) approach. He identified some principles that can be summarized as follow:

1. ʻAlamātiyyah or Sign-Based Knowledge
   The first characteristic of the epistemology of the Maqasid Quran is that it is based on signs/verses or evidence or signs. Verses in the Quran were many that instruct the believers to find signs/ evidence of the presence of God through nature, social relations and from within themselves.
2. Comprehensive, rooted, and integrated knowledge
   This principle is negating the partiality in knowledge building. In the Quran, we can find more verses related to existence than the stated signs (that is the verses from the Quran). The message brought by the Prophet is to understand the signs that show the beautiful and perfect names and attributes of God. The signs are related to the universe, natural environment, psycho-social nature, as well as the material/ man made environment. The integration will involve the thorough observations by different means pertaining to human modalities, as well as different faculties of human intellect, such as analyzing and synthesizing, all the way to achieving *hikma* (wisdom and understanding).
3. Muzakkāh- purified knowledge that allows for growth
   Building knowledge in Islam must allow for growth *(tazkiyah-tazakkah)* for the individual and communities at large. The verb "zakā" in Arabic has two related meanings (1) to grow, (2) to purify. These two meanings can be

interpreted as two complementary processes, to grow in sustainable ways, the development process must periodically be purified/purified.

Tazkiyah is basically an ideal relationship between humans and their psychological environment. For knowledge to grow, knowledge must be purified otherwise it will be like bubbles/foam that will be easily loosened/ broken. A heart that is less pious is more likely to fail in making knowledge that is sign-based, rooted, comprehensive and purified.

4. *'Arabiyyah*, Arabic-based knowledge

Auda (2021) stated that the arabic requirement in developing knowledge has nothing to do with race and ethnicities, but it represents language with systematic characteristics. In the Maqasid perspective, Muneim (2018) exposed that Arabic supports three characteristics of Quranic Science, namely: 1) Sign understanding: Bayaan (exposition), ilm (comprehending signs) and tafsil (differentiation). 2). 'Aql (confirming relationship), especially when it comes to formulating and integration of knowledge. 3) Taqwa (to keep away/ avoid wickedness and to engage in goodness), and hikma (to gain wisdom), as it relates to the third principle of muzakka (purified knowledge). In one of the discussion series of prophetic science at Gadjah Mada University (Masjid Kampus UGM, 2021), Bagus Riyono stated that the reference to Arabic is important so that concepts in science can describe a clear meaning and represent a reality in its essence. However, dissemination of knowledge is a different area that will need to consider the local language, so that the new understanding would connect to the particular contexts and issues.

2. The Nafs, the Core Concept in Islamic Psychology

An important concept that is understood in Islam as a concept that represents human psychology is Al Nafs (The Nafs). In Arabic the words Nafs means the following: most essential identity, precious and sought after and at the same time it has the same root as breath/ breathing (Nafas), a very basic sign of living in the life of human as explained by Muneim in one discussion series of Maqasid Institute in December 2019. Muneim's explanation is deemed important as his competency as a linguist, a native Arabic and a Maqasid scholar of today. Therefore, understanding the Nafs is something very important, which is essentially related to biological state, and defines the identity of a person. The literal definition of the word Nafs is the Soul/ Self. It is interesting to know that the word Psyche, Bakhtiar (2002) revealed, means soul. Psychology, coming from the Greek words Psyche (the Soul) and logos (the word of God). In its original meaning, it is the study of the word of God within the human soul.

In studying the Nafs in the Islamic scientific tradition, one does not stop at Nafs as an object. Like many other disciplines that are based on the Quran, in the Maqasid approach, Psychology would serve a higher purpose of building and strengthening the society and civilization. Humans with their Nafs will eventually interact with the environment, influence, and respond to, and are affected by the external context from the environment. Helping the people to build sound Nafs for such a purpose and existence then is very valuable. Thus, in Islamic Psychology the next task is formulating principles on how to develop the Nafs. From here, the term Tazkiat Al Nafs (Tazkiyatun Nafs) emerges, a very important concept in Islamic Psychology related to self-development/ growth which was already discussed above and will be explained more in the next part. Furthermore, the establishment of Akhlaqul Karimah, the Moral excellence, is the goal of fostering oneself through tazkia.

3. Structuring the Study of Nafs

In the many disciplines that the Quran and Sunnah becomes their basis and provide guidance in their understanding, the following three elements taken from Auda (2021), and Muneim (2018) need to be considered, to produce sign based, integrated – deeply rooted, and purified knowledge:

- **Maudhu/Object**

Maudhu, is the object of the study. This will have to be clearly defined. Understanding of the object of the study requires that one will delve into it in depth (tafaqquh) and comprehensively. Object of the study would extend to areas that are observed in the people. One thing is certain that Quranic based knowledge will always see the Nafs in relations within its context, namely with God, with the natural environment, with her/himself, with others and with the material/ man-made environment. Comprehensiveness, when using the Quran as the inspiration for conceptual formulation may be achieved when the concept is based not only on a few verses, but all of the relevant verses that are related to the issue being studied. For this purpose, the researcher needs to read thoroughly from cover to cover as they try to find out on how the Quran explains the specific issue/s.

- **Method/Manhaj**

Islamic Psychology allows for at least three areas of development and observation namely: theoretical and conceptual building, observation of phenomena and application of theories and concepts.

When moving at the conceptual level, placing the Quran as a source for model development is highly recommended. However, it requires discipline to understand its network of concepts, and thus mastery in Arabic Quran becomes necessary. Problems will arise when interested Islamic Psychology researchers do not have sufficient Arabic language skills. To complement such a situation, the concept development is done in collaboration with experts of the Quranic language.

Some will ask why then it becomes so important to extract Quranic concepst. This brings us to the basic belief about science/ signs-based knowledge in Islam: that the verses of the Quran are the spoken signs from God, and in the end the One perfect in knowledge is Allah, so that the Book that He revealed needs to be understood at all times by knowing the tools to understand it correctly. Tracing the Quran without sufficient knowledge as the basis, in the belief of Muslim scholars, could lead to misunderstandings. This is regrettable, because this is what often happens to this day so that mistakes in understanding the religion of Islam occur. In detail, Auda (2021) explained that different levels of effort are suited to the level of knowledge that a researcher would like to produce.

- **Maqasid/Purpose**

It is about purpose. Every scientific endeavor will bear a certain goal. At the beginning of starting his scientific endeavors, a Muslim scholar should have a clear intention. In the process of learning and producing knowledge, the orientation towards Maslaha (principle of beneficial outcome for the larger entities, or common good) need to be there to begin with. The type of knowledge that is produced, learned, and practiced, thus must be rightly and thoroughly formulated, and is oriented to common good. Knowledge that harms life and the balance of the living environments should be avoided, because in the end someone who has knowledge will be responsible for it in front of his Lord. The intent will also become the basis for justification as to whether what the scientist is doing really has significance, shows necessity, and answers well the problems of his communities. We will find that some psychological research may not answer the important, critical, and fundamental questions in life and the problems of the people that live in it.

Further explanation of benefits and common goods may relate with the following principles: 1) The benefits for the many can only be achieved when knowledge offers its application element. The application of knowledge is essential as the foundation for building beneficial knowledge. It is even become the famous mission of Universitas Islam Indonesia, that is "To gain knowledge to emulate them in our acts/ conduct, and to act on the foundation of evidence/ sign-based knowledge." 2) The right application should be based on sound conceptual ground. For the knowledge learner and producer to rightly apply the knowledge, then practices/ applications need to be based on a sound and comprehensive concept. And lastly 3) A right and comprehensive concept will not be produced unless the scholar and scientist engage in Tazkiyatun Nafs, a process of self-purification that would impact the quality of the knowledge produced.

4. Al Nafs: A Concept in Context

In the Maqasid approach, an object of study will never stand alone, but it will have a relationship with the context it faces. Something is present in a system; this system is interdependent and has a purpose. Al Nafs as a concept of Psychology derived from the scriptures, cannot be seen as a stand-alone concept in our efforts to understand it. Al Nafs exists within the context of the environment and interrelationships that can be complex. An individual will always be faced with a relationship to 1) God, the creator; 2) Natural environment; 3) Himself; 4) Other people/ social relations; and 5) Relationships with objects/ material or man-made environments.

These relations will build a dynamic context that will influence and be influenced by human beings. Muslim's highest and utmost relation is their relationship with God that implies the duty to worship as a way to show gratitude for all His blessings. Gratitude is not a static state, and the best manner of showing gratefulness is when a person willingly follows His orders. The second relations imply a task for taking care of the environment (*Immara-arabic).* It is at the hand of the believer to treat the environment with respect, because it's a gift from God, for them to live in. The third relation leads to a task for self-purification (*tazkia),* a process that people will have to go through in their life, for the seeds of goodness, learning and attaining knowledge, of doing good to grow. Tazkia leads to success, yet unfortunately many people tend to do the opposite, torturing their own soul, so that it leads them to different states of psychological imbalance. It has always been fascinating to define the role of a psychologist in this context, that is to do tazkia for themselves and to help others do *tazkia,* to enable them to grow as a person. The fourth relation is relationship with others, or social relation. The keyword of the critical role in this relationship is *khilafa,* which can mean exchanging roles, helping each other and succession/ regeneration. From this explanation, we can see that problems of leadership, cooperation, cohesiveness, and conflicts will be present in the context of this relationship. Finally, the relationship with material/ man-made objects. This relationship has to do with our relationship with material entities, which of course should not be regarded as our "master" or most important, but as the means/ support for performing other roles in the above relationships. If the orientation to the material environment is misplaced, problems in people's lives start to occur, to name one is our environmental degradation. To fulfill our wants for various material supplies, man created industries, and these industries have taken up so much of our environmental resources. Many conflicts, mental anxiety occur because of our mistakes in placing our relationship with the material environment as our priority.

Very interestingly, Muneim (2018) mentions that the existence of the Nafs can be described as 1) Bearing internal dynamics (within the Nafs); and 2) Facing various realities (from its external environment). The internal dynamic is a struggle or test between being Taqwa (obedient) and Fujuur (crossing the limit set by God), between Freedom of Will and Reason/ intellect, Needs and Wants etc. Within their external environment, humans face realities that are plural. This plurality can include time and space, gender, social status, life and death, religion, and school of thought. They can form differences in degrees *(darajat)* as one reality might overpower/ take domination over the others. The purpose of a person's life is that in dealing with the plurality in this system, and being tested by it, people train themselves (the Nafs) to remain in its sound qualities. Each successful encounter between the Nafs and its internal and external environment will lead him/ her to be purified and to grow (Tazakka). This is also supported by Lang's (2011) study of the Quran which found that three important concepts relevant for the purpose of life will be interrelated, namely: intellect, choice, and suffering. These three elements are needed for the human to grow. What is meant by success and to grow, is that their relationship with God continues to be improved and strengthened. And the impacts they give to their surroundings are at best for maslaha (beneficial/ bring greater good). Consequently, with the betterment of the affair with God, his/ her other affairs will follow the improvements. This is a continued struggle (jihad) throughout a person's life until the day will come when he/ she must return to the Creator (Ajaal/ death).

In Arabic this test is called Ibtila. Not all self can successfully face this test. And a healthy soul is one that remains peaceful in this dynamic and challenging environment, because he understands that this test is given to determine who is the most devout of them. With this, the person is moving to the important life purpose, that is to grow and to be beneficial. Once again, in the context of such an environment, the highest status that can be obtained for a person is not on the achievement of one or several of these degrees, but on the status of his devotion as a sign of gratitude to God Almighty.

5. Tazkiyatun Nafs

Tazkiyatun Nafs, is a word that has a semantic network with tazakka (to grow and purify), in other words self-purification and growth, and Dzikr (remembrance), shalah (Prayer) and Ibtila (test). All Muslim scholars agree on this concept of Tazkiya as the concept of developing the human soul, and this purification is meant to purify the soul from anything that pollutes and makes it unable to grow properly, and most importantly from all that hinders it from worshiping and recognizing its Lord. Like in farming, tazkia is an effort to fertilize, cultivate and grow one's soul. In one of the many discussions of Islamic Science including in his work (2018), Muneim often stated that knowledge agents are subjects to tazkiya, in order to produce purified knowledge. He further explained that the soul is like soil, when it is fertile and pure, the seeds of goodness will grow. It is interesting that in this regard, the role of a psychological scientist and a practitioner of psychology can be authentically formulated, namely, to purify and let grow of oneself, and to help others to grow and be purified. This goal contains in it the value of humility because as a person, a psychology scientist is not someone who is perfect, but he/ she does tazkia for him/ herself and with that he can help others to achieve a better state from when he/ she came for advice or help.. Tazkia is a central process that will help people expand the capacity to do the task as khalifa (vicegerent of God) in this earth, to do Imara (caring for the environment), khilafa (exchange roles and supporting each other), and to properly place the material environment/ reality in their life.

In his Quranic discovery, Lang (2011) stated that tazkia is *"a personal duty of a believer,"* which is carried out to grow and achieve excellence in character. The characters which pertain to the devout believers are loved by God, these are: doing good, showing compassion, merciful, forgiving, just, protecting, defending the weak, seeking knowledge, generous, truthful, peaceful, loving others, wise etc. Interestingly, these characters also belong to God the Almighty, the one who orders the people to go through sufferings as the means to grow and equip them with the intellect to make choices. These are: The Most Compassion and Merciful, Most and Oft Forgiving, Most Just, Protector, Defender of the weak, All Knowing, Most Generous, the Real One, the Truth, in Him we find peace, Most loving, Most Wise. Thus, he concluded that what God asked for from the people and what He offers to the people are in fact in concordance.

It is widely accepted by the learned Muslim that Islam has prescribed for them the method and rituals to achieve Tazkia. This is where the other related terms like Dzikr (remembrance) and the understanding of Ibtila (life test) come into play. A Tazkiyat-ed person will see the need for remembrance of God, thus they conduct prayers and extra prayers, charities and doing good for others. This is good for their own soul and brings them closer to the blessings from the Almighty God. A tazkiyat-ed person will not see life challenges as bad, because it can become the means for them to grow. Yet towards these tests, a person might appraise them differently. As stated in the Quran:

> *We dispersed them through the land in groups—some were righteous, others were less so. We tested them with prosperity and adversity, so perhaps they would return 'to the Right Path'. (7:168)*
> *Every soul will taste death. And We test you 'O humanity' with good and evil as a trial, then to Us you will 'all' be returned (21:35)*

Prophet Muhammad, peace be upon him, said about this life tests and how the believers would appraise and benefit from them:

> *"How wonderful is the case of a Believer. There is good for him in whatever happens to him -and none, apart from him, enjoys this blessing. If he receives some bounty, he is grateful to Allah and this bounty brings good to him. And if some adversity befalls him, he is patient, and this affliction, too, brings good to him" (A Hadist — the saying and examples from Prophet Muhammad, narrated by Muslim).*

The Quran also explains the opposite status of the Self, that is Tadsiya, the opposite of purified and growth (Tazkia), meaning defilement, polluted, or tarnished. The Quran described:

> *And by the soul and the One Who fashioned it, then with the knowledge of right and wrong inspired it! Successful indeed is the one who purifies their soul, and doomed is the one who corrupts it, (91: 7–10). Successful indeed is the one who purifies their soul.*

Thus, doing tazkia will help people (as the chosen being by Allah) to expand the capacity to carry out the noble tasks and duties, that is to perform the essential roles in the relationship mentioned above with the noble intens and through the right processes. Thus with tazkia they personally grow and become purified, and so is the surrounding contexts that they live in.

6. Justification of the Integrity of Knowledge

The efforts made by many Muslim psychologists in the world to build and develop Islamic psychology demand the presence of standards/criteria that can be used to judge whether a construction of knowledge shows its validity, especially when the word Islam is mentioned in the name of this "new area". Regarding these criteria, the Maqasid Quran approach sets a standard to accept or reject a scientific effort as valid science. There is a saying in Arabic which goes "to understand something, you have to know its opposite." In this regard, the principles stated above will have their opposites, which are the principles to negate or affirm something as a true knowledge. Thus, science is less acceptable when it is not based on signs or evidence, in the Islamic paradigm the signs are not only accessible from observations, but it can also include the verses in the Quran, as the words from the One whose knowledge is All Encompassing. Furthermore, it also cannot be said to be true when its formulation is partial, not comprehensive, and integrated. Third, a scientific endeavor will be rejected as true when it has been polluted with interests and thus is not purified. Muneim (2018) explains in detail regarding the affirmation and negation of knowledge based on signs/verses/evidence. At least, the Quran eliminates 3 types of non-sign-based knowledge, they are clouded by: (1) al-hawā or toppling desire, (2) al-zhann or speculation (3) al-itibā 'li al-itibā' or imitation for the purpose of imitation without supporting signs. The last type, Imitation, in the Quran can be further classified into 3 sub-categories; (1) imitate those who are arrogant, or in the Qur'anic phrase referred to as 'those who misrepresent themselves as greater than themselves' (al-mustakbirīn). This reminds us of the importance of humility in our scientific endeavors, and to realize that the ideas in science that may seem dominant or the mainstream discourse existing, are not necessarily the ones that best suit our issues. This will open differing ideas and alternatives to flourish (2) imitate the ancestors (al-ābā'), this can also include the predecessor in the science as we know today, as it might close the door of reforms at times when it is needed (3) imitating the majority (al-akṡariyyah), as this could close off critical judgment essential to come into sound and purified knowledge.

7. The Current and Future Direction of Islamic Psychology

Until today, the science of Psychology in Islam continues to grow and develop. At least two paths are noticeable in its development. One path is more oriented towards revitalizing the classical concepts from earlier Muslim scholars. The classic work of Abu Zaid Al Balkhi, that talks about how people could develop him/ himself and to maintain a healthy and balanced life physically and mentally (Masalikh Al Abdan wal Anfus) was rewritten for today's reader. In fact, Malik Badri, the founder of modern Islamic Psychology translated the psychological parts of the book that was written 1000 years ago. He found that what Al Balkhi did provide a grand basis for Cognitive behavioral therapy (Badri, 2013). One paper after another was written in trying to understand Al Balkhi's concept on sustenance of the body and soul, one of them is by Awaad and Ali (2015) of Stanford University. Al Balkhi went deep into explaining phobias, rooted in a Psychological state of Al Fazaa, classified it as a specific primary psychological disorder that could manifest together with physical symptoms, and detailed its management (Awaad and Ali, 2016) . Some works are also centered on Al Ghazzali's work to understand the structure and dynamic of the soul (Fachrunisa & Chizanah, 2020). The application of classical methods that allow people to maintain balance in their souls is also widely developed based on classical concepts that have been practiced in Islamic tradition for a long time. Practices such as reflection on Syukur (gratefulness), Muraqaba – reflective moment (Hartanti, Huwaida, Adriwiguna, Qudsyi, 2021), Repentance/ Tauba and forgiveness (Uyun, Kurniawan & Jaufalaily, 2019), and Dzikrullah or remembrance of God (Frager, 1999) are developed into structured intervention. With this being researched and applied, Muslim Psychologists can have the basis to integrate beliefs, religiosity, and spirituality in their understanding of human being and thus need to be recognized and well addressed for their study of human being, and for the prevention of illness as well as the effective process of psychological treatment/ intervention.

The second path of developing Islamic Psychology involves exploration of the texts written in the Quran and Sunnah to formulate and extract new concepts related to humans in the context of their lives today. Today this effort found its philosophical undrpinning in the Maqasid approach, one of an approach in understanding Islam, managing affairs, and developing strategy. The belief that the purpose of the Quran revelation is to give guidance and to enlighten, encourages Islamic Psychology scientists to continue to ground the principles described by the Creator into the real problems of human life, to this day. This approach is still newly born and shed new lights on the integration of Islam and science (Auda, 2021), including on Islamic Psychology. Besides classical works that have been existing and practiced over one thousand years in the Muslim tradition, today we can hope for new conceptual and theoretical development based on revelations. Some theories are developed, for example by Riyono (2012) on motivation, Rusdi (2017) on *radhy* or acceptance (2019), Budiharto and Himam (2006) on Prophetic leadership, or Zulaifah (2019) on Quranic work ethic. With todays' challenge in the world, especially in the Muslim world, going back to the Quran allows Muslim scholars to formulate knowledge with guidelines and principles that are important for integrated, rooted problem solving as well as strategies for the growth of their communities. Quran is the book of statements of the Creator of the universe, for the caretaker of His creations – namely the thinking/ intelligent human. Thus, when the life shows obvious signs of damage, imbalance, downfall, or losses instead of growth, balance, and beneficence (*maslaha*), the Muslim scholars will need to check and see whether our concepts and practices are already in concordance with the higher purpose of the creation.

8. Research Studies in this Edition

In this edition, research related to Islamic psychology shows more diverse themes from various areas/ sub-discipline of Psychology: education, clinical and industrial/ organizational, developmental, community, and post-disaster psychology. In reading the titles and abstracts entered by the authors, we can see that some studies try to portray phenomena that occur in Muslim societies by accommodating concepts obtained from the mainstream psychology, others use concepts that resemble the concepts in Islam such as spirituality. Several studies try to raise the authentic concepts that were taken from Islamic literature. In the future, the birth of new concepts related to Islamic Psychology will continue to occur, if we look at the works of Islamic Psychology enthusiasts around the world. The birth of new concepts of Islamic Psychology will enable the community to understand their reality in accordance with the beliefs they have. It also encourages the Islamic Psychology community to produce knowledge, not only to use knowledge. The "Khazana" (good literature of knowledge) of Islamic Psychology, with its richness, substantiality, and comprehensiveness at the face of the current crisis of modernity, finds a path to expose its benefits. As quoted by one of the early Muslim scholars, Ibnul Qayyim al-Jauziyah, the purpose of the message of Islam can be summarized in these few key words, namely: Justice, Mercy, Wisdom and Common good. Islamic Psychology is one discipline that shows the potential to answer such noble purposes. In the end, Allah is All-Knowing, and to Him we ask for mercy and guidance.

References

Auda, J. (2021). *Reenvisioning Islamic Scholarship. Maqasid Methodology as a New Approach*. Caritas Books, Swansea, United Kingdom Milpitas.

Auda, J. (2021). *Understanding the Quran*. [Video]. Muslims Association of Canada. https://etarbeyah2018.appspot.com/understanding_quran/course

Awaad, R., & Ali, S. (2015). Obsessional Disorders in al-Balkhi's 9th century treatise: Sustenance of the body and soul. *Journal of Affect Disorder*. doi: 10.1016/j.jad.2015.03.003

Awaad R., & Ali, S. (2016). A modern conceptualization of phobia in Al-Balkhi's 9th century treatise: Sustenance of the body and soul. *Journal of Anxiety Disorder*, *37*, 89–93. doi: 10.1016/j.janxdis.2015.11.003.

Badri, M. B. (1979). *The Dilemma of Muslim Psychologists*. MWH Publishing: London

Badri, M. B.(2013). *Abu Zayd al-Balkhi's Sustenance of the Soul: The Cognitive Behaviour Therapy of a Ninth Century Physician*. IIIT. London.

Badri, M. B. (2020). The Islamization of psychology: its why, its what, its how and its who. International *Journal of Islamic Psychology*, *3*(1), 22–33. http://jour nal.iamphome.org/index.php/IJIP/article/view/15/16

Bakhtiar, L. (2002). An Introduction to Alchemy of Happiness by Abu Hamid Muhammad Ghazzali. In Nasr, S.H (ed). *Alchemy of Happiness* (Pp 23–28). Great Books of the Islamic World.

Budiharto, S., & Himam, F. (2006). Konstruk teoritis dan pengukuran kepemimpinan profetik [Theoretical Construct and Measurement of Prophetic Leadership]. *Jurnal Psikologi. 33* (2), 133–146.

Masjid Kampus UGM (2021). Nilai dalam Paradigma Profetik "Transendensi".*Diskusi Serial Profetik #3*. accessed on Oktober 5, 2021, From www.youtube.com/watch?v=

Fachrunisa, R.A., & Chizanah, L. (2020). Al Ghazzali's psychological construct of Nafsu. International *Journal of Islamic Psychology, 4(1),* 19–25. http://jour nal.iamphome.org/

Frager, R. (1999). Heart, Self and Soul, The Sufi Psychology of Growth, Balance and Harmony. Quest Books. Wheaton, Illinois.

Hartanti, W.S., Huwaida, R., Adriwiguna, N.S., Qudsyi, H. (2021). Muraqabah intensification therapy (MIT): An alternative Islamic therapy for social media addiction. *International Journal of Public Health Science.* 11(1). http://doi.org/ 10.11591/ijphs.v11i1

Iqbal, M. (2009). *The Making of Islamic Science.* Islamic Book Trust, Malaysia

Khattab, M. (2018). *The Clear Quran. English Translation of the Quran.* https:// quran.com

Koenig, H.G., & Shohaib, S.A. (2014). Health and Well-Being in Islamic Societies. Springer. Heidelberg

Lang, J. (2011). The Purpose of Life. *https://www.youtube.com/watch?v=ifll gTA2pmY*

Muneim, A. A. (2018). Towards Islamic maqasid education philosophy for sustainable development: quranic perspective with special attention to indonesia *Millah: Jurnal studi Agama, 17*(2), 221–266, dOI: 10.20885/millah.vol17.iss2. art4

Riyono, B (2012). *Motivasi dengan Perspektif Psikologi Islam. Edisi Pertama.* (Motivation in Islamic Psychology Perspective, 1st Edition). Quality Publishing, Yogyakarta, Indonesia. https://repository.ugm.ac.id/id/epr int/36108

Rusdi, A. (2017). Ridha dalam psikologi islam dan konstruksi alat ukurnya [acceptance in islamic psychology and its measurement construction]. *Jurnal Psikologi Islam*, *4*(1), 95–117

Saliba, G. (2007). *Islamic Science and the Making of the European Renaissance*. The MIT Press. Cambridge.

Uyun, Q., Kurniawan, I.K., Jaufalaily, N. (2019). Repentance and seeking for forgiveness: The effects of spiritual therapy based on Islamic tenets to improve mental health. *Mental Health, religion, and Culture,* 22:2, 185–194, 10.1080/13674676.2018.1514593

Zulaifah, E. (2019). Work ethic from Qur'anic Maqasid approach: an introduction and preliminary theoretical development. *Minbar. Islamic Studies, 12*(1): 251–266. https://doi.org/10.31162/2618-9569-2019-12-1-251-266

Marcus Stueck

PREFACE II
Psychology of the Four Directions: The Biocentric Health Theory as a "Bridge" between Western and Islamic Psychology

The connection with the divine is in the Islamic world and in the western world of a holistic development, in which spirituality plays a major role for the health sciences. Even Einstein expressed this fact in his famous phrase "God does not play dice". Religions have always populated the natural space and thus influence the inner experience of humans. In 2020 to 2022, a theory, the Biocentric Health Theory, was developed by Stueck (2020, 2021, 2022), which was the basis for a study, led by the DPFA Academy of Work and Health, with 8 universities and institutions, collecting data from all 5 continents, on the topic of "Covid-19 and Mental Processing". The goal was to develop a "Biocentric Vision of Being Human after COVID-19", which includes the integration of Islamic Psychology and Western Psychology. The biocentric paradigm could represent a framework, in which closed systems open up and find points of contact, lowest common denominators. This is especially necessary in times when there are devaluations and discriminations in the western countries concerning Islam (Islamophobia), but also missionary acts of Islamic institutions in western countries and a time which is characterized by wars, natural catastrophes, an increase of mental illnesses, etc.

1. What is Biocentrism?

Biocentrism is about seeking connection and enduring aualities. In this respect, this book is intended to help make connections and promote understanding in relation to Islamic Psychology and in relation to so-called Western Psychology.

If terms were to be used to describe the Biocentric Model, they are:

- Adaptation and acceptance
- Showing humanity
- Leaving comfort zones, opening to others, to new things
- Dismantling of protective mechanisms and armor
- Allowing instabilities and experiencing one's own vulnerability

- Perceiving and allowing developmental leaps
- Seeking connections, the goal of biocentricity is connection
- Integration of dualities, e.g., pain and joy
- Loving, affective relationship orientation
- Awareness and spiritual development
- Compassion and tolerance for all life forms
- Development of humility and wonder
- Ethics centered on aesthetics and compassion
- Intentionlessness and presence in the here and now
- Respect for all that lives
- Respect for the space another living being needs to express its life ("I am life in the midst of life that wants life", Schweitzer, 1999),
- Acting from the "heart", sharing, giving, and receiving love, being able to see the divine in the other person
- Observing situations or inner feelings without judging
- Experiencing e.g., nature without judgment, being part of nature, experiencing the divine

The biocentric approach (bios = life, centrum = at the center) considers human beings as a component of the natural realm, among many other life forms. It is an inclusive approach that asks for the smallest common characteristics between the living beings of the habitat earth, wants to make them conscious to the human being and thus calls him to cooperate with the components of the natural space, to respect the life in it and to act compassionately with the community of all living beings, but also to act lovingly with himself and with other people, and with nature.

2. Biocentric Boundaries

In Biocentric Health Theory (Stueck, 2020 a,b; 2022), various biocentric boundaries have now been defined that make it impossible to connect to self, others, and nature. Biocentric boundaries were first formulated in Pandemic Management Theory by Stueck (2021), which formed the basis to a study "Covid 19 and Psyche" (Stueck, Bidzan, Faroki, Kankeh, 2020; Bidzan-Bluma, Bidzan, Jurak, Bidzan, Knietzsch, Stueck, Bidzan, 2020). These are behaviors of humans that separate them from life: These include:

- Affective pathologies, such as devaluation of others, lack of self-love (self-destruction).
- Chronic states of stress and exhaustion

- Anxiety boundaries (fear of loving, fear of living, fear of expressing oneself, fear of the primitive)
- Dysregulative situation evaluations and lack of coping
- Hypersensitivity
- Physical and social dissociation

Social dissociations, i.e., separations of parts that actually belong together, include (Toro, 2010):

- Separation of life and work
- Separation of the sacred and the profane

In the above-mentioned study "Corona and Psyche" a multitude of other separations were uncovered. Among others, separation of people from touches, separation of instinct from rational, separation of ethics and morals, separation of inner and outer natural space, etc. (Stueck, 2021a). The separation of the profane and the sacred will be described in the following, which has a relation to religion.

3. Separations in the Religion

The basic principle is that every religion, as long as it is lived from the heart, is compatible with the biocentric approach. It means the daily practice of the connection to God achieved through prayer and thus to love and mercy with all living beings and the transfer to the practical life, but also professional and scientific areas. In the religions there is an esoteric and an exoteric side (Stueck, 1993). The esoteric side also includes the fact that one does not necessarily need a church or a "place of worship" in order to enter into contact with God.

Figure 1. The profane and the sacred. Tree as altar in the Treviso region, Italy

In Figure 1, a tree in the Treviso region of Italy was discovered, by the author of this book, to serve as an ecclesiastical altar for the inhabitants. I can perform sacred acts in profane settings, just as I can perform sacred acts in sacred places. The separation of the profane and the sacred was postulated by Toro (2010) and Dürkheim (2005) and scientifically described in relation to Islamic prayer by Raharjo (2014) at a 2014 Bionet meeting in Riga (Latvia). It ultimately reflects the separation of body and mind, the separation of humans from life and nature.

Some religions put out the human being as a representative of God and call all other living beings as creatures which have not reached this level. Also, there are Koran interpretations that do not really have anything to do with the theological meaning of this scripture, but rather with ideological intentions. These are examples of generated moral concepts of religions, i.e., the exoteric side, which do not have much to do with the deeper meaning of religions, namely the connection with divinity.

This connection is always first an esoteric connection, i.e., an intimate connection between human and God. It can be experienced spiritually, but also physically. In this connection, trust arises, which is then very helpful in living through difficult situations. There are numerous studies also in this book on the relationship of faith to people's coping. With the esoteric side of a religion, biocentrism is well compatible, as it promotes life and an ethic of human relational behavior that is based on a capacity for love. With the exoteric side of a religion, biocentricity is less familiar, as there are examples of how the powerful rules of a religion are not sufficient to protect life and aliveness in the natural realm. The scientific findings on the abuse of children by priests are a frightening example of this.

- As part of a research project[1], personnel and hand files of 38,156 clergy from 27 dioceses from 1946 to 2014 in Germany were reviewed, and evidence of sexual abuse of 3,677 children and adolescents was found in 1,670 clergy (4.4 %) of the Catholic Church.
- From the analysis of the criminal files, it can be deduced that most of the acts were based on a planned commission of the crime (83 %) and were not spontaneous or one-time so-called breakthrough acts.
- Those affected miss a credible confession of their own guilt and remorse, both on the part of the accused and on the part of the church as an institution.

1 "Sexual Abuse of Minors by Catholic Priests, Deacons and Male Religious in the Area of the German Bishops' Conference". Prof. Dr. med. Harald Dreßing, Central Institute of Mental Health, Mannheim (Network Coordinator)

The Roman Catholic Church has not yet released figures on how many children in total have reported abuse worldwide, how many priests are accused of having committed abuse, and how many accused priests have been dismissed. Estimates put the number of abused children worldwide in the hundreds of thousands. Moral-normative categories have not been sufficient to end these criminal acts in the Catholic-Roman Church system. This realization leads to the following basic biocentric assumption:

> *Where sensual bodily experience is suppressed, where the living out of a sexuality based on compassion and love is suppressed, acts of unimaginable cruelty, beyond the imagination of common sense, can occur. These acts cannot be prevented by a normative set of rules called morality, which creates feelings of guilt that contribute to the cover-up of the atrocities, but only by ensuring a healthy sensual, psycho-sexual development based on love, which makes it clear to every human being that he lives in the here and now in "paradise", in a wonderful nature. Only through the interaction of esoteric and exoteric religious practices can an ethical orientation of behavior, triggered by religions, take place. Where the exoteric side (morality) of the religions and the interpretation of their scriptures by clergymen, not the scriptures themselves, spread beliefs, such as animals are creatures that help humans to get in touch with God, the biocentric orientation and ethics ends. Animals, plants, and the elements of nature are just as divinely imbued as humans. There is no discriminatory distinction between higher and lower in biocentricity* (basic biocentric assumption, Stueck, 2022).

4. Fundamental Works on the Biocentric Health Theory

Fundamental work on this approach has been presented by Toro (2004, 2005, 2010), with the development of Biodanza, the Biocentric Principle and Biocentric Education, and Schweitzer (1999), with his work on the ethics of human beings in the natural realm ("I am life in the midst of life that wants to live"). Toro (2010) shares the visionary thinking of Schweitzer (1999, Schweitzer, Campion, 1961) and develops a practical approach to implement this with Biodanza: "When I meditate on life, I feel the obligation to respect any will of life around me because it is equal to mine." (Toro, 2004). But also, Cavalgante and Wagner (2018), mainly the concept of living corporeality as a biocentric field of action and many other fields of action in the social pedagogical field, also inspired by works of Freire (Education and Hope, 2007) and Morin (2012).

The deep nature centered approach of Naess (1989, 1998, 2007) also belongs to a biocentric basic theory, which states that it would be better to speak of a community or complex of all living beings when defining nature, than to speak of nature as something separate from humans. Humans are part of it. The influence of parts of nature, namely by cosmic timers, like moon circulation and the light-dark activation by the sun on the living beings is examined by the chronobiology. This connection of the human being with the cosmic space has been completely disregarded in anthropocentric theories. Here, work has been presented on chrono-biopsychology by Balzer and Stueck that is part of biocentricity and demonstrates that humans are a bio-cosmic entity as suggested by Toro (2010). Toro (2010) also shaped the experiential approach to discovering and experiencing the divine in oneself, the other, and nature in the here and now. But his own work on "Complete Science" is also part of this, proposing to integrate the experience or self-experience as a scientific method, alongside qualitative, quasi-experimental and experimental research methods. This way of looking at scientific self-experimentation and experience was already proposed by Husserl (1965) and Diltey (1986) at the beginning of the 20th century and by then not considered. It was not until Toro (2010) that experience was reintroduced as a method of cognition, and by Stueck (2015) it was included in the set of research approaches. The Biocentric Health Theory (Stueck, 2020 a,b, 2022) was developed by the author during 20 years of research, especially the biological and psychological foundations of biocentricity (Stueck, 2009, 2020, 2021, 2022) on the Inner and Outer Natural Space (Stueck, 2022), on the Penguin and Polar Bear Parable (Stueck, 2015), on the concept of Biopoiesis (Stueck, 2021b), on the scientific evaluation of Biodanza (Stueck & Villegas, 2008, 2021; Stueck, 2009) and on the Concept of the School of Empathy (Stueck, 2013) and on inclusion and connection to Islamic psychology (Psychology of the 4 cardinal points, Stueck, 2022).

5. Biocentrism as a Bridge between Western and Islamic Psychology

Ultimately, the biocentric paradigm is about regaining respect for life, the "sanctity of life" as Toro (2010) puts it, without having to belong to any religion, and developing a capacity for love in all areas of life and work that allows us to get in touch with everything that lives and to protect that life. Also, the approach described by Zulaifah in the preface 1.

Toro describes it in his Biocentric Principle (Toro, 2004) as follows: The fundamental idea of good is that this consists in preserving and favoring life, leading it to its highest value, and that evil consists in destroying life, harming it, and hindering its flourishing. A very rare field of research allows us to experience this description, namely there is violence in delivery rooms in Germany, where, by action of midwives, women experience psychological and physical violence (among other things, derogatory remarks during childbirth, lack of communication with the expectant mother, but also loveless encroachments into the vagina of women). Another example is the above-mentioned abuse of priests. Possibly, good and evil will always be in this world, as two basic forces. But there should be awareness and empathy about it. In this respect, the biocentric approach could be a bridge between Islamic psychology and Western psychology. This is urgently necessary, that two systems with different languages and symbols understand and approach each other. That is why we organized the Bionet conferences in Latvia 2012, 2014, 2016 and then also in Yogyakarta in 2018. Because increasingly the world is globalizing. There is an increasing mixing of ethnicities, the different ways of thinking associated with them, and the different religious and cultural backgrounds. To act anthropocentrically means that one direction dominantly prevails. To be biocentric in the coexistence of religions and ways of thinking also means to consider the culture- and religion-specific approaches in science and pedagogical or psychological practice.

6. God and Science? How Does it Fit Together?

From the point of view of Zulaifah (see preface 1), it is unthinkable that Muslims in the context of Islamic psychology subject their God or the Koran to critical reflection. Zulaifah (see page 2), writes about this in the book Islamic Psychology in the first preface:

> *"In Islam, the perspective on the self and the surrounding environment has clear theological foundations, can be traced in their holy book, and are described in the narrations about attitudes, actions and examples given by the Prophet Muhammad- peace be upon him.... Alienating the Supreme Being from these relationships will eventually stripped the essence of their faith. Furthermore, it has always been clear for every devout Muslim that scientific inquiry as an attempt to understand the law and work of nature and life does not have to put aside the Creator".*

God and science, how does that fit together? To understand the Qur'an as a guideline for Muslims and to use it theologically scientifically is understandable for various reasons. However, this does not release Islamic-psychological scientists from using the body-related survey instruments of the:

- Physical-sensory experience without evaluation
- Self-reflective observation without evaluations

And to describe the results, initially without interpretations. This step of introducing two old new scientific survey methods of self-experience and self-reflection without evaluation (qualitative research) is the only conceivable way to scientifically justify Zulaifah's statement (see above). These two scientific methods of inquiry existed before (Husserl and Dilthey introduced them), but they disappeared again from the scientific context.

Unfortunately, this aspect of connecting cognitive understanding and experience is hardly considered in the scientific context. In the Biocentric Health Theory (Stueck, 2020, 2021, 2022), in the Biocentric Paradigm (Toro, 2004), "Life and Ethics" by Schweitzer (1999) it is a basic condition for scientific research and for dealing with oneself, others and nature. Therefore 3 levels should be distinguished and used in scientific research, no matter from which cultural context someone originates:

- Loving physical experience without evaluation, without guilt and shame.
- Loving reflection, without evaluation and without guilt and shame.
- Reflecting on a scientific level with evaluations, including qualitative content analysis of the Qur'an and research on issues related to it based on empirical data.

As Zulaifah states additionally in her preface: "Furthermore, it has always been clear for every devout Muslim that scientific inquiry as an attempt to understand the law and work of nature and life does not have to put aside the Creator. Islamic Psychology is an endeavor that answers the concerns of many Muslim psychologists in the world (Badri, 1979) who feel that modern science could isolate them from their belief related to their core identity as God's creation…"

If this basic constant is valid, that the holy scripture cannot be subjected to a critical reflection, this means that theology and science are linked here. Then also the experience and the self-reflection without evaluation from a biocentric perspective must be introduced into the scientific discourse. Einstein described: that the experience of the miracle is a question of training.

For the Islamic psychology it means that the orientation to the Qur'an must be accompanied by an experiential level, because then the emotional and behavioral level of the human being becomes visible and can be examined, without filters. This connection of cognitive analysis and the experience can be trained. In the 2018 Bionet conference, both levels of experience were present, although it was controversial:

- The recitation of the Qur'an.
- And the physical sensual experience by means of Biodanza for children.

7. Experiences of the Western Scientists During the Bionet-Conference 2018

Unfortunately, besides the content-related occupation and interpretation of the Qur'an also the experience level was practiced, which is the basic idea of the Bionet conferences, was experienced by some as disturbing. Not by the participants, because they had so much joy in it. Ultimately, the conflict between the cognitive debate and the experience reveals a deep rift that is visible everywhere in the world at the moment, in the separation between body and mind, in the separation between the profane and the sacred, in the separation between religion and science, between the subjective and the objective, man and nature, in wars, natural disasters, and so on. First, representatives of Islamic psychology must decide whether the connection with Western psychology is desired and by what means should this connection be achieved? An integration of the western scientific methods, as it is described in the preface of Zulaifah, is not sufficient, without the empathic question or awareness of the problem position, that the western science has nothing to do with the Qur'an and is also not interested in an integration of the Qur'an into its scientific procedure. Culturally, the link between theology and the state, and theology and science has been severed for good reasons. The Inquisition of the Middle Ages led to powerful derailments of the church against Galilei and Copernicus. In this regard, the Nafs (Tazkiyatun Nafs) that Zulaifah (see preface 1) mentions could be important inspirations for research questions on spirituality. And spirituality is a concept also accepted by the West (see point 9).

There are two factors that promote the separations, first is the lack of focus on love, which is scientifically completely unreflective and secondly the reflection on human egocentrism, which prevents connections and is also responsible for the separation of man from nature (Biocentric Health Theory, Stueck, 2020 a, b,; 2022).

8. Human Egocentrism as Its Factor for Separations

The question "who has the best approach?" is ultimately an entanglement in human egocentrism, which prevents the inner natural space of man and the outer natural space from connecting. The definition of an inner and outer natural space first occurred in Biocentric Health Theory (Stueck, 2020 a, b; 2022) and the integration between inner and outer natural space is a goal of Biocentrism. It is all about the connection. One factor that separates it is the human ego. The ego (the ME) was defined by Gislon and Canevese (Stueck, 2020, a, b; 2022) in connection with the intellect and with control. Egocentrism is a personality trait (Becker, 1989, cit. in Stueck, 2022) that increases the so-called ego. Ultimately, the elevation of the ego, i.e., the "inflation of the ego" prevents connection to life and to loving actions and connections, as this process makes it impossible to leave one's own perspective and to enter into connections or to form interactional couplings with others (the "we") or one's environment or nature. The ego (Latin = Myself) stands in psychology for the I, the self. When inflating the ego, offenses of the ego play a role, which can start with the childhood by reference persons, which prevent it from taking other perspectives. Therefore, it is important to pay some attention to the issue of mortification in one's own life and at work, as it prevents normal relationship formation and ultimately necessary spiritual development. Likewise, with unprocessed grievances, it becomes more difficult to develop biocentric attitudes. Self-esteem deficits and personality disorders or the separation of rational evaluation from physicality also play a role in "inflated egos." Transcending one's ego into an "ego-reduced," i.e., trust-based loving connection to others and to nature is a lifelong task. It is, according to Erikson (1959, Theory of the Psychosocial Development of the I, Stage 7: Ego Integrity), the last developmental task a person should accomplish at the end of life before death. This developmental task is closely related to the development of wisdom and spirituality, as well as closeness to nature. The concept of spirituality (lat.= breath, spirit) describes the lifelong search of a transcendent reality, which lies behind the material world, and which is only with difficulty accessible to rational explanations. Spiritual experiences are connected with questions of meaning and values of existence, with the experience of the wholeness of the world, the experience of the connectedness with something "holy" or the perception of the soul. Likewise, a person's spirituality is connected with the integration of the "inexplicable" and the "ethically valuable" into one's life, which cannot be expressed in language. These are very personal states, independent of religion, which have an impact on the conduct of life, and are difficult to access to logic or communication about them. They are accessible only to the experience.

In Table 1 are shown some symptoms of the human ego from the Biocentric Health Theory (Stueck, 2021b), which hinders a connection between human to God, human to nature, human to others. The following exercise would be interesting, namely, to check how strong one's ego is, or the view of a discipline, e.g., Islamic Psychology or Western Psychology disciplines.

Table 1. Symptoms of ego

Symptomatology of a strong ego, which does not allow man to connect with his inner and outer natural space.	**Symptomatology of biocentric features of man, which allow to connect with his inner and outer natural space.**
By always wanting to have more	It is enough what I get
I always have to have things alone and am concerned about my own advantage	I am good at sharing
It always has to be the way I envision it	I accept
By devaluing others or entering into competition	I take everything
By masking feelings	Expression of feelings
excessive doing, hyperactivity and thus avoid introspection	Slowing down
Little presence (a lot of thinking about the past, future, not being able to live in the here and now).	Presence
By looking for explanations and excuses for my behavior	It is like it is
Feel guilt	I say what has to be said
Being upset, anger	Acceptance
Controlling and Manipulating situations, Others	I let it free
Feeling shame, being embarrassed	It just happens and must be reflected
Everything needs to be perfect	Be perfect in imperfection, everything is perfect as it is
Often want to be right	We share and there are different points of view
Having fixed thoughts about myself with evaluations, having excuses about my behavior	Thinking in which I take different positions, look at something from all sides, without evaluation, perceive and accept
Rigidity in thoughts, ideas and feelings about oneself in the inner space of nature.	Nature changes every four months in the outer natural space
I identify with roles, have masks and merits "I am the one or the …. "	I am authentic without role, without mask, I don't need merits
I can't stand doing nothing or certain states of being and have to fill inner empty spaces with activity or substances.	I endure doing nothing and enjoy it

A form of life for overcoming the human ego is named in the Biocentric Health Theory (Stueck, 2021b) the turning to the spiritual development of a human being and to the development of the ability to love.

9. Proposal 1: The Concept of Spirituality as a Bridge between Islamic Psychology and Western Psychology

Following Hoffmann (2009, cit. in Stueck, 2022), who elicited these forms in a study of psychotherapy patients in Germany, at least seven factors could be differentiated as expressions of spirituality and derived as relevant for Biocentric Health Management Theory:

- Faith (prayer and "trust in God") and a sense of security.
- Knowledge and insight based on wisdom
- Overcoming the "I" position and achieving transcendent experiences
- Compassion, generosity and tolerance
- Conscious, present interaction with others, oneself and the environment
- Reverence and gratitude
- Presence and acceptance of what is.

> *Meditation is the best-known method of developing spirituality in the West. However, there are many other directions or factors that develop spirituality: strong experiences of nature, near-death experiences, Sufi traditions, prayer, biodanza, age of life, etc. However, the development of spirituality has primarily nothing to do with the application of a specific method or religion. Rather, spirituality has to do biocentrically with the development of an inner attitude and spiritual, transcendental experiences, especially the experience of the wholeness of the world and the connectedness with the "sacredness" of life, the ability to give and receive love to all beings, beginning with the human being. This is a lifelong task of moving from egocentrism to the attitude of love, which is made more difficult by certain lifestyles of Western civilization* (basic biocentric assumption).

In biocentrism, the human thus looks behind the classifications. And this lets him see the miraculousness of life, because the classifications are man-made, the biological mechanisms of action behind them are not. It is a miracle, which occurs everywhere in nature, if one experiences and reflects it, without rash interpretations.

Already Einstein and Wheeler pointed out these connections:

> "If we find once in the center of the universe, what drives this universe and its evolution causally, then it will be after everything what we know today, less a chrome shining mechanism, but rather something, which we would call colloquially a miracle. We will be able to detect this miracle, but it will remain a miracle."
> Prof. John Wheeler: Nobel Laureate, "Father of the New Quantum Physics"

> "Amazement is our approach to the universe, humility is our approach to our fellow man.",

> "The progress of scientific development is, in the final analysis, a constant flight from amazement.", "Those who have lost the ability to marvel are largely dead.", "One must look at the impossible until it becomes an easy matter. Wonder is a matter of training."
> Prof. Albert Einstein: Nobel Prize winner, "father of the theory of relativity":

Here it becomes clear once again how important experiencing and reflecting is for scientific advancement.

10. Why Is There a Feeling of Isolation of Islamic Psychology from the Rest?

So why "Muslim psychologists" feel that modern science isolates them from their beliefs? (Zulaifah, Preface 1). The reason may lie in their own concept of scientific research, i.e., in themselves:

a) **One reason is that modern science has created an artificial separation between the subjective and the objective.** By means of various research designs, it is supposed to ensure that the examined object of a scientific study is also examined objectively. However, since Heisenberg and Einstein (Copenhagen Conference, 1916), since the development of quantum physics, we know that the subject, the observer, always changes and influences what is observed. So, it is not possible to examine something objectively. If everything is subjective, then one should also accept the above-mentioned investigation instruments of self-experience, without evaluation and self-reflection without evaluation as scientific methods. Husserl (1965) introduced this approach of self-reflection without evaluation and Dilthey (1986, cit. in Stueck, 2022) the experience without evaluating into the scientific discourse at the beginning of the 19th century. Unfortunately, these approaches have disappeared.
b) **A second reason, which is related to the experience, is the artificial theological separation between the esoteric and the exoteric side of a religion.** In Christianity this happened in the Middle Ages, when one of the last mystics (Meister Eckhart) was "banned" by the Church. The esoteric mystical side of the religion is the above-mentioned subjective experience of the connection with God and the self-reflection about it, without evaluation. The exoteric side is the interpretation of the holy scriptures and the setting of moral boundaries.
c) **A third reason is the "loving"-transmission of the contents:** What we scientists of the "West" have experienced at the Bionet meeting 2018 were powerful presented "exoteric" Quran interpretations, the adherence to a dogma, which was alienating for us Western scientists, who are very open to Islamic psychology. One component was missing, namely love and the possibility of freely experiencing the recited Qur'an. In science, love appears in the possibility of free thinking and creativity of the scientist. Not in moral dogma, which is the opposite, namely control. Control and science should not go together. Thus, the bridge of Islamic psychology to the West cannot

succeed either. Something has been missing, which can be summarized as freedom of thought and the possibility of individual experience and description with this theological writing. Science is free as the thinking process it's a free process. At the same time, the Islam has a mystical side that is very deeply rooted. In the scientific public, this mystical side is unfortunately rejected as well in the West. In private, it is done. We have met so many loving, spiritual colleagues at the Islamic University of Yogyakarta and admired their approach to God in prayer.

What to do? Scientific work should not be separated if one wants to be real and present, as subject and object, observer and observed are also not separated. And here the Islamic psychology can be a pioneer of a too developed modern science, if it just does not separate the mysticism and the scientific work, the ethics, which is based on sensual-aesthetic experience and the morals, which is based on the setting up of rules. Unfortunately, according to our experiences, it is to be feared that it does. With it a chance would be lost, because the western science has already accomplished it and therefore there is also a painful separation of the human being from nature, as it is described in the biocentric health theory (Stueck, 20 a, b; 2022). The Islamic Psychology has the chance to develop a "Complete Science" and by doing it, to integrate and to heal this planet. This needs consciousness.

11. Proposal 2: Necessity of a "Complete Science"

The following can be deduced from the previous thoughts: If Islamic psychology follows this path of separating the level of experience and reflection without evaluation from the level of scientific reflection based on empirical data, without formulating scientific criteria and methods to holistically examine the contents of its underlying guiding scripture, the Qur'an, then it becomes dogmatic and thus incomprehensible to the West, even when it uses Western methods and terms. The intelligible absence of critical reflection from God and moral dogma are two different things to be distinguished. If Islamic psychology becomes aware of this conflict, it can even become a pioneering model for a healthy and peaceful world. So far, unfortunately, it is not aware of this force. The solution would be simple. In the Biocentric Health Theory (Stueck, 2020 a, b: 2022), in the chapter "Complete Science", it is proposed to use the following research gates, both in Islamic and so-called Western psychology:

1. The experience, without language and evaluation, in the here and now, only description of what is experienced

2. Self-reflection on inner processes in the here and now, with language, but without evaluation, merely description of what is reflected upon
3. Descriptive, qualitative methods (describing, ordering, evaluating, and classifying)
4. Quasi-experimental methods (measuring, testing hypotheses and evaluating in the field)
5. Experimental methods (measure, testing hypotheses, and evaluate in the laboratory).

Also, in addition to this variety of scientific methods, holistic psychology should be interdisciplinary. And it should include cultural contexts, including religious contexts. This concept was implemented as a research concept at the DPFA University of Saxony until 2018.

12. Proposal 3: Necessity of a Psychology of the Four Directions

Therefore, besides the research gates, which secure the connection between personal experience and reflection with the object of investigation and the empirical-scientific reflection and investigation, a second proposal is interesting. Here the division of a psychology into the 4 cardinal points (directions) is proposed:

- **The psychology of the north**: it was founded by the experimental works of Wundt (1900) in Leipzig. It is the academic psychology we know, in which many psychologists feel at home, having studied it. It then spread to the West. Wilhelm Wundt had 150 PhD. students from all over the world at the University of Leipzig, the first psychological institute in the world, founded in 1879. Basic subjects of experimentally based psychology, of which Wundt is the father, are general psychology, social psychology, personality psychology, etc. In this northern view subjectivity is conceived as something separate from objectivity. Wundt also tried to develop the psychology of the 4 cardinal points with the description of the psychology of peoples, although he did not call it like that and tried to standardize the psychology[2] with a "north-western"

2 Between 1900–1920, he published a ten-volume psychology of peoples with standardized studies of language, myth, and mores, covering areas such as art, society, law, culture, and history. These works are basic works of cultural psychology. In them, Wundt analyzed spiritual-cultural and cultural-psychological processes and classified them according to a system of psychological and epistemological principles.

way of thinking, in which he ordered and classified ways of life of the 4 cardinal points according to certain criteria by so-called mental objectivators, which describe and classify social processes of community, art and culture of different cultures. Wundt highlights about 20 fundamental motives of cultural development. Examples are: Life care and division of labor, child care and community, self-education motive, making and imitation motive, ensoulment and magic motive, rescue and redemption motive, play instinct and jewelry motive, and values such as freedom and justice. The psychology of the North naturally includes Sigmund Freud from Vienna, the founder of psychoanalysis, Ebbinghaus who studied memory, Neumann who introduced psychotechnology. To the psychology of the North belongs the Russian psychology of Leontjev and Pavlov, the psychologists of learning. Likewise, the developmental psychologist Vygotsky, who described the zones he next develops, which plays a role in this pandemic management theory or biocentric health theory.

- **The psychology of the West:** has been founded mainly in the Anglo-Saxon area and is related to the psychology of the North and, like the psychology of the North, works with the approaches of the experiment, quasi-experimental research, and qualitative paradigms. If as many variables as possible are controlled in the experiment, then the finding is more objective and valid (high internal validity, validity). This comes at the cost of practicality (low external validity). This is a dilemma, because without the inclusion of the experience, achieving high external validity becomes difficult. Western psychology is now guiding action throughout the world. The above-mentioned research paradigms shape the applied disciplines as we know them: educational and clinical psychology or psychotherapy, industrial and organizational psychology. Here, too, subjective experience and objective comprehension of states are separate from each other. Psychologists like Seligman (positive psychology), Beck (cognitive behavioral therapy) and Lazarus (stress psychology) also play a role in the Biocentric Health Theory. The psychology of the North and West are according to the penguin and polar bear concept according to Stueck (2015) directions, the polar bear archetype represented (Stueck, 2022, Biocentric Fields of Action).
- **The Psychology of the South** is a diametrically different psychology, because it consists of work that focuses on experience and the subjective construction of reality that is thereby set in motion. There is no separation of objective and subjective worlds. The experience is a research method. Toro (2010) refers to the experience as vivencia and the royal road to psychic health. Representatives here are: Castaneda (1967, cit. in Stueck, 2022), Naranjo

(2005, cit. in Stueck, 2022), Toro (2010), Maturana (2002, cit. in Stueck, 2022). Included in southern psychology is the work of shamans in South America and Africa. These are partly methods that work through the experience and engagement with the method (trust in the shaman's medicine). This also includes the work with Ayawaska in psychotherapy, with Biodanza, etc. (Stueck, 2022, Biocentric Fields of Action).
- **The psychology of the East** includes Islamic psychology, as described above. But also, the self-awareness systems, e.g., of Yoga and related works (Patanjali, cit. in Stueck, 1993). The Yoga Sutras of Patanjali (Blitz, cit. in Stueck, 1993), are the first psychology book of the world, because in the Sutras (verses) the verses summarized by the Rishis (seers) about the interaction of body and mind were written down for the first time. But also, the Sufis (eastern mystics) belong to it beside many further self-experience disciplines of the Orient, which the Occident (the west and north) did not take up at all into its psychological understanding. The psychology of the East also includes holistic medicine with its "resounding" effects of Indian medicine (Ayuveda), Chinese medicine (acupuncture). Here not every effect is measurable. For example, the energy pathways (meridians) in Chinese medicine are only partially detectable, as are the chakras (energy centers) and the aura (so-called astral body) of Indian medicine. But they exist because they can be experienced in the application of the methods. Here meditation, praying and psychoactive substances help as well in perception (psilocybin, Stueck, 2022, Biocentric Fields of Action, connection with the wholeness). The tradition of the Sufis and their insights (laid down in various writings) also belong to the psychology of the East.

It is only through the teaching and practice of the psychologies of the North, West, South, and East, as proposed in Biocentric Health Theory, that one can claim to teach and practice a holistic psychology or science of human psychological processes that is connected to life and is a true-life science. Focusing on the North-Western psychology tradition as it is practiced at the moment is not sufficient for this. It lacks connection to cultural and religious contexts, body-oriented self-awareness, and observation, without judgment. Too much is taught and too little is experienced, or these experiences are recognized as significant knowledge of the individual, as his truth, in the form of casuistic scientific value.

13. Examples of Successful Integration

In the past, there have been several successful examples of how Islamic and Western psychologists can work together:

- For example, between 2009 and 2013, course instructor trainings on empathy were conducted. This included training psychologists at the Islamic University of Yogyakarta on the dance-oriented program with Biodanza (Empathy School nonverbal) and Nonviolent Appreciative Communication (Empathy School verbal)
- These evidence-based programs developed at the University of Leipzig were then implemented and evaluated in Islamic educational institutions in Yogyakarta.
- Establishment of a laboratory with chronobiological measurement instruments used in Islamic psychological research.
- Finally, the doctoral thesis at the University of Leipzig (Prof. Witruk).
- Several scientific articles have been produced

References

Cavalgante, R., Wagner, C. (2018). *Biocentric Principles.* Editiones CDH

Diltey, W. (1986). *Poetry and Experience.* Princeton University Press

Durkheim (2005). *The Elementary Forms of Religious Life.* Cambrigde University Press

Erikson H. (1959). Identity and the Life Cycle. New York: International Universities Press

Freire, P. (2007). *Education and Hope (*Vol. 2). Muenster: Waxmann.

Husserl, E. (1965). *Philosophy as Rigorous Science, Phenomenology and the Crisis of Philosophy.* New York: Harper and Row

Morin, E. (2012). *The Way for the future of human beings.* Hamburg: Krämer.

Naess, A. (1998). *Life's philosophy: reason and feeling in a deeper world.*Athens: The University of Georgia Press.

Naess, A. (1989). Ecology, *Community and Lifestyle.*Cambridge: CUP.

Naess, Ar. (2007). *The selected works of Arne Naess* (Vol. 1). New York: Springer Science & Business Media.

Qudsyi, H., Kusumaningrum, F. A., Utami, D., Fahmi, A., Afsari, N. Iqbal, M., Stueck, M. (2020). Adaptation of avem (arbeitsbezogenes vehaltens- und erlebensmuster) test to measure work-related behavior and experience patterns. *International Journal of Scientific & Technology Research,* 8 (6), ISSN 2277-8616

Qudsyi, H., Trimulyaningsih, N., Novitasari, N., Stueck, M. (2017). Developing module of nonviolent communication among children in yogyakarta. *Proceeding of International Conference on Child-Friendly Education,* Universitas Muhammadiyah Surakarta. ISSN: 2503-5185. 159–180

Raharjo. (2014). The Profane and the Holy in Islam. Presentaton at Bionet-Conference 2014

Schweitzer, A. (1999). Die Weltanschauung der Ehrfurcht vor dem Leben: Kulturphilosophie III (Vol. 1). München: C.H. Beck.

Schweitzer, A., & Campion, C. T. (1961). The Decay and the Restoration of Civilization. London: Unwin Books.

Stueck, M., & Villegas, A. (2021). Science and Biodanza. Peter Lang: submitted

Stueck, M., & Villegas, A. (2008). Dance towards Health. Strassburg: Schibri.

Stueck, M. (1993). The influence of the Eastern traditions in the western psychology. University of Leipzig: unpublished Diplom Work

Stueck, M. (2009). The stressreduction under the use of Yoga ad Biodanza with teachers. Evaluation of a holistic stress management concept in schools. Strassburg: Schibri

Stueck, M. (2013). Introducton in the School of Empathy. In Witruk, E. (2013). Learning disorders. Peter Lang.

Stueck, M. (2015). *The Pinguine- and Polarbear Modell.* Trogome

Stueck, M. (2019). The Health Cube. In E. Witruk & D. S. Utami, *Educational and Rehabilitation Psychology (vol. 8): Traumatic experiences and dyslexia.* Berlin: Peter Lang2

Stueck, M. (2020a). *The Biocentric Health Management Theory.* In: Witruk, E. (2020). Berlin: Peter Lang (accepted, in press)

Stueck, M. (2020b). *Conception of a test battery for psychometric measurement of biocentric acting.* In: Witruk, E. (2020). Berlin: Peter Lang (accepted, in press)

Stueck, M. (2022). Biocentric – a vision of being human after COVID19 and War. *Introduction in the Biocentric Health Theorie.* Strassburg: Schibri submitted.

Stueck, M. (2021). The Pandemic Management Theorie. COVID 19 and Biocentric Development. *Psychological Health Report.*

Stueck, M., Sakti Kaloeti, D. V., Villegas, A., & Utami, D. S. (2018). The influence of Biodanza and School of Empathy verbal – respectful communication on the ability to express emotions and needs: a pilot study among adults in Indonesia. *Health Psychology Report*, 7(4), 334–340. https://doi.org/10.5114/hpr.2019.88665

Stueck, M., Villegas, A., Bauer, K., Terren, R., Toro, *V. & Sack, U. (*2010*). Psycho-immunological process evaluation of Biodanza. Signum Temporis,* 2(1), 99.

Toro, R. (2004). *The Biocentric Principle.* International Biocentric Foundation (IBF), Biodanzaschule Leipzig. Unpublished Material.

Toro, R. (2005). *The Biocentric Education.* International Biocentric Foundation (IBF), Biodanzaschule Leipzig. Unpublished Material.

Toro, R. (2011). *Progetto Minotauro.* Torino: Pintore.

Toro, R. (2010). *Das System Biodanza.* Hannover: Tinto-Verlag.

Utami, D.S., & Stueck, M. (2016). Relations of spirituality, family hardiness, and wellbeing to understand parent`s life quality in Indonesia. *Anthropological Research and studies.* p. 86 ISSN 2344-2824

Widiasmara, N., Novitasari, R., Trimulyaningsih, N., Stueck, M. (2017). School of Empathy for Enhancing childrens wellbeing. *International Journal of Social Science and Humanity*, Vol. 8, No. 8, 230–234

Table of Contents

List of Contributors

Zhazha Fifi, Afiyah
Institution: Islamic University of Indonesia
Address: Jalan Kaliurang km 14,5, Sleman, Special Region of Yogyakarta, Indonesia
E-mail: zafiyah.yah26@gmail.com

Ike Agustina
Institution: Universitas Islam Indonesia
Address: Jalan Kaliurang km. 14,5 Sleman, Yogyakarta, Indonesia
E-mail: ike.agustina@uii.ac.id

Talitha Quratu Aini
Institution: Universitas Islam Indonesia
Address: Yogyakarta, Indonesia
E-mail: talithaquratuaini@gmail.com

Libbie Annatagia
Institution: Islamic University of Indonesia
Address: -
E-mail: libbie.annatagia@gmail.com

Putra Dyah Arminingtyas
Institution: Islamic University of Indonesia
E-mail: -

Rahkman Ardi
Institution: Universitas Airlangga
Email: rahkman.ardi@psikologi.unair.ac.id

Bintang Ilham Avicena
Institution: Universitas Islam Indonesia
Address: Bronggang, Argomulyo, Cangkringan, Sleman, Yogyakarta
Indonesia, 55583
E-mail: hamcena@gmail.com

Dinie Ratri Desiningrum
Institution: Faculty of Psychology, Diponegoro University
Address: Jl. Prof Soedarto, SH, Kampus Undip Tembalang, Semarang, Indonesia 50275
E-mail: diniedesiningrum@lecturer.undip.ac.id

Raden Rachmy Diana
Institution: Sunan Kalijaga State Islamic University
E-mail: Raden.diana@uin-suka.ac.id

Siti Fauziah
Institution: Master of Science in Psychology, Faculty of Psychology Airlangga University Surabaya
Address: Jl. Airlangga 4–6, Surabaya, East Java – 60286.
Email: 2018@psikologi.unair.ac.id

Nailul Fauziah
Institution: Faculty of Psychology, Diponegoro University
Address: Jl. Prof Soedarto, SH, Kampus Undip Tembalang, Semarang, Indonesia 50275
E-mail: nailul_f@yahoo.com

Rika Fitriyana
Institution: Faculty of Psychology, Universitas Bhayangkara Jakarta Raya
Address: Kampus II, Jl. Perjuangan Raya, Marga Mulya, Bekasi Utara, Indonesia
E-mail: rika.fitriyana@dsn.ubharajaya.ac.id

Ricky Firmansyah
Institution: Islamic Studies and Psychology, University of Indonesia, Indonesia
Address: Jl. Salemba Raya No.4, RW.5, Kenari, Senen, Kota Jakarta Pusat, DKI Jakarta 10430, Indonesia
E-mail: ricky.firmansyah@ui.ac.id

Nabila Ayu Gumilang
Institution: Universitas Islam Indonesia
Address: Jalan Kaliurang km. 14,5 Sleman, Yogyakarta, Indonesia
E-mail: -

Siti Hajar Halili
Institution: University of Malaya
Address: Department of Curriculum &Instructional Technology, Faculty of Education, Kuala Lumpur.
Email: siti_hajar@um.edu.my

Seger Handoyo
Institution: Academic Staff at Universitas Airlangga, East Java
Email: seger.handoyo@psikologi.unair.ac

Ila Nurlaila Hidayat
Institution: Fakultas Psikologi UIN Sunan Gunung Djati Bandung
Address: Jalan AH. Nasution, No. 105, Bandung (40614)
E-mail: ila.nurlaila@uinsgd.ac.id

Baiq Nurul Hidayati
Institution: Stikes Yarsi Mataram
Address: Mataram, West Nusa Tenggara, Indonesia
E-mail: baiqnurulhid16@gmail.com

Andi Holilulloh
Institution: UIN Sunan Kalijaga, Yogyakarta
Address: Sukasari, Cilegon, Banten Province
Email: andiekholilullah@gmail.com

Yohanis Franz La Kahija
Institution: Pusat Pemberdayaan Keluarga (Center for Family Empowerment), Universitas Diponegoro
Email: franzlakahija@gmail.com

Dian Veronika Sakti Kaloeti
Institution: Faculty of Psychology, Universitas Diponegoro
Address: Jl. Prof. Soedarto Tembalang Kota Semarang
Email: dvs.kaloeti@live.undip.ac.id

Norfaezah Md Khalid
Institution: University of Malaya
Address: Department of Educational Psychology & Counseling, Faculty of Education, Kuala Lumpur.
Email: norfaezah@um.edu.my

R. Edi Komarudin
Institution: Fakultas Adab dan Humaniora UIN Sunan Gunung Djati Bandung
Address: Jalan AH. Nasution, No. 105, Bandung (40614)
E-mail: edikomarudin@uinsgd.ac.id

Wanadya Ayu Krishna
Institution: Islamic University of Indonesia
Address: -
E-mail: wanadya_akad@uii.ac.id

Ayu Kurnia
Institution: Master of Psychology, Universitas Diponegoro
Email: ayukurnias@gmail.com

Erin Ratna Kustanti
Institution: Faculty of Psychology, Diponegoro University
Address: Jl. Prof Soedarto, SH, Kampus Undip Tembalang, Semarang, Indonesia 50275

Citra Indriani Mandala
Institution: Department of Psychology, Islamic University of Indonesia
Address: Jl. Kaliurang KM 7, Kp Kolombo Kav.008
E-mail: citraindrianim@gmail.com

Rosleny Marliani
Institution: Fakultas Psikologi UIN Sunan Gunung Djati Bandung
Address: Jalan AH. Nasution, No. 105, Bandung (40614)
E-mail: roslenymarliani@uinsgd.ac.id

Sarita Candra Merida
Institution: Faculty of Psychology, Universitas Bhayangkara Jakarta Raya
Address: Kampus II, Jl. Perjuangan Raya, Marga Mulya, Indonesia
E-mail: sarita.candra@dsn.ubharajaya.ac.id

Ahmad Shamsuri Muhamad
Institution: University of Malaya
Address: Department of Educational Psychology & Counseling, Faculty of Education, Kuala Lumpur.
Email: shamsurimuhamad@um.edu.my

Muwaga Musa
Institution: School of Psychology, Kampala University
Address: PO Box 176, Iganga, Uganda
Email: muwagamusa@gmail.com

Fuad Nashori
Institution: Islamic University of Indonesia
Email: fuadnashori@uii.ac.id

Fuad Nashori
Institution: Islamic University of Indonesia
E-mail: fuadnashori@gmail.com

Nur Pratiwi Noviati
Institution: Department of Psychology, Islamic University of Indonesia
Address: Jl. Kaliurang KM 10, Sleman – Yogyakarta
E-mail: nur.pratiwinoviati@uii.ac.id

Resnia Novitasari
Institution: Islamic University of Indonesia
Address: -
E-mail: resnia.novitasari@gmail.com

Annisaa Miranty, Nurendra
Institution: Islamic University of Indonesia
Address: Jalan Kaliurang km 14,5, Sleman, Special Region of Yogyakarta, Indonesia
E-mail: annisaa.miranty@uii.ac.id

Anne Octavia
Institution: Psychology Master Program, University of Persada Indonesia YAI, Jakarta, Indonesia
Address: Jl. Pangeran Diponegoro No.74, RT.2/RW.6, Kenari, Senen, Kota Jakarta Pusat, DKI Jakarta 10430, Indonesia
E-mail: anne.octaviaa@gmail.com

Olga Pavlova
Institution: Moscow State University of Psychology and Education, Russia
Address: -
E-mail: os.pavlova@mail.ru

Anggun Resdasari Prasetyo
Institution: Faculty of Psychology, Diponegoro University
Address: Jl. Prof Soedarto, SH, Kampus Undip Tembalang, Semarang, Indonesia 50275

Ratna Syifa'a Rachmahana
Institution: Universitas Islam Indonesia
Address: Kemuning St. No. 5, Pandeansari, Condongcatur, Depok, Sleman, Yogyakarta, Indonesia, 55283
E-mail: ratnamyn@yahoo.com

Mira Aliza Rachmawati
Institution: Universitas Islam Indonesia
Address: Yogyakarta, Indonesia
E-mail: 003200102@uii.ac.id

Shukran Abd. Rahman
Institution: International Islamic University Malaysia, Malaysia
Address: -
E-mail: shukran@iium.edu.my

Ratna Azkia Rakhmandari
Institution: Islamic University of Indonesia
E-mail: ratnaazkiar@gmail.com

Norsafatul Aznin A. Razak
Institution: University of Malaya
Address: Department of Educational Psychology & Counseling
Email: safatul@um.edu.my

Zulmi Ramdani
Institution: Fakultas Psikologi UIN Sunan Gunung Djati Bandung
Address: Jalan AH. Nasution, No. 105, Bandung (40614)
E-mail: zulmiramdani@uinsgd.ac.id

Fitri Romadonika
Institution: Stikes Yarsi Mataram
Address: Mataram, West Nusa Tenggara, Indonesia
E-mail: romadonika.fitri@gmail.com

Arina Dina Rusyda
Institution: Faculty of Psychology, Diponegoro University
Address: Jl. Prof Soedarto, SH, Kampus Undip Tembalang, Semarang, Indonesia 50275
E-mail: dinaarina33@gmail.com

Rias Pratiwi Safitri
Institution: Stikes Yarsi Mataram
Address: Mataram, West Nusa Tenggara, Indonesia
E-mail: rias_dangkem@yahoo.co.id

Normeilina Sari
Institution: Islamic University of Indonesia
E-mail: -

Iswan Saputro
Institution: Islamic University of Indonesia
E-mail: iswansaputro@gmail.com

Salma
Institution: Pusat Pemberdayaan Keluarga (Center for Family Empowerment), Universitas Diponegoro
Email: salmaibrahim1707@gmail.com

Tri Setiani
Instiution: Islamic University of Indonesia
E-mail: -

Hamidah Sulaiman
Institution: University of Malaya
Address: Department of Educational Psychology & Counseling, Faculty of Education, Kuala Lumpur.
Email: hamidah4804@yahoo.com

Suryanto
Institution: Master of Science in Psychology, Faculty of Psychology Airlangga University Surabaya
Address: Jl. Airlangga 4–6, Surabaya, East Java – 60286.
Email: suryanto@psikologi.unair.ac.id

Melati Sumari
Institution: University of Malaya
Address: Department of Educational Psychology & Counseling, Faculty of Education, Kuala Lumpur.
Email: melati@um.edu.my

Dewi Retno Suminar
Institution: Universitas Airlangga
Email: dewi.suminar@psikologi.unair.ac.id

Endang Retno Surjaningrum
Institution: Universitas Airlangga
Email: endang.surjaningrum@psikologi.unair.ac.id

Marcus Stueck
Institution: DPFA Academy of Work and Health, Germany
Address: -
E-mail: marcus.stueck@dpfa-hs.de

Valentino Marcel Tahamata
Institution: Master of Science, Mind Brain and Consciousness, Taipei Medical University
E-mail: -

Muhammad Novvaliant Filsuf Tasaufi
Institution: Islamic University of Indonesia
Address: -
E-mail: 103200102@uii.ac.id

Dian Sari Utami
Institution: Islamic University of Indonesia
Address: -
E-mail: dian.utami@uii.ac.id

Nur Widiasmara
Institution: Islamic University of Indonesia
Address: -
E-mail: nurwidiasmara@uii.ac.id

Emi Zulaifah
Institution: Department of Psychology, Islamic University of Indonesia
Address: Jl. Kaliurang KM 10, Sleman – Yogyakarta
E-mail: emi_zulaifah@uii.ac.id

Annisaa Miranty Nurendra & Zhazha Fifi Afiyah

Work-Family Conflict, Job Satisfaction, and Organizational Commitment among Indonesian Dual Career-Women in Banking Industry

Abstract. The purpose of this research is to explore the role of work family conflict to organizational commitment with job satisfaction as a mediator variable among dual career women. The participants in this study were 134 women who work in the banking industry in Yogyakarta, Indonesia. The research instruments used in this study were: a) organizational commitment scale, adapted from Allen & Meyer (1990), b) work family conflict scale, adapted from Greenhaus and Beutell (1985), and c) job satisfaction scale, adapted from Luthans (2005). The data were analyzed using SEM mediation analysis with *JASP for Mac*. The study results showed that: a) work-family conflict can predict organizational commitment level, b) work-family conflict can predict job satisfaction level, c) job satisfaction can predict organizational commitment level, d) job satisfaction has a mediating effect in the relationship between work family conflict and organizational commitment.

Keywords: work family conflict, job satisfaction, organizational commitment, dual career women.

1. Introduction

In line with the times and the increasingly advanced globalization era, intense competition occurs in the business world, both in the domestic market and in the foreign market. The impact of this phenomenon cannot be avoided, including in the banking industry. Competition has become increasingly sharp along with the entry of foreign banks competing for customers in the same market. The dynamics of fierce competition in the banking sector require early anticipation in the field of human resources as an effort to maintain the company's existence (Sakina, 2009). Especially in the banking industry, women play a significant role. More than 52 percent of banking employees are female workers. The dual-career woman is a terminology to describe a married and working woman.

Based on previous research by Naido and Jano (2002), dual career women may face high potential stressor. The existence of two different roles, in work life and household, will cause conflict in a dual career woman so it will affect her role in work. Whereas the work demands can make employees overwhelmed with fulfilling their roles so that she does not have the energy to meet all the needs of her family members. In addition, the relatively long number of working hours will cause employees to be unavailable when their children or spouses need them (Buhali & Margareta, 2013). A research study conducted by Apperson (Buhali & Margareta, 2013) found that there are several levels of role conflict between men and women, that women experience role conflict at a higher level than men. This is because women see family as their main obligation and should get more attention than their job roles.

A study by Namasivayan and Zhao (Rantika & Sunjoyo, 2010) states that organizational commitment will be influenced by work family conflicts, which will have a negative influence on employee organizational commitment. Work family conflict is a form of conflict between roles where the pressure is from work and taking care of the family. An employee will be confused with focusing on work or their family at home. Work family conflicts arise among employees who are mostly married and have children. Work family conflict is an inter-role conflict (conflict between roles), conflict arises when roles in work and roles in the family require each other to be fulfilled, fulfilling one role will make it difficult to fulfill the other's roles (Soeharto, 2010).

Work-family conflicts can also affect employee job satisfaction. According to Ammiriel (Yuliana & Yuniasanti, 2013) work-family conflict is one of the internal factors that can affect job satisfaction of an employee. Work family conflicts arise because of the imbalance between the role of a worker and the role of a family member. Meanwhile, Spector (Yuliana & Yuniasanti, 2013) stated that work family conflicts are negatively correlated with job satisfaction, that is, employees who experience a lot of conflict tend to have a low level of job satisfaction.

Job satisfaction according to Spector (Mangundjaya, 2012) is a description of a person's feelings about his job. It is an extension of liking (satisfied) or disliking (dissatisfied) with their work. Job satisfaction is an attitude that reflects the employee's feelings of pleasure or happiness to work (Hidayat, 2013). A person will bring with him a set of wants, needs, desires and past experiences that combine to form work expectations when joining an organization as an employee. Job satisfaction in the organization concerns the attention of superiors, work environment, appropriate rewards and the level of work difficulties that affect employee performance. So even though the work is risky or has a high enough level of pressure and when the employees are satisfied with the company, everything that is done will produce maximum results (Amilin & Dewi, 2008). According to Judge (Puspitawati & Riana, 2014) job satisfaction must be maintained to improve organizational performance. People who are relatively satisfied with their work will be more committed to the organization (Mathis & Jackson in Puspitawati & Riana, 2014).

Organizational commitment is the degree to which the employee believes, accepts the goals of the organization, and will remain in the organization. Someone who has a strong organizational commitment will influence employees to work hard in achieving organizational goals (Hastuti, 2013). Commitment of organizational members becomes important, so that the organization can continue to run and achieve the goals of the organization. Commitment shows the employee's desire to stay and work and dedicate themselves to the organization. Organizational commitment is important since if enough employees leave, it will cause considerable losses in organizational activities (Sumarto, 2009). Gaylor (Hidayat, 2013) states that organizational commitment is not only loyalty to the organization but a process that runs with employees who express their concern for the organization in the form of success and high achievement. The success of an organization and pursuing quality does not only depend on how the organization improves the competence of its employees, but also how to stimulate employees to have commitment to the organization (Azeem, 2010).

Rohman (2009) examines job satisfaction and desire to move which is influenced by organizational commitment. The research objective was to determine whether organizational commitment affects job satisfaction and influences the desire to move and job satisfaction affects the desire of employees to move. The result of the research is that affective commitment has a significant positive effect on job satisfaction and continuance commitment has a significant negative effect on job satisfaction.

Another study was conducted by Rantika and Sunjoyo (2010) who examined organizational commitment, work family conflicts and job satisfaction in nurses. The result of the research is to find that job satisfaction affects organizational commitment positively. Sumarto (2009) also examines organizational commitment and job satisfaction. The results obtained from the research are that organizational support has no effect on organizational commitment. Puspitawati and Riana (2014) examined the effect of job satisfaction on organizational commitment and service quality of workers. The results showed that job satisfaction has a positive effect on organizational commitment and service quality. Anafarta (2011) examines work family conflicts and job satisfaction using a structural equation modeling approach. The results showed that work family conflicts did not affect job satisfaction.

The mixed findings lead to an assumption that the criteria of the participants will affect the result. In this study, we assume that among dual career-women who work in the banking industry, work family conflict will affect their job satisfaction and organizational commitment. The hypothesis to be explored and tested was that job satisfaction served as a mediator variable in the relationship between work family conflict and organizational commitment as stated in Figure 1.

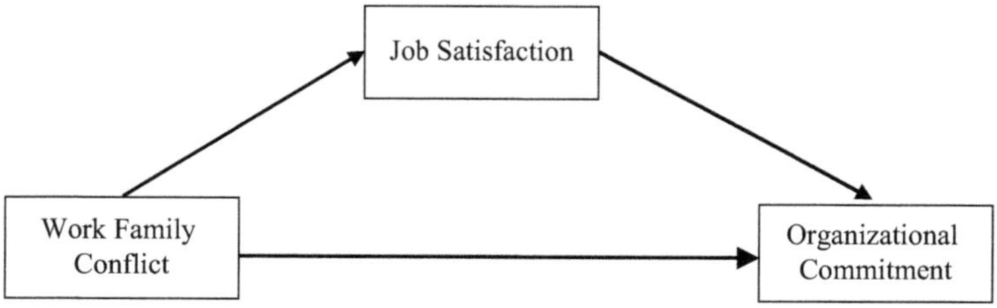

Figure 1. Proposed model

2. Theoretical Review

2.1 Organizational Commitment

Mayer and Allen (Pramadani & Fajrianthi, 2012) reveal that organizational commitment is a psychological manifestation that characterizes the work relationship with the organization and has implications for the decision to continue or discontinue membership in the organization. Luthans (2005) defines organizational commitment as a strong desire to remain as a member of a particular organization, a desire to strive according to organizational desires and certain beliefs and acceptance of organizational values and goals. In other words, attitudes that reflect employee loyalty to the organization and a continuous process in which organizational members express their concern for the organization and its success and continuous progress.

Mayer and Allen (Supriati, 2013) formulate aspects of commitment in organization, namely: 1) Affective Commitment, relates to the emotional relationship of members to the organization, identification with the organization, and involvement of members with organizational activities; 2) Continuance Commitment, related to the awareness that organizational members will suffer losses if they leave the organization; 3) Normative Commitment, describes a feeling of attachment to continue being in the organization. Organizational members with high normative commitment will continue to be members of the organization because they feel they must be in the organization.

2.2 Work Family Conflict

Frone, Rusell and Cooper (Buhali & Margareta, 2013) define work family conflicts as role conflicts that occur in employees, where on the one hand they have to do work in the office and on the other hand must pay attention to the family as a whole. Meanwhile, according to Greenhaus and Beutell (1985) work family conflict is a form of role conflict in which the demands of work and family roles simultaneously cannot be aligned according to Natemeyer (Roboth, 2015) defines work family conflict as a form of conflict in which general demands, time and tension arising from work interfere with employees' responsibilities to the family.

Work family conflict contains several aspects according to Greenhaus and Beutell (1985), namely: 1) Time-based Demands, the limited time a person has, the time used for work often results in limited time for family and vice versa, 2) Strain-based Demands, tensions in one role that ultimately affect the performance of other roles, 3) Behavior-based Demand, difficulty changing behavior alternately from one role to another.

2.3 Job Satisfaction

Mathis and Jackson (Sopiah, 2008) define job satisfaction as a positive emotional statement which is the result of an evaluation of work experience. According to Howell and Dipboye (Munandar, 2012) job satisfaction is the overall result of the degree of liking or dislike of workers towards various aspects of their work. Meanwhile, according to Spector (Laksmi & Hadi, 2012) job satisfaction is an attitude variable that reflects how individual evaluations feel about their work, both as a whole and from various aspects of the job.

According to Luthans (2005) there are several dimensions in job satisfaction, namely: 1) The work itself, where the job provides interesting assignments, opportunities to learn and opportunities to accept responsibility as various source of satisfaction; 2) Salary, where employees see salary as a reflection of how management views employees' contributions to the company; 3) Promotion opportunity, perceived as opportunities for advancement in organizations where employees accept greater responsibility in terms of work; 4) Supervision, it is supervisor's ability to provide technical assistance and behavioral support; 5) Co-workers, the degree to which a colleague is technically clever at doing work and is able to provide social support.

3. Method

3.1 Sample

The participants in this study were 134 women employees who were married, with a minimum tenure of 1 year. The age of the participants ranged between 25 to 55 years old, meanwhile their marriage ranged between 1 to 40 years. The tenure also varies from 1 to 40 years.

3.2 Measurement Tools

Questionnaires used in this study were: a) organizational commitment scale, b) work family conflict scale, and c) job satisfaction scale.

3.2.1 Organizational Commitment Scale

The scale adapted from Mayer and Allen (Supriati, 2013). The dimensions to be measured were the affective commitment, the continuance commitment, and the normative commitment. The scale consists of 24 items. The total item correlation moves between 0.308 to 0.832 with alpha Cronbach 0.920.

3.2.2 Work Family Conflict Scale

Work family conflict is adapted from Greenhaus and Beutell (Juariyah & Harsono, 2011). The dimensions to be measured were time-based demands, strain-based demands and behavior-based demands. This scale consists of 26 items. The total item correlation moves between 0.348 to 0.769 with Alpha Cronbach 0.938.

3.2.3 Job Satisfaction Scale

The job satisfaction scale is adapted from Luthans (2005). The dimensions to be measured were satisfaction to the job itself, salary, promotion opportunities, supervision and co-workers. The job satisfaction scale has 35 items with total item correlation moves between 0.343 to 0.840 and Cronbach's alpha of 0.964.

4. Results

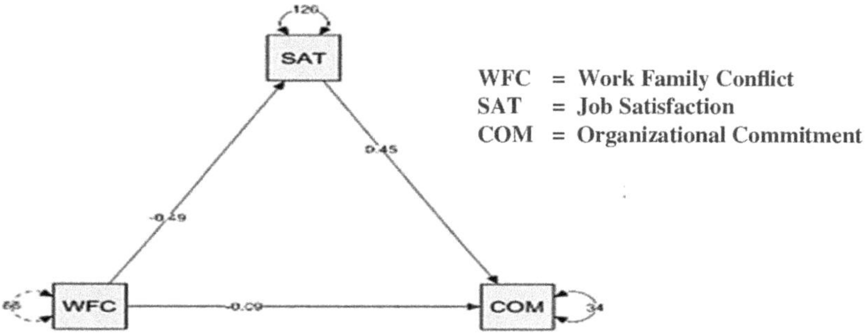

Figure 2. Empirical model

Data analysis result illustrated in Figure 2. As seen on Table 1, work family conflict can be a predictor of organizational commitment. The correlation between work family conflict and organizational commitment is negative with R = -0.3061. This means that the higher the work family conflict, the lower the organizational commitment, and vice versa. Work-family conflict can also be a predictor for job satisfaction variables. The correlation of work-family conflict with job satisfaction is negative with R = -0.4908. This means that the higher the work-family conflict, the lower the job satisfaction and vice versa. Job satisfaction can be a predictor for organizational commitment variables. The correlation between job satisfaction and organizational commitment is positive with R = 0.7887. This means that the higher the job satisfaction, the higher the organizational commitment and vice versa.

Table 1. Correlation between variables

Variables	M	SD	1	2	3
1 Work Family Conflict	40,2	6,6	-		
2 Job Satisfaction	76,8	7	-0.4908**	-	
3 Organizational Commitment	70,6	11	-0.3061**	0.4448**	-

**correlations are significant at p< 0.01

Table 2 shows that the direct effect from work-family conflict to organizational commitment was not significant (p>0.05), meanwhile the indirect effect of work-family conflict through job satisfaction to organizational commitment was significant ($p<0.01$) and not including 0 value in its LLCI and ULCI. This means that high work family conflicts can reduce organizational commitment by reducing job satisfaction first.

Table 2. Direct, indirect and total effect

Variables	Estimate	SE	Z	p	LLCI	ULCI
Direct Effect						
WFC * Commitment	-0.086	0.065	-1.316	0.188	-0.264	0.087
Indirect effect						
WFC * Satisfaction * Commitment	-0.220	0.058	-3.814	0.000	-0.418	-0.015
Total Effect						
WFC * Commitment	-0.306	0.081	-3.578	0.000	-0.544	-0.028

The results of this study are in line with the research of Buhali and Margaretha (2013) which stated that work-family conflicts have a significant effect on organizational commitment. The negative relationship between work-family conflicts and organizational commitment shows that individuals who have difficulty harmonizing their roles in the family and at work will feel less committed to their organization. Theoretically, work family conflicts affect organizational commitment according to Chusmir (Buhali & Margaretha, 2013) because one of the factors that affect an employee's organizational commitment is individual characteristics. It is known that self and family have a strong influence on employee organizational commitment. Employee attitudes, values, and needs show directly or indirectly their commitment to the organization. From their personal characteristics, there will be two external circumstances that will affect the commitment process, namely the work situation and the family situation.

In addition, this study is in line with Sumarto's research (2009) which states that job satisfaction has a positive effect on organizational commitment and vice versa. This means that the higher the job satisfaction obtained by employees, the higher their organizational commitment. Job satisfaction is achieved through proper wages, satisfaction with the work performed, a conducive work environment, and adequate management treatment, so that they have a commitment to the organization. Job satisfaction may affect organizational commitment because the relationship between job satisfaction and organizational commitment is very strong. According to O'Driscoll (Sumarto, 2009) satisfaction and commitment always go hand in hand, employees who are more involved with work will feel satisfied and will increase their organizational commitment. Mathis and Jackson's study (Puspitawati & Riana, 2014) showed that people who are relatively satisfied with their work will be more committed to the organization.

5. Conclusion

In this study, it appears that job satisfaction has a mediating effect on the relationship between work-family conflict and organizational commitment. Therefore, it is necessary to increase employee job satisfaction, organizations can implement HR strategies or policies that aim to reduce employee work-family conflicts, for example by increasing a supportive climate in the organization, reducing workloads or demands whenever possible.

Work-family conflict also appears to have a significant direct role on job satisfaction. Therefore, organizations can help employees to have better work family conflicts by providing self-development techniques for employees to be able to manage their time and self in relation to office and home duties, and enforce family friendly organizational policies, such as flexible working hours and so on. Further research may explore the antecedents of work family conflict related and job satisfaction variables for working women, such as working culture across organization.

6. References

Allen, N., & Meyer, J. (1990). The measurement and antecedents of affective, continuance and normative commitment to the organization. *Journal of Occupational Psychology, 63*(1), 1–18.

Amilin., & Dewi, R. (2008). The effect of organizational commitment on public accountant job satisfaction with role stress as a moderating variable. *JAAI, 12*(1).

Anafarta, Nilgun. (2011). The Relationship between work-family conflict and jobsatisfaction: a structural equation modeling (SEM) approach, *International Journal of Business and Management, 6 (4),* 168–177.

Azeem, S. (2010). Job satisfaction and organizational commitment among employees in the sultanate of oman. *Scientific Research, 1*(4), 295–300. .

Buhali, G. A., & Margaretha, M. (2013). Effect of work-family conflict on organizational commitment: Job satisfaction as a mediation variable. *Journal of Management, 13*(1).

Greenhaus, J. H., & Beutell, N. J. (1985). Sources of conflict between work and family roles. *The Academy of Management Review, 10*(1), 76–88.

Hastuti, R. T. (2013). Organizational commitment and leadership style in implementing performance-based budgeting for public service bodies. *Integrated Journal of Health Sciences, 3*(1).

Hidayat, R. (2013). The influence of leadership on communication, job satisfaction and organizational commitment in the banking industry. *Makara Journal Series Sosial Humanities, 17*(1).

Juariyah, L., & Harsono. (2011). The effect of work-family conflict on the withdrawal behavior of working married couples. *Journal of Business Economics, 16*(1).

Laksmi, N. A., & Hadi, C. (2012). The relationship between work family conflict and job satisfaction at karayan in the production section of PT.X. *Journal of Industrial and Organizational Psychology, 1*(2).

Luthans, F. (2005). *Organizational Behavior*, 10th edition. Yogyakarta: Publisher ANDI

Mangundjaya, W. (2012). Perceptions of organizational support versus job satisfaction and its role on organizational citizenship behavior. *Journal of Social Psychology, 8*(7).

Munandar, A. S. (2012). *Industrial and Organizational Psychology*. Jakarta: University of Indonesia (UI-Press)

Pramadani, A. B., & Fajrianthi. (2012). Relationship between organizational commitment and readiness to change in Telkom Ketintang surabaya enterprise service (DES) employees. *Journal of Industrial and Organizational Psychology, 1*(2).

Puspitawati, N. M. D., & Riana, I. G. (2014). The effect of job satisfaction on organizational commitment and service quality. *Journal of Strategic Management and Entrepreneurship, 8*(1).

Rantika, R., & Sunjoyo. (2010). The effect of work-family conflict on organizational commitment mediated by job satisfaction in the nurse profession at the regional general hospital (RSUD) Dr. Moewardi Surakarta

Roboth, J. Y. (2015). Analysis of work family conflict, organizational commitment, and performance of women with multiple roles at the east indonesia compassion foundation. *Journal of Business Research and Management, 3*(1).

Rohman, A. (2009). The effect of organizational commitment on job satisfaction and desire to move (Studies on employees of public accounting firms in Central Java). *FE Unsil Accounting Journal, 4*(1).

Sakina, N. (2009). Employee organizational commitment at PT. Bank "X" in Jakarta. *Journal of Psychology, 7*(2).

Soeharto, T. N. (2010). Work-family conflict with job satisfaction: Meta analysis. *Journal of Psychology, 37*(1).

Sopiah. (2008). *Organizational Behavior*. Yogyakarta: Publisher ANDI

Sumarto. (2009). Increase commitment and satisfaction to reduce intentions to leave. *Journal of Management and Entrepreneurship, 11*(2).

Supriati. (2013). The influence of organizational commitment on lecturer turn-over intention at Bengkalis Polytechnic. *Inovbiz's Journal,1*(1).

Yuliana, E. S., & Yuniasanti, R. (2013). Relationship between work-family conflict and job satisfaction of female police at Polres Kulon Progo. *Journal of Socio-Humanities, 4*(5).

Citra Indriani Mandala, Emi Zulaifah & Nur Pratiwi Noviati

The Mediating Role of Psychological Well-Being on the Relation between Work-Family Balance and Job Satisfaction

Abstract: The aim of this study is to examine the relationship between work-family balance and job satisfaction with psychological well-being as a mediating variable. Using data from 71 working mothers, the results showed a positive relationship between work-family balance and psychological well-being of the working mothers. Then, there is a positive relationship between psychological well-being and job satisfaction level of working mothers. Furthermore, psychological well-being is shown to be an effective mediating variable, bridging between work-family balance and job satisfaction. Finally, the key finding of this study was that psychological well-being mediated the effect of work-family balance and job satisfaction. The study showed that there was full mediation of psychological well-being in the relation between work-family balance and job satisfaction.

Keywords: Work-family balance, job satisfaction, psychological well-being, working mother

1. Introduction

One of the determinants of an organizational effectiveness is job satisfaction (JS) (Aziri, 2011). Singarimbun (2011) revealed that women's job satisfaction was lower than male employees. The Indonesian Statistical Bureau (Badan Pusat Statistik [BPS], 2016) surveyed the conditions of the labor force. The results showed that there was an increase of female workers by 3,799,735. The data showed that most of the female workers were married, or in other words, they were working mothers. When married women choose to work, this leads her to have multiple roles. The dual role triggers a more complex problem because of the demands in both roles. This is a dilemma for working mothers because of the difficulty in balancing these two roles. These difficulties can have a negative impact on both work and family life (Ermawati, 2016). Job satisfaction is a component of life satisfaction for working mothers, only when she can achieve a life balance of family and work (Anuradha & Pandey, 2016). Yadav and Dabhade (2014) revealed that work-life balance is important because it can affect the job satisfaction of mothers.

While the relationship between work-family balance (WFB) and job satisfaction were confirmed in previous studies, it is not yet clear through which variables such relations occur; if mediation from other variables does exist, it needs to be examined if the mediation is a full or partial mediation, for a firm conclusion. Thus, it is important to test which variables play a role in bridging the relationship of the two. Psychological well-being (PWB), from its definition, implies its importance for job satisfaction. Ryff (1989) defined PWB as a full achievement of psychological potential where a person can accept strengths and weaknesses, has a purpose in life, develops positive relationships with others, becomes an independent person, can adapt, and continues to grow personally. Tasema (2018) states that PWB can lead to a sense of feeling calm when working, so it allows one person to achieve job satisfaction even when he/she faces hectic work. The role of WFB and PWB towards job satisfaction triggers the idea to examine the relationship between the three variables with PWB as the mediating variable. Thus, this study is to see whether there is a mediating effect of PWB on the relationship between WFB and job satisfaction, especially among working mothers. This is due to the increasing number of female workers who tend to have lower job satisfaction than male workers (Singarimbun, 2011). With the increasing numbers of women involving themselves in professional work and career in Indonesia, this fact of the less satisfied working mothers is important to be known. Does experiencing WFB influence their satisfaction with their job? If yes, how would PWB play a role in this relationship?

2. Theoretical Review

2.1 Job Satisfaction

Spector (1997) describes job satisfaction as employees' feelings for their work and various aspects of their work. This feeling shows the extent to which employees feel satisfied or dissatisfied with their work. Employees who are satisfied with their jobs tend to approach their work with a positive attitude or to survive within their jobs. While employees who are not satisfied with their work tend to avoid their work. Aspects of job satisfaction according to Spector (1997) are: 1) The nature of the work itself, which refers to the level of satisfaction with the type of work performed, 2) Supervision, refers to the level of employee satisfaction with superiors, 3) Colleagues, refer to the level of satisfaction with coworkers, 4) Appreciation, refers to the level of satisfaction with non-monetary rewards, where this reward is given to employees who have good performance, 5) Working conditions, referring to the level of satisfaction with applicable regulations and procedures, 6) Communication, referring to the level of satisfaction with communication that exists in the organization, 7) Salary, refers to the level of satisfaction with salary and increase in salary received, 8) Promotion, refers to the level of employee satisfaction with opportunities for promotion or development, 9) Benefits, referring to the level of satisfaction with the benefits provided. Mullin (2005) explains the factors that influence job satisfaction as follows: 1) Personal factors, including employee personality and marital status. In fact, the focus in this study namely work-family balance and psychological well-being belong to this category 2) Social factors, including relationships with co-workers, 3) Cultural factors, including the underlying values and principles for behaving among employees, 4) Organizational factors, including organizational size, formal structure, personnel policies, and procedures, and 5) Environmental factors, including economic, social, technical actors as well as government policies.

2.2 Work-Family Balance

Greenhaus, Collins and Shaw (2003) define work-family balance as the extent to which individuals are involved and feel satisfied with the role in work and family. There are three aspects of WFB according to Greenhaus, Collins and Shaw (2003), namely: 1) time balance, referring to the same amount of time to carry out roles in work and family, 2) balance of roles, referring to the same level of psychological involvement between roles in work and family, 3) balance of satisfaction, refers to the level of satisfaction felt in the roles at work and family.

2.3 Psychological Well-Being

Ryff (1989) defined PWB as the full achievement of psychological potential where a person can accept strengths and weaknesses, has a purpose in life, develops positive relationships with others, becomes an independent person, can adapt, and continues to grow personally. Aspects of PWB according to Ryff (1989) are: 1) Autonomy, the ability to determine one's life choices (self determination), regulate behavior, not to seek other people approval but to do self-evaluation by personal standards and to be independent 2) Environmental mastery, a person's ability to choose or create an environment following psychological conditions so as to be able to develop themselves creatively through physical and mental activities, 3) Personal growth, the need to actualize themselves to be, open to experience and a desire to continue to develop, 4) Positive relations, the ability to love, have a strong and great sense of empathy and affection for others and have deeper friendships, 5) Purpose in life, someone who has a purpose in life has a feeling that life today and the past have meaning and believe to achieve life goals, 6) Acceptance of self, have a positive attitude towards oneself, acknowledging weaknesses and strengths that are inside and having a positive outlook on the past.

3. Method

The study used a quantitative research method that is correlational to examine the relation between WFB and JS with PWS as a mediating variable. There are three hypotheses proposed in this study, namely: a) There is a positive relationship between work-family balance and psychological well-being b) There is a positive relationship between psychological well-being and job satisfaction and c) The relationship between work-family balance and job satisfaction is mediated by psychological well-being.

3.1 Sample

The respondents involved in this study were 71 female workers from the production and administration department of a garment industry, who were married and were parents. The industry is located in southern central Java, in the province of Yogyakarta. The work schedule is 5/24 from 8 to 4 pm.

3.2 Research Instruments

The study uses three Likert scales which have six responses with scores ranging from 1 (totally disagree) to 6 (totally agree). The three scales were Job Satisfaction Scale, Work-Family Balance Scale and Psychological Well-Being. The Job Satisfaction was a 36 items scale developed by the authors referring to the job satisfaction theory by Spector (1997). The internal consistency coefficient shows Cronbach alpha of 0.966 and the item-total correlation ranged between 0.293–0.818. The Work-Family Balance scale is a modification of a WFB scale from the study of WFB by Alinaksi, Nashori and Zulaifah (2016) with 28 items. The value of the Cronbach alpha is 0.913 and the item-total correlation ranged between 0.291–0.725. The Psychological Well-Being scale used a scale from Ryff (1989) with 31 items. The Cronbach alpha is 0.925 and the item-total correlation range between 0.258–0.779.

4. Results

Table 1. Coefficients for the mediating effect

Testing Path	Unstandardized Coefficient		*t*	Sig.	Bootstrapping	
	Coefficient	Std. Error			LLCI	ULCI
IV – M (a)	0.4567	0.1136	4.0212	0.0001	0.2301	0.6832
M – DV (b)	0.6962	0.1693	4.1120	0.0001	0.3583	1.0340
IV-M-DV (c')	-0.2726	0.1774	-1.5362	0.1291	-0.6267	0.0815
IV – DV (c)	0.0453	0.1772	0.2559	0.7988	-0.3081	0.3988
Indirect Effect	0.3179	0.1203			0.1342	0.6140

Data were analyzed using bootstrapping procedures in SPSS. The results of the analysis show that WFB has a significant relationship to PWB with $p = 0.001$ and a path score of 0.457, so that the first hypothesis is accepted. This result is in line with the study by Sanoveriana and Fourianalistyawati (2016) which shows that there is a relationship between WFB and PWB. WFB showed a high contribution in improving PWB. A study by Lumbangaol and Ratnaningsih (2018) showed a significant negative relationship between work-family conflict and psychological well-being with an effective contribution of 45.4 %. When family conflict occurs, it will reduce psychological well-being, and vice versa. WFC occurs when a person is unable to balance their work and family life. The low level of WFC shows that there is a relative balance between work-family life where a person can divide time, energy, and roles in both domains so that there is suitability and harmony that encourages high psychological well-being. The current study is also in line with Sianturi and Zulkarnain's research (2013) which shows that there is a negative relationship between WFC on psychological well-being. The things that underlie the relationship are first, a happy employee is an employee who has a positive relationship based on trust, empathy, and compassion. The positive relationships are obtained through interaction with family and co-workers. Second, WFC is one of the determinants of one's happiness. The conflict occurs because of the inability to balance the two roles.

The next analysis is to examine the relationship between PWB and JS. The results of the analysis show that PWB has a significant relationship to JS with $p = 0.001$ with a path score b of 0.696, so that the second hypothesis is accepted. In line with Tasema's study (2018) which shows a significant positive relationship between PWB and JS. When PWB increases, JS will be higher. PWB can increase job satisfaction as its presence enables a person to build good relationships with other people, important for the quality of interpersonal relationships at work. A person is called to be well psychologically when they can accept strengths and weaknesses, build relationships, become an independent person, control the environment and to continue to grow personally. With all these psychological capacities, it will not be too difficult for him/her to find satisfaction with work. Experiencing PWB will bring a feeling of calm at work that enables a person to face the pressure of work and to be able to create achievements. Good psychological well-being can help individuals to achieve a good level of job satisfactionThe last analysis was conducted to examine the relationship of WFB to job satisfaction with PWB as a moderating variable. The results of the analysis indicated that an indirect effect of WFB on JS via PWB was significantly positive, with an indirect score of 0.317 and a confidence interval of 95 % ranging from 0.134–0.614. Specifically, there wasn't a significant total effect with total effect score of 0,045, p = 0.798, and direct effect score of -0,272 with p = 0,129. These results indicated a full-mediation model of WFB and JS through PWB. The imbalance of work and family shows that a person is unable to divide time, energy and role in both domains resulting in mismatches and disharmony that encourage low PWB (Lumbangaol & Ratnaningsih, 2018). Maurya and Agarwal (Lumbangaol & Ratnaningsih, 2018) added that someone who can carry out their functions and responsibilities optimally will experience PWB so that they can produce a good performance. Wright and Bonett (2007) stated that when someone's PWB is low, it will have an impact on low job satisfaction. This situation, when taking place, might have an impact on the intention to move to other organizations, with the hopes of increasing their personal improvement or simply experience. Tenggara, Zamralita, and Suyasa (Lumbangaol & Ratnaningsih, 2018) said that PWB plays a significant role in the level of individual satisfaction with work. Tasema (2018) underlined that PWB brings a feeling of calmness when working so that a person can deal with work pressure. When a person is unable to balance their work and family it will lead to work-family conflicts that have an impact on the low psychological well-being. Low psychological well-being makes a person work with less sense of growth, meaning, competencies, thus reduce job satisfaction.

5. Conclusion

The result of this study showed a positive relationship between work-family balance and psychological well-being of the working mothers. There is a positive relationship between psychological well-being and job satisfaction level of the working mothers. It also showed that there is no direct relationship between work-family balance and job satisfaction. This indicates that there is a full-mediation effect of psychological well-being on the relationship between work-family balance and job satisfaction. The results of this study give us the following theoretical and practical implications. On the theoretical side, the mechanism on how work-life balance affects job satisfaction, is now known from the current study, that is through the role of psychological well being. On the practical side, as PWB shows a consequential effect on job satisfaction, we can say that an attempt to improve job satisfaction in an organization through work-life balance intervention needs to, first of all, examine whether or not the program has resulted in the increase of psychological well-being of the employees.

6. References

Alinaksi, A. N., Nashori, F., & Zulaifah, E. (2016). Konseling work family balance untuk menurunkan tingkat stres kerja karyawan di PT. JFL Yogyakarta [Work-family balance counselling to reduce employees job stress at PT JFL Yogyakarta]. *Thesis* (unpublished). Yogyakarta: Fakultas Ilmu Sosial Budaya Universitas Islam Indonesia

Anuradha, & Pandey, M. (2016). Impact of work life balance on job satisfaction of women doctors. *Problem and Perspective in Management, 14*(2), 319–324

Aziri, B. (2011). Job Satisfaction: A Literature Review. *Management Research and Practice, 3*(4), 77–86

Badan Pusat Statistik. (2016, February). *Keadaan Angkatan Tenaga Kerja di Indonesia* [The State of the Labor Force in Indonesia]. Retrieved on April 19th 2017 from https://www.bps.go.id/publication/2016/06/01/bd60570a94b7dc84053e2be9/keadaan-angkatan-kerja-di-indonesia-februari-2016.html

Ermawati, S. (2016). Peran ganda wanita karier (konflik peran ganda wanita karier ditinjau dalam perspektif islam) [Dual roles of career women (Dual role conflicts of career women in islamic perspective)]. *Jurnal Edutama, 2*(2), 59–69

Greenhaus, J. H., Collins, K.M., & Shaw, J.D. (2003). The Relation Between Work Family Balance and Quality of Life. *Journal of Vocational Behavior,* 63, 510–531 DOI: 10.1016/S0001-8791(02)00042-8

Lumbangaol, E. E., & Ratnaningsih, I. Z. (2018). Hubungan antara konflik pekerjaan-keluarga dan kesejahteraan psikologis pada wartawati radio. [The relation between work-family conflict and psychological well being of radio reporters]. *Jurnal Empati, 7*(1), 221–226.

Mullin, L. J. (2005) *Management and organizational behavior* (7th Ed). FT Prentice Hall.

Ryff, C. D. (1989). Happiness is everything, or is it? Explorations on the meaning of psychological well-being. *Journal of Personality and Social Psychology, 57*(6),1069–1081.

Sanoveriana, A., & Fourianalistyawati, E. (2016). Work family balance, trait mindfulness and psychological well-being in middle-aged working parents. *Proceedings on Social Science and Humanities, 1,* 1–9.

Sianturi, M. M., & Zulkarnain. (2013). Analisis work family conflict terhadap kesejahteraan psikologis pekerja. *Jurnal Sains dan Praktik Psikologi, 1*(3), 207–215.

Singarimbun, J. B. (2011). Analisis kepuasan kerja karyawan berdasarkan perbedaan karakteristik jenis kelamin.[Analysis of job satisfaction based on gender differences] *Jurnal Murni Sadar, 1*(2), 63–76.

Spector, P. E. (1997). *Job satisfaction: application, assessment, causes and consequences.* California: SAGE Publication.

Tasema, J. K. (2018). Hubungan antara psychological well being dan kepuasan kerja pada karyawan di kantor x [Relationship between psychological well-being and job satisfaction at office X]. *Jurnal Maneksi, 7*(1), 39–46.

Wright, T. A., Bonett, D. G. (2007). Job satisfaction and psychological well being as nonadditive predictors of workplace turnover. *Journal of Management, 33*(2). 141–160.

Yadav, R. K., & Dabhade, N. (2014). Work life balance and job satisfaction among the working women of banking and education sector – A Comparative Study. *International Letters of Social and Humanistic Sciences,* 21, 181–201.

Dian Veronika Sakti Kaloeti, Salma, Yohanis Franz La Kahija,
Ayu Kurnia & Valentino Marcel Tahamata

The Assessment of Psychological Distress among Incarcerated Men

Abstract: This study examined the psychological distress among incarcerated men and investigated the construct validity of the instruments on targeted samples. To accomplish this goal, a total of 510 incarcerated participants aged 25–34 (SD = 0.98) from three men's correctional facilities located in Central Java and Yogyakarta took part in the study. Participants completed the 12-item General Health Questionnaire (GHQ-12) and sociodemographic data. The mean GHQ-12 score for the total sample was 3.31 (SD = 3.49). The internal consistency of the GHQ-12 showed satisfactory results (Cronbach's α = 0.88). Results showed that more than half (63 %) of the inmates scored low on the GHQ-12, and more than a quarter proportion (37 %) of them scored high, indicating an unhealthy psychological state. Further, the construct validity and factorial structures were tested through Exploratory Factor Analysis (EFA) These findings have some important theoretical implications for mental health promotion in prison and offer several opportunities for more future research.

Keywords: Psychological Distress, Mental Health, Screening, Incarcerated Men

1. Introduction

The population of prisoners in Indonesia is approximately 200,000 prisoners according to the latest available data in 2012 (United Nations Office on Drugs and Crime,2017). The number of incarcerated men of the Correctional Institution in Central Java, Semarang-Indonesia was 12,411 (Ministry of Law, 2018). This is incomparable with the capacity of prisons which can only accommodate 8,215 people. Situations of overcapacity and limited available resources, have an impact on inmates' mental health. The regimentation of incarceration predisposing offenders to mental health issues (Massoglia & Pridemore, 2015; Schnittker, Massoglia, & Uggen, 2012; Turney, Wildeman, & Schnittker, 2012).

The mental health problems experienced by prisoners are anxiety and depression (Kaloeti et al., 2018; WHO, 2005; Yi, Turney & Wildeman, 2016). There are more than 10 million convicts worldwide, and the prevalence of all investigated mental disorders is higher than general population comparison (Fazel et al., 2016). These situations become a risk factor for the emergence of self-injury (Blaauw, Kerkhof & Hayes, 2005; Lekka, Argyriou & Beratis, 2006), and suicidal behavior (Palmer & Connelly, 2005; Lohner & Konrad, 2007). Specifically, suicide is a leading cause of death in prisons (Baillargeon, et.al., 2009; Fazel, Cartwright, Norman-Nott & Hawton, 2008; Jenkins, Kendall et al., 2005; Suto & Arnaut, 2010). Furthermore, offenders with mental health issues may be at a higher risk of adjustment inside the prison and experience future recidivism (Baillargeon et al., 2009; Mears, Cochran, & Bales, 2012).

Furthermore, Baillargeon et. al. (2009) in their study found incarcerated persons with mental health disorder were 70 % more likely to return to prison at least once than were those who were not. Research shows that individuals with an incarceration history, compared to those without an incarceration history, have a significantly greater likelihood of emotional distress, depression, life dissatisfaction (Massoglia & Pridemore, 2015; Schnittker et al., 2012; Turney et al, 2012).

The incarceration conditions like lack of privacy, support, and solitary have been identified as strong correlations for self-harm and adaptation challenges for those with mental health conditions in prison settings (Olley, Nicholls & Brink, 2009). Psychological distress can often lead to more serious mental health consequences. Research showed psychological distress is associated with offenders' adaptation and their mental health condition (Olley et al., 2009; Assari et al, 2018). Then, the routine assessment and implementation of mental *health screening* and assessment of prisoners are necessary for holistic rehabilitation planning, evaluation and possible treatment. Given the substantial consequences in the conditions of confinement, in most of the prisons of Indonesia, yet there is a lack of information about the prevalence of mental health symptoms among prisoners. Despite their high prevalence, mental disorders often go unrecognized in health care settings among prisoners (Gonzalez & Conell, 2014). About 26 % of the prisoners were diagnosed with a mental health condition at some point during their lifetime, and a very small proportion (18 %) were taking medication for their conditions (Gonzalez & Conell, 2014).

This study used the twelve-item version of the General Health Questionnaire (GHQ-12). The GHQ-12 is a self-administered screening tool designed broadly to measure psychological distress in the general population (Goldberg, 1972). The GHQ has been translated into 38 languages. The General Health Questionnaire (GHQ) is one of the most widely used screening tests to assess the mental health of a population and is designed as a structured, brief and self-administered questionnaire (Goldberg et al., 1997; & Kim et al., 2013). In Indonesia, reliability and validity studies on the GHQ-12 have been conducted (Indiani & Suhardi, 2006; Primasari & Hidayat, 2016). GHQ-12 has been widely used as a unitary measure (Martin & Newell, 2005), but two or more underlying factors have been identified in previous studies based on factor (Campbell, Walker & Farrel, 2003; Penninkilampi-Kerola, Miettunen & Ebeling, 2006).

The purpose of the study is, first to derive an assessment of the psychological health of incarcerated men in Semarang, Indonesia and the second is to determine the reliability and factor structure of the screening measurement in an Indonesian prison setting.

2. Theoretical Review

2.1 Psychological Distress

Psychological distress is a state of emotional suffering typically characterized by symptoms of depression and anxiety. These symptoms often coexist and co-occur with common somatic complaints and a wide range of chronic conditions. There are five characteristics of patients living with psychological distress, they are perceived inability to cope, changes in emotional status, discomfort, communication of discomfort, and harm (Arvids Dotter et al., 2016). Psychological distress is described as a number of uncomfortable subjective states, encompassing the mood and bodily states associated with depressive (e.g. sadness and worthlessness) and anxious states (e.g. worry and restlessness) (Mirowsky & Ross, 2003).

Higher levels of psychological distress are associated with various fixed factors, such as female gender, lower educational status, and increased age after 75 years of age (Baidawi & Trotter, 2015). Apart from being influenced by fixed factors, psychological distress is also influenced by modifiable factors such as the level of support and social involvement, level of physical activity, sleep cycle, functional status and physical health burden (Baidawi & Trotter, 2015). Arvids Dotter et al. (2016) stated that psychological distress is an imbalance between self and ideal self, which slowly breaks up individual self-esteem. The imbalance is described in three dimensions, namely struggling to cope with everyday life, feeling inferior to others, and losing one's grip on life.

2.2 Psychological Distress among Incarcerated

The level of psychological distress among prisoners was found in England and Wales, which showed that 63 % of the total prisoners had psychological distress (Brooke et al., 1996). Then in Ghana as much as 70 % (Ibrahim et al., 2015), and 63 % of prisoners in Zambia (Nseluke & Siziya, 2011), and 61.9 % of psychological distress that occurs in prisons is caused by a stressful prison environment than in other institutions. due to overcrowding, loss of privacy, lack of meaningful activity, many forms of violence, isolation from social relationships, and inadequate mental health services in prison. Psychological conditions in prisons are generally in the form of anxiety, boredom, discomfort, isolation, and stressful situations (Handayani & Fitri, 2014). Furthermore, Baidawi and Trotter (2015) stated psychological distress in older prisoners, including personal and demographic factors such as age, cognitive ability and educational level, and physical health conditions. Next are sentence factors, the initial period of imprisonment is the most distressing time for inmates the older ones, then prison factors, such as a stable environment, activities, and ministry in prison. The last one is social factors, namely social interactions that occur in prison. Interaction with prison staff causes distress to older inmates. It was also found that psychological distress was significantly associated with prison service satisfaction. The psychological distress level is 3 times higher for inmates who are not satisfied with prison services compared to inmates who are not satisfied with prison services (Dachew et al., 2015).

3. Method

3.1 Sample

The present study involved 510 incarcerated men at 3 correctional facilities in Yogyakarta and Semarang, Central Java. All participants gave their written informed consent after the purpose of the investigation and the procedure to be followed had been explained, and a declaration on the anonymity and confidentiality of their data and their freedom to participate or to withdraw at any time were guaranteed.

3.2 Measurement Tools

GHQ-12 was used in this study. This instrument is a screening tool which was used to identify the severity of psychological distress experienced by an individual within the past few weeks. GHQ-12 is already adapted into the Indonesian version and has good validation (Primasari & Hidayat, 2016). It focuses on two major areas: 1) the inability to carry out normal functions and 2) the appearance of new and distressing phenomena. Each item on the scale has four responses from "better than usual" to "much less than usual." (Bimodal responses: 0-0-1-1). The scores were summed up by adding all the items on the scale ranging from 0 to 12. The cut-off points 3/4 was used in this study to determine the respondents' level of psychological well-being (Patel et al, 2007).

In this study, the GHQ-12 produced Cronbach's α value of .88. To verify the utility of the instrument to assess distress in incarcerated men, the psychometric characteristics of the GHQ-12 must be analyzed. For this purpose, exploratory factor analysis was conducted, internal consistency was analyzed, and subsequently. The analyses were performed using SPSS AMOS v.21.

4. Results

4.1 Descriptive Statistics

The mean obtained in the GHQ-12 in the total sample was 3.31 (SD = 3.49). In Table 1, it's shown there are 509 (100 %) men in the study with majority are incarcerated adults aged between 25–34 years (37 %), Muslim (92 %) and Javanese (88 %). More than half of the participants reported finishing junior high school and are married (54 %). More than 60 % are sentenced above 3 years, 53 % convicted of narcotics, 44 % to general crimes, 3 % to corruption cases. Based on the ¾ cutoff score, more than half (63 %) of the inmates scored low on the GHQ-12 or normal, and more than quarter proportion (37 %) of them scored high, indicating an unhealthy psychological state.

Table 1. Demographic characteristics of the subjects

Variables	Frequency	%
Age (Years)		
18–24	118	23
25–34	191	37
35–44	125	25
45–54	52	10
>54	24	5
Religion		
Islam	468	91,7
Christian	40	7,8
Budha	2	0,4
Ethnic Group		
Javanese	448	88
Sumatran	27	5
Borneo	11	2
Sulawesi	2	1
Others	22	4
Education		
Did not pass Elementary	33	7
Elementary	71	14
Junior High	349	68
Senior High	57	11
Marital Status		
Single	148	29
Married	277	54
Separated/divorced	85	17
Cases		
Narcotics	270	53
Corruption	14	3
Crimes (e.g.,murder, fraud, burglary,sexual)	226	44
Verdict		
Life sentences	1	0,19
>3 years	336	65,88
1–3 years	120	23,53
Less than 1 year	53	10,4

4.2 Exploratory Factor Analysis

The results of Bartlett's sphericity test and the Kaiser-Meyer-Olkin (KMO) sample adequacy test showed values of 2048.216 ($p<0.001$) and 0.91 respectively, so the suitability of the correlation matrix structure was verified, and consequently the feasibility of using factor analysis was confirmed.

Factor analysis of the scale with principal component extraction method with a maximum likelihood procedure solution yielded a two-factor model, explaining 51.36 % of the variability of the model. The factor structure of the GHQ-12, eigenvalues and the percentage of explained variance of each of the two factors are shown in Table 2. Items 2, 5, 6, 7, 9, 10, 11 and 12 are grouped into the first factor (8 items: psychological distress/general dysphoria). Items 1, 3, 4, and 8 loaded on the second factor (4 items: social dysfunction). The items that make up each factor came from loading equal to or higher than .40.

Table 2. Exploratory factor analysis: factor loadings for the GHQ-12, principal components, varimax rotation, eigenvalues, and percentage of explained variance

No	Items	Factor I	Factor II
1	Able to concentrate	--	.79
2	Loss of sleep over worry	.54	--
3	Playing a useful part	--	.60
4	Capable of making decisions	--	.73
5	Felt constantly under strain	.73	--
6	Couldn't overcome difficulties	.60	--
7	Able to enjoy day-to-day activities	.58	--
8	Able to face problems	--	.55
9	Feeling unhappy and depressed	.73	--
10	Losing confidence	.70	--
11	Thinking of self as worthless	.74	--
12	Feeling reasonably happy	.55	--
	Eigenvalue	5.10	1.06
	Explained variance%	42.54	8.82
	Cumulative%	42.54	51.36

It has been shown the GHQ-12 were rich and potential for mental health screening purposes and could apply in a prison setting. Also, its brevity may have practical advantages for scaling and clinical purposes. The data indicated two-factor fit and have adequate reliability rates. The two factors are Factor I-related to anxiety/ depression, and Factor II-related to social dysfunction, testing the ability to perform daily activities and to cope with everyday problems.

Furthermore, being stereotyped as a criminal has an impact on incarcerated self-stigma (Moore, Tangney, & Stuewig, 2016). As a result, they tend to experience various symptoms of mental disorders, such as anxiety, stress, and depression (Moore, et al., 2016). The rising tide of mental disorder may be related to factors such as economic change related to life satisfaction level before imprisonment, social support, and types of prison (Beyen, Dadi, Dachew, Muluneh, & Bisetegn, 2017). Specifically, Sinha (2010) found that a number of negative emotions arose due to imprisonment, including psychological distress, anxiety, depression, and being unable to enjoy life. Furthermore, social dysfunction can occur because of the feeling of insecurity and lead to adaptive disability in the prison environment (Hairston, 2018). This study found, more than a quarter of the incarcerated men experienced psychological distress. But on the other hand, surprisingly, the prisoners do not face difficulties in carrying out daily activities. This is related to rehabilitation programs for the offenders which facilitated them to work in daily activities. These skills provide an essential contribution for their social function when returning to the public. In addition, family and significant others' support become meaningful sources for the prisoners. Scanlon, et al. (2018) showed that a positive relationship with family or significant others are very prominent for the assisted to return to the society.

Collectivistic culture delivers the importance of the roles of community. Several studies showed that the community as an intervention method is essential to enhance the mental health status among the incarcerated (McKenna et al., 2015). The positive atmosphere called the prison in-reach model of care, built inside the prison through the rehabilitation program, peer support from other incarcerated members, psychosocial rehabilitation program which is delivered by the wardens and family visits helps their positive psychological state. Ungar (2006) specified culture plays an important role in how individuals react to problems, such as emotion expression (Harrel, Kafetsios & Hess, 2015), and emotion regulation (Leersynder, Boiger, & Mesquita, 2013). Furthermore, Lim (2016) found that internalized cultural values will shape a person's attitude in facing life's challenges. Javanese ethnicity has several local wisdoms that reflects collectivistic culture. People with Javanese ethnicity have a strong tendency to instill social values that influence their mental health status (Kurniawan & Hasanat, 2007). One of the fundamental values is '*guyub*'. The term '*guyub*' refers to togetherness, where Javanese people must create harmony, and respect the existence of others (Hardjowirogo, 1989). Most of the participants are Javanese, which allows them to provide mutual support in prison. McGowan et al (2017) revealed that social support fosters resilience in people exposed to negative emotions (depression, anxiety, stress) and increases psychological well-being. In addition, Wells, Avers, and Brooks (2012) found community social support given to vulnerable groups is associated with resilience in the face of psychological distress and implications for physical and mental health.

Beside that, *'narimo ing pandum'* is another necessary value that the Javanese hold. '*Narimo ing pandum*' is a state of complete acceptance of every event experienced, both now, past, and in the future (Koentjaraningrat,1990). This attitude has a strong spiritual value, where Javanese believe that every problem comes from God. The internalized value makes the prisoners tend to be aware of their conditions. Further, gratitude, patience, and acceptance as part of these values make the incarcerated accept their imprisonment. In line, Russo-Netzer and Moran (2018) discovered that self-acceptance allows a person to make peace with their problems and has implications for growth.

5. Conclusion

Based on this study, routine mental health screening becomes imperative. This study also has some limitations. The generalizability of the results is limited due to the sample and to the fact that it was a convenience sample. Future, we recommend collecting data from incarcerated women and conducting experimental research that might support the findings. The involvement of local values will provide an essential approach in leading prisoners' mental health.

6. References

Arvidsdotter, T., Marklund, B., Kylén, S., Taft, C., & Ekman, I. (2016). Understanding persons with psychological distress in primary health care. *Scandinavian Journal of Caring Sciences, 30*(4), 687–694. September, 25 https://doi.org/10.1111/scs.12289

Assari, S., Lankarani, M., & Caldwell, C. (2018). Does discrimination explain the high risk of depression among high-income African American men? *Behavioral Sciences, 8*(4), 40. Doi: 10.3390/bs8040040

Baidawi, S., & Trotter, C. (2015). *Psychological Distress Among Older Prisoners : A Literature Review. September.* https://doi.org/10.1080/1936928X.2015.1075166

Baillargeon, J., Penn, J. V., Thomas, C. R., Temple, J. R., Baillargeon, G., & Murray, O. J. (2009). Psychiatric disorders and suicide in the nation's largest state prison system. The journal of the American Academy of Psychiatry and The Law, 37(2), 188–93

Beyen, T. K., Dadi, A. F., Dachew, B. A., Muluneh, N. Y., & Bisetegn, T. A. (2017). More than eight in every nineteen inmates were living with depression at prisons of Northwest Amhara Regional State, Ethiopia, a cross sectional study design. Beyen et al. BMC Psychiatry, 17(31), 1–9. Doi: 10.1186/s12888-016-1179-9

Blaauw, E., Kerkhof, A. J. F. M., & Hayes, L. M. (2005). Demographic, criminal, and psychiatric factors related to inmate suicide. *Suicide and Life-Threatening Behavior, 35*(1), 63–75. Doi:10.1521/suli.35.1.63.59268

Brooke, D., Taylor, C., & Maden, J. (1996). Point prevalence of mental disorder in unconvicted male prisoners in England and Wales. BMC Medical Research Methodology, 313.

Campbell, A., Walker, J., & Farrell, G. (2003). confirmatory factor analysis of the ghq-12: Can I see that again? *Australian & New Zealand Journal of Psychiatry, 37*(4), 475–483. Doi:10.1046/j.1440-1614.2003.01208.x

Dachew, B. A., Fekadu, A., Kisi, T., Yigzaw, N., & Bisetegn, T. A. (2015). Psychological distress and associated factors among prisoners in Northwest Ethiopia: Cross-sectional study. *International Journal of Mental Health Systems, 9*(1), 1–6. https://doi.org/10.1186/s13033-015-0033-7

Fazel, S., Cartwright, J., Norman-Nott, A., & Hawton, K. (2008). Suicide in prisoners: A systematic review of risk factors. Journal of Clinical Psychiatry, 69(11), 1721–1731

Fazel, S., Hayes, A.J., Bartellas, K., Clerici, M., & Trestman, R. (2016). Mental health of prisoners: prevalence, adverse outcomes, and interventions. *Department of Psychiatry,* 16, 30142–30150. Http://dx.doi.org/10.1016/S2215-0366(16)30142-0

Goldberg D.P., Gater, R., Sartor Ius, N., Ustun, T.B., Icc Inelli, M.P., Gureje,0., Rutter, C. (1997). The validity of two versions of the GHQ in the WHO study of mental illness in general health care. *Psychol. Med, 27*(1), 191–197. Doi: 10.1017/S0033291796004242

Goldberg, D. (1972). *The detection of psychiatric illness by questionnaire: A technique for the identification and assessment of non-psychotic psychiatric illness.* London, New York: Oxford University Press.

Gonzalez J. M. R., & Conell, N. M. (2014). Mental health of prisoners: Identifying barriers to mental health treatment and medication continuity. *American Journal of Public Health,* 104 (12), 2328–2333. Doi: 10.2105/AJPH.2014.302043

Hairston, C. F. (2018). Family relationships during incarceration and when fathers return home. *Journal of Offender Rehabilitation, 57*(2), 67–68.

Handayani, P., & Fitri, M. (2014). Pemetaan problem-problem psikologis narapidana di lapas kelas II A Jember [Mapping of the psychological problems of prisoners in prison class II A Jember]. *Insight, 10*(2), 159–171.

Hardjowirogo, M. (1989). *Manusia Jawa*. Jakarta: Haji Masagung

Harrel, S., Kafetsios, K., & Hess, U. (2015). A cross-cultural study on emotion expression and the learning of social norms. *Frontiers in Psychology, 6,* 1501. Doi: 10.3389/fpsyg.2015.01501

Ibrahim, A., Esena, R., Aikins, M., O'Keefe, A., & McKay, M. (2015). Assessment of mental distress among prison inmates in Ghana's correctional system: a cross-sectional study using the Kessler Psychological Distress Scale. *International Journal of Mental Health Systems, 9*(17).

Indiani, S., & Suhardi. (2006). Validity and reliability of the general health questionnaire for psychological distress and social dysfunction screening in the community. *I'enel Kesehatan, 34*(4), 161–173. Retrieved from http://ejournal.litbang.depkes.go.id/index.php/BPK/article/view/1204.

Jenkins, D. J., Kendall, C. W., Marchie, A., Faulkner, D. A., Wong, J. M., de Souza, R., … Connelly, P. W. (2005). Direct comparison of a dietary portfolio of cholesterol-lowering foods with a statin in hypercholesterolemic participants. *The American Journal of Clinical Nutrition, 81*(2), 380–387. Doi:10.1093/ajcn.81.2.380

Kaloeti, D. V. S., Rahmandani, A., Sakti, H., Salma, S., Suparno, S., & Hanafi, S. (2018). Effect of childhood adversity experiences, psychological distress, and resilience on depressive symptoms among Indonesian university students. *International Journal of Adolescence and Youth,* 1–8. Doi:10.1080/02673843.2018.1485584

Kim, Y .J., Cho, M. J., Park, S., Hong, J. P., Sohn, J. H., Bae, J. N., Jeon, H. J., … Park, J. I. (2013). The 12-item general health questionnaire as an effective mental health screening tool for the general Korean adult population. *Journal Of Neuropsychiatric,* 10, 352–358. Http://dx.doi.org/10.4306/pi.2013.10.4.352

Koentjaraningrat. (1990). *Kebudayaan Jawa*. Jakarta: Balai Pustaka.

Kurniawan, A. P., & Hasanat, N. U. (2007). Perbedaan ekspresi emosi pada beberapa tingkat generasi Suku Jawa di Yogyakarta [Differences in emotional expression at various levels of Javanese generation in Yogyakarta]. *Jurnal Psikologi*, 1–17.

Leersynder, J. D., Boiger, M., & Mesquita, B. (2013). Cultural regulation of emotion: individual, relational, and structural sources. *Frontiers in Psychology*, 1–11.

Lekka, N. P., Argyriou, A. A., & Beratis, S. (2006). Suicidal ideation in prisoners: Risk factors and relevance to suicidal behavior. A prospective case-control study. *European Archives of Psychiatry and Clinical Neuroscience, 256*(2), 87–92. Doi:10.1007/s00406-005-0606-6

Lim, N. (2016). Cultural differences in emotion: differences in emotional arousal level between the East and the West. *Integrative medicine research, 5*(2): 105–109.

Lohner, J., & Konrad, N. (2007). Risk factors for self-injurious behavior in custody: Problems of definition and prediction. *International Journal of Prisoner Health, 3*(2), 135–161. Doi:10.1080/17449200701321654

Martin, C. R., & Newell, R. J. (2005). The factor structure of the 12-item General Health Questionnaire in individuals with facial disfigurement. *Journal of Psychosomatic Research, 59*(4), 193–199. Doi:10.1016/j.jpsychores.2005.02.020

Massoglia, M., & Pridemore, W. A. (2015). Incarceration and Health. *Annual review of sociology, 41*, 291–310. https://doi.org/10.1146/annurev-soc-073014-112326

McGowan, J. A., Brown, J., Lampe, F. C., Lipman, M., Smith, C., & Rodger, A. (2017). *Resilience and Physical and Mental Well-Being in Adults with and Without HIV. AIDS and Behavior, 22*(5), 1688–1698.

McKenna, B., Skipworth, J., Tapsell, R., Madell, D., Pillai, K., Simpson, A., . . . Rouse, P. (2015). A prison mental health in-reach model informed by assertive community treatment principles: Evaluation of its impact on planning during the pre-release period, community mental health service engagement and reoffending. *Criminal Behaviour and Mental Health*, 25, 429–439.

Mears, D. P., Cochran, J. C., & Bales, W. D. (2012). Gender differences in the effects of prison on recidivism. *Journal of Criminal Justice, 40*(5), 370–378. Doi:10.1016/j.jcrimjus.2012.06.009

Ministry of Law. (2018). *Status Pelaporan Jumlah Penghuni Lembaga Pemasyarakatan*. Retrieved from http://smslap.ditjenpas.go.id

Mirowsky, J. & Ross, C. E. (2003). *Education, social status, and health* (New York, Aldine de Gruyter).

Moore, K. E., Tangney, J. P., & Stuewig, J. P. (2016). The self-stigma process in criminal offenders. *Stigma Health, 1*(3), 206–224.

Nseluke, M., & Siziya, S. (2011). Prevalence and socio-demographic correlates for mental illness among inmates at lusaka central prison, Zambia. *Medical Journal Zambia, 38*(2).

Olley, M. C., Nicholls, T. L., & Brink, J. (2009). Mentally ill individuals in limbo: obstacles and opportunities for providing psychiatric services to corrections inmates with mental illness. *Behavioral Sciences & The Law, 27*(5), 811–831. Doi:10.1002/bsl.899

Palmer, E. J., & Connelly, R. (2005). Depression, hopelessness and suicide ideation among vulnerable prisoners. *Criminal Behaviour and Mental Health, 15*(3), 164–170. Doi:10.1002/cbm.4

Patel, V., Araya, R., Chowdhary, N., King, M., Kirkwood, B., Nayak, S., ... Weiss, H. A. (2007). Detecting common mental disorders in primary care in India: a comparison of five screening questionnaires. *Psychological Medicine, 38(02).* Doi:10.1017/s0033291707002334

Penninkilampi-kerola, V., Miettunen, J., & Ebeling, H. (2006). A comparative assessment of the factor structures and psychometric properties of the GHQ-12 and the GHQ-20 based on data from a Finnish population-based sample. *Scandinavian Journal of Psychology, 47(5),* 431–440. Doi:10.1111/j.1467-9450.2006.00551.x

Primasari, I., & Hidayat, R. (2016). General Health Questionnaire-12 (GHQ-12) sebagai instrumen skrining gangguan penyesuaian. *Jurnal Psikologi, 43*(2), 121–134. Retrieved from https://jurnal.ugm.ac.id/jpsi/article/view/9155/15173

Russo-Netzer, P., & Moran, G. (2018). Positive growth from adversity and beyond: Insights gained from cross-examination of clinical and nonclinical samples. *American Journal of Orthopsychiatry, 88*(1), 59–68.

Scanlon, F. A., Scheidell, J. D., Cuddeback, J. S., Samuelsohn, D., Wohl, D. A., Lejuez, C. W., . . . Khan, M. R. (2018). Depression, executive dysfunction, and prior economic and social vulnerability associations in incarcerated African American men. *Journal of Correctional Health Care,* 1–14.

Schnittker, J., Massoglia, M., & Uggen, C. (2012). Out and down. *Journal of Health and Social Behavior,* 53(4), 448–464. Doi:10.1177/0022146512453928

Sinha, S. (2010). Adjustment and mental health problems in prisoners. *Industrial Psychiatry Journal, 19*(2), 101–104.

Suto, I., & Arnaut, G. L. Y. (2010). Suicide in prison: A qualitative study. *The Prison Journal, 90*(3), 288–312. Doi:10.1177/0032885510373499

Turney, K., Wildeman, C., & Schnittker, J. (2012). As Fathers and Felons. *Journal of Health and Social Behavior, 53*(4), 465–481. Doi:10.1177/0022146512462400

Ungar, M. (2006). Resilience across Cultures. *British Journal of Social Work, 38*(2), 218–235.

United Nations Office on Drugs and Crime. (2017). UNODC Indonesia country programme 2017–2020. Retrieved from http://www.unodc.org/documents/indonesia//publication/2017/UNODC_Country_Programme_2017_-_2020.pdf

Wells, M., Avers, D., & Brooks, G. (2012). Resilience, Physical Performance Measures, and Self-Perceived Physical and Mental Health in Older Catholic Nuns. *Journal of Geriatric Physical Therapy*, *35*(3), 126–131.

World Health Organization. (2005). *Information sheet: Mental health and prisons*. Retrieved from https://www.who.int/mental_health/policy/mh_in_prison.pdf

Yi, Y., Turney, K., & Wildeman, C. (2016). Mental health among jail and prison inmates. *American Journal of Men's Health*, 1–10

Hamidah Sulaiman, Siti Hajar Halili, Melati Sumari, Norfaezah Md Khalid, Norsafatul Aznin A. Razak, Ahmad Shamsuri, Muhamad & Andi Holilulloh

The Relevance of Emotional Intelligence in Urban Poverty among Secondary School Students in Malaysia

Abstract: Poverty has various definitions, which start from inadequate diet, financial issues, and the life hardship within a social context. Various agendas have been introduced to address the problem of urban poverty for triggering social problems to families in the city. Among the problems are increasing rate in crime, rape, incest, murder, degradation of health, security as well as the neglecting of education and health of children. This study aims to identify the category of families in urban poverty, the level of emotional intelligence among adolescents, to determine the categories of urban poverty and to explore the critical issue of urban poverty families. The approach used is based on Fuzzy Delphi technique to gather experts' opinions in a workshop. The results list the five categories of poverty, four critical issues related to urban poverty communities and the setting of seven resolutions to overcome these critical issues by consensus of the expert group.

Keywords: Urban poverty, social problems, adolescents, social context, Fuzzy Delphi techniques.

1. Introduction

According to the Malaysian Ministry of Women, Family and Community Development (2015), the population living in poor condition in urban areas is also referred to as the population of urban poverty, in which poverty is described as the status of being marginal and underprivileged. Adolescents living in metropolitan areas of poverty are populations of metropolitan disadvantage generally identified with underprivileged circumstances (Alegre, 2012). Several studies have shown that radical urban slum development is a source of urban poverty (Hamidah, 2020). As a result, these problems are not capable of absorbing all workers for job opportunities which generate unemployment problems and the provision of basic facilities in the region.

2. Theoretical Review

2.1 Models of Emotional Intelligence

There are two theoretical approaches to emotional intelligence today that are defined as the paradigm of capacity and mixed models (Darling & Steinberg, 1993) . The capacity model recognizes emotional intelligence as a normal intellect and claims that the structure follows conventional intelligence standards. Capacity model proponents evaluate emotional intelligence as an analytical skill with performance tests that have a consistency parameter. Mix models are so-called because they integrate capacity growth with personality traits and abilities such as trust, self-esteem and cognitive self-effectiveness. Emotional intelligence theory influences the effectiveness of peer-to-peer networking staff, and overall job performance (Kazemi et al., 2012).

2.2 Emotional Intelligence in Everyday Life

Several studies have produced evidence indicating different domain-wide consequences involving cognitive and social growth, psychiatric well-being, psychological disorder, academic performance, and organizational leadership and other behaviors (Mitlin, 2003). Mental fitness and security were the only cognitive wisdom. Anxiety and depression are the most common symptoms in this area which lead to psychotherapy for people. The skills associated with emotional intelligence can also enable individuals to effectively deal with depressive thoughts and promote constructive emotions to enhance both personal growth and health. Second, emotional intelligence is social functioning. Asnawi, Sombuling, and Madlan (2017) reported that among teenagers with lower emotional intelligence were rated as more aggressive in one sample than others and tended to be engaged in more inconsistent behavior than their peers who scored higher in emotional intelligence. Third, emotional intelligence is academic performance. It suggests that other aspects of school achievement will influence emotional intelligence. Another research suggests that students with higher scores on the MSCEIT YV were less likely to have pessimistic feelings towards the school and its staff. Last, emotional intelligence is workplace performance that contributes significantly to many facets of success at the workplace. Thus, the objective of this study is to identify the level of emotional intelligence among adolescents in urban poverty, specifically on the critical issues faced by the urban poverty families.

3. Method

This research collected data using the Delphi Fuzzy Method (FDM). Murray, Pipino and Gigch implemented FDM in 1985 and Kaufman and Gupta reviewed the FDM (Adler & Ziglio, 1996) in 1988. The reasoning for using FDM is to overcome the limitations of the standard Delphi system. Experts are chosen for the FDM panel based on many factors, such as the psychology and counseling degree, a program that directly exposes students to the applications and practices in this area. They may also have experience as course coordinators who are in charge of the program development and revision process. It prioritizes teacher educators with more than 20 years of experience teaching the curriculum. They may have expertise in developing and assessing the area of counseling and therapy. They are chosen to have in-depth views on case collection to identify and the topic of urban poverty groups. In this research, a total of 30 experts were chosen to define and categorize urban poverty problems in different fields. They were interviewed using the Fuzzy Delphi Method.

4. Results

A total of thirty experts were interviewed using the Fuzzy Delphi process. They identified five types of major problems in urban poor families, such as: (1) Financial poverty, which includes employment, wages and liabilities; (2) Family, physical, health and nutrition status poverty; (3) Participation poverty, which includes the transit infrastructure and systemic factors; (4) Poverty capacities, which implies information and skills; (5) Cultural poverty, which includes philosophy, faith, belief, globalization and economic competition.

Table 1. Mean score in the level of emotional intelligence among adolescents in urban poverty

No	Categories	Mean scores	Interpretation
1	Empathy skills	3.418	Moderate
2	Social skills	2.246	Low
3	Self-awareness	2.536	Moderate
4	Leadership	2.397	Low
5	Emotional management.	2.377	Low

From the results of the Delphi Fuzzy Process, seven proposals were addressed by the panel of experts to resolve problems for families in urban poverty, such as: (1) Architecture and preparation in the field of human resource growth for poor communities, such as delivering or offering skills training, home management training, and clinic to enhance their quality of life; (2) Include poverty eradication services by the Ministry of Housing and Local by providing assistance and preparation for urban disadvantaged populations; (3) develop policies to safeguard the human resources of poor people, such as the rights of children, schooling and the idea of community schools; (4) Offers nutritious help to disadvantaged people, such as flour and food relief, and is free of charge for children; (5) Constructing theme parks in urban communities is important and will offer access and oversight to the poor members community; (6) Offer special research grant to prospective family-related scholars, in particular urban poverty; (7) create a Hub for Professional Intervention focusing on community-based rehabilitation and schooling.

5. Conclusion

Further research is suggested to arrange a workshop that involves experts to establish a problem-solving paradigm in urban poverty among teenagers focused on experiences relevant to the key issues found in this report. Education plays a significant role in boosting the economic development of a nation, as well as growing the awareness and skills for a better life, according to Asnawi, et al. (2017). Furthermore, a review workshop should be undertaken to generate books in family education, teenage developmental psychology, and family growth from the Islamic viewpoint to ensure that these books will have positive influence and advice to urban poor parents and communities.

6. References

Adler, M., & Ziglio, E. (1996). Gazing into the oracle: The Delphi method and its application to social policy and public health. London: Jessica Kingsley Publishers.

Alegre, A. (2012). Is there a relation between mother's parenting Styles and Children's Trait Emotional Intelligence? *Electronic Journal of Research in Educational Psychology, 10*(1), 005–034.

Asnawi, A, A., Sombuling, A., & Madlan, L. (2017). Penerimaan gaya keibubapaan dalam kalangan remaja dan kesannya terhadap perkembangan kecerdasan emosi [Acceptance of parenting style among adolescents and its impact on emotional intelligence development]. *Jurnal Psikologi Malaysia, 31*(2), 78–89.

Chang, P. L., Hsu, C. W., & Chang, P. C. (2011). Fuzzy Delphi method for evaluating hydrogen production technologies. *International Journal of Hydrogen Energy*, *36*(21), 14172–14179.

Darling, N., & Steinberg, L. (1993). Parenting Style as Context: An Integrative Model. Psychological Bulletin, 113, 487–496

Hamidah, S. (2020). *Psikologi Perkembangan Anak dan Remaja Pengasuhan Anak Lintas Budaya [Child and Adolescent Developmental Psychology: Child Parenting across Cultures]*. Bandung: Remaja Rosdakarya.

Kazemi, A., Solokian, S., Ashouri, E., & Marofi, M. (2012). The relationship between mother's parenting style and social adaptability of adolescent girls in Isfahan. Iranian *Journal of Nursing and Midwifery Research, 17*(2), 1–6.

Malaysian Ministry of Women, Family and Community Development. (2015). *Definisi miskin*. Retrieved from http://www.kpwkm.gov.my/nkra/definisi

Mitlin, D. (2003). Addressing urban poverty through strengthening assets. *Habitat International*. *27*,393–406.

Rika Fitriyana & Sarita Candra Merida

The Implementation of Islamic Cognitive Restructuring through CBT for Depression: A Case Study

Abstract: As the largest Muslim population globally, Indonesia needs mental health services to support its religious society. The role of religion and spirituality in clinical practice has been studied extensively in the last few decades, with significant research results indicating substantial progress in integrating spirituality and religion into clinical practice. Furthermore, this study aimed to illustrate how psychotherapy, in this case, Cognitive Behavioral Therapy (CBT), helps Muslims who seek treatment to deal with depression. Implementing the Islamic cognitive restructuring method is one way to ensure ethical and effective treatments for Muslim clients. By developing Islamic perspective psychotherapy, integration of Islamic belief in practicing CBT for Muslim clients can be done. This research uses the small-N experimental design and generated results providing arguments that Islamic-CBT could help patients with depression to heal. Continued clinical replication series is needed to improve broader claims about the effectiveness of the treatment tested.

Keywords: CBT, cognitive restructuring, muslim, psychotherapy

1. Introduction

According to the Center Board of Statistics, Indonesia's total population has reached 261.890 by the year 2018, and 87 % of them are Muslims (Statistik, 2018). As the largest Muslim population in the world, Indonesia needs mental health services to support its religious society. Research shows that the role of religion and spirituality in clinical practice has been studied extensively in the last few decades, with significant research indicating substantial progress in the successful integration of spirituality and religion into clinical practice. Previous studies found that Muslims who seek treatment in mainstream psychotherapy tend to have difficulty connecting to and trusting their therapist formulation of treatment goals (Inayat, 2007). In the last ten years, many research reports showed trends in how Islamic traditions are integrated into modern psychology (Haque, Khan, Keshavarzi, & Rothman, 2016).

In Indonesia,through its Center of Data and Information, the Ministry of Health revealed that 6 % or almost 14 million people are diagnosed with depression (Manafe, 2018). This data showed the urgency for the government or health institutions to provide treatment for depression. One of the depressive disorder characteristics is discrete episodes of at least two weeks' duration involving clear-cut changes in affective, cognition, and neuro-vegetative functions and interepisode remissions (American Psychiatric Association, 2013). It also causes distressing symptoms that affect how someone feels, thinks, and handles daily activities, such as sleeping, eating, or working (National Institute of Mental Health, 2016). Multiple studies showed that depression is related to various diseases such as heart disease, cancer, stroke, bone health, and diabetes (Sotelo & Nemeroff, 2017).

2. Theoretical Review

2.1 What Is Depression?

Depression is an emotional condition with suffering feelings such as deep sadness, guilty feeling, meaningless life (Kring, Johnson, Neale, & Davison, 2013). Besides that, the person with depression syndrome avoids relating to another person in a social setting. They choose to withdraw from another person. They fail to participate in social activity with others, and they feel sad continuously for an extended period. Depression also has behavioral definitions such as demonstrating sad or flat affect, having a preoccupation with the subject of death, having suicidal thoughts, exhibiting mood irritability, and isolated oneself from others, such as their families and their peers. Low academic motivation, lack of interest in many activities, refusing to communicate openly with others, little or no eye contact with others, frequently expressing negative self-statements, and exhibiting low appetite are also some indications of depression (Jongsma, Peterson, & Bruce, 2014).

2.2 What Is Cognitive Behavior Therapy (CBT)

Donald Meichenbaum developed a therapeutic technique called Cognitive Behavior Modification (CBM) that later transformed into Cognitive Behavior Therapy, which focuses identifying dysfunctional self-talk to change unwanted behaviors. For many years, depression has been treated using medication or other commonly employed treatments, such as CBT, which are standard handling for patients with depression (Rosenberg & Kosslyn, 2011). Moreover, CBT has become one of the most widely used models for people with religious orientations (Hodge, 2011). Some therapists found challenges when working with religious clients and applying scripture in psychotherapy proved useful in handling this problem (Garzon, 2005). It is essential for professionals who work with Muslim clients to understand the Islamic faith and Islamic practices in daily life (Hamdan, 2008).

2.3 What Is Islamic Cognitive Behavior Therapy (CBT)

Beck's theory about depression, known as the "cognitive triad," tells us that depressed people tend to have:(a) a negative view of self, (b) a negative view of the world, and (c) a negative view of the future (Rehm, 2015). In Islamic-CBT, the depression patient works together with their therapist to restructure his/her cognitive distortion, using Islamic perspective and value. The therapist guides the patient to overcome his/her depression based on the Quranic hope and drive, such as stated in the Holy Qur'an verses below (Khan, 2016):

> *"God does not change the condition of a nation until they first change itself."* (Qur'an, 13: 11)
> *"God does not burden any person but to allow him to develop his potential."* (Qur'an, 2:286)
> *"With hardship comes ease. Indeed, with hardship comes ease."* (Qur'an, 94: 5–6)

Table 1. Islamic cognitive restructuring session (Khan, 2016)

Session	Topic	Explanation
1	Good Rapport and Problems Identification	Conducting depth-interview and listing significant problems in a patient's life.
2	Cognitive restructuring with Qur'anic verse (13: 11)	Therapists help patients find strength by looking at problems from the Islamic view.
3	Cognitive restructuring with Qur'anic verse (2: 286)	Patient learns about the problems and creates new ways to solve them by realizing Allah does not lay responsibility on anyone beyond his capacity.
4	Cognitive restructuring with Qur'anic verse (94: 5–6)	Discussing hard situations that ever occurred in life and with every hardship comes ease afterward.
5	Evaluation	Therapist guides the patient in evaluating all the sessions before and sees the difference after implementing new thinking ways.

Using this part of the session and topic, the patient learns to deal with cognitive distortion that occurs in his/her mind. He/She realizes that whatever form of hardship or difficulty a person is experiencing, he/she has the resources to overcome it. In short, the therapist needs to help clients identify their strengths and inner potentials to overcome psychological problems like depression. Intervention with CBT can help patients to develop a healthy cognitive pattern and rational beliefs about themselves. This intervention also prevents them from relapsing in the longer term. Besides that, CBT also improves healthy interpersonal relationships and regains positivity in their daily lives (Jongsma et al., 2014). The Islamic CBT helps patients to recover faster than usual CBT, show better treatment compliance, leads to lower rates of relapse, and also reduces treatment disparities (Husain & Hodge, 2016).

3. Method

3.1 Sample

This research used Small-N design, characterized by frequently administered measurements and the experimental manipulation of an intervention, in which participants serve as their control (Barker, Pistrang, & Elliott, 2015). In this case, we also involve repeated measurements, which allow monitoring any changes in the patient closely. This research uses two patients diagnosed with depression as research participants, who joined the CBT session as part of treatment.

A single case study, especially the implementation of psychoanalysis therapy, can describe the gap between academic research and clinical practice. Clinically, the result has given relevant insight into how Islamic CBT as part of psychotherapy works on patients (Meganck, Inslegers, Krivzov, & Notaerts, 2017).

3.2 Measurement Tools

The standardly used measurement in assessing depression for this study was the Beck Depression Inventory (Beck, 2018). It is a self-report evaluation that is performed approximately 10 minutes at the beginning of the first session as a baseline and the last session after the intervention.

4. Results

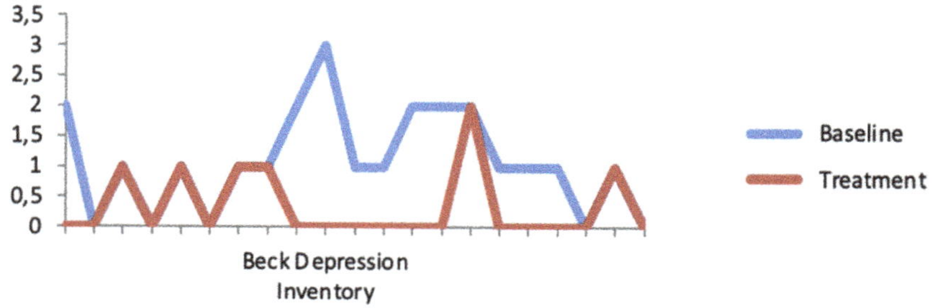

Figure 1. Pre-post test (CT)

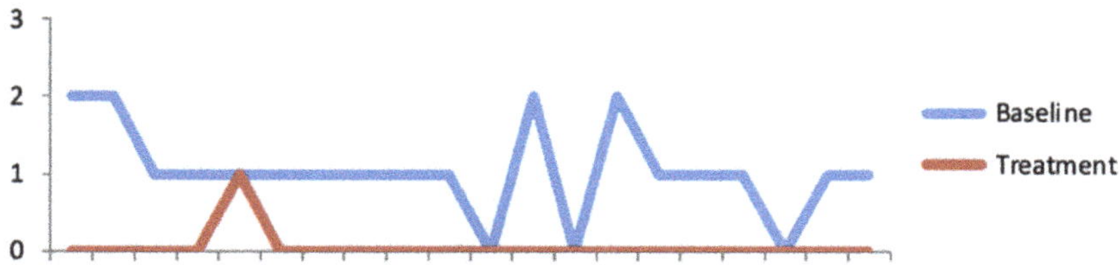

Figure 2. Pre-post test (PT)

The result above shows that there were differences in subject conditions before and after treatment. Figures 1 and 2 described the condition using the BDI tool. Both subjects showed positive recovery after treatment with Islamic CBT. From this result, we can conclude that CBT with Islamic cognitive restructuring helped patients decrease their depression levels. This result gives a similar result with a previous study that showed that CBT affiliated with positive religious statements could decrease compulsive disorder symptoms (Aouchekian, Karimi, & Naja, 2017). Their study designed for religious CBT single group study without a control group, is similar to the current study. According to Mehraby, Islamic beliefs and traditions can provide meaning for the individual who faces loss and grief. By conducting cognitive restructuring, therapists facilitate patients to recover from significant loss and dislocation (Mehraby, 2003).

Based on each aspect of BDI, the subjects (CT and PT) have a high score that indicates depression symptoms such as deep sadness, guilty feeling, and meaningless life. For example, at the beginning of the session, CT showed a profound effect, difficulty in communicating with others, and crying during the sessions. The other case, PT, also cried and had the same problem in the communication with the therapist, just like CT. Both had irrational thoughts, which was "should thinking," which made them feel depressed. After treatment, they managed to reconstruct their thoughts with Islamic values and positive beliefs. The therapist guided them with Qur'anic drive and hope through the sessions.

5. Conclusion

This study confirmed that cognitive restructuring with Islamic values and beliefs positively impacted patients with a psychological disorder. Especially those who suffered depression showed better results with less possibility of relapse, faster recovery, more positive interpersonal relationships, and higher quality of life. This result was similar to the previous study result that giving brief CBT helped patients with depression, somatization disorders, and obsessive-compulsive disorders (King et al., 2002).

6. References

American Psychiatric Association. (2013). *Diagnostic and Statistical Manual of Mental Disorders DSM 5* (5th ed.). American Psychiatric Publishing. October, 25. https://doi.org/10.1176/appi.books.9780890425596.744053

Aouchekian, S., Karimi, R., & Naja, M. (2017). Effect of religious cognitive behavioral therapy on religious obsessive-compulsive disorder (3 and 6 months Follow-up), 1–6. https://doi.org/10.4103/abr.abr_115_16

Barker, C., Pistrang, N., & Elliott, R. (2015). *Research Methods in Clinical Psychology: An Introduction for Students and Practitioners* (3rd ed.). Wiley-Blackwell.

Beck, A. (2018). *Beck Depression Inventory-II (BDI-II)*. Psych Congress Network.

Garzon, F. L. (2005). Interventions that apply scripture in psychotherapy. *Journal of Psychology*, *33*(2), 113–121.

Hamdan, A. (2008). Cognitive restructuring: An Islamic perspective. *Journal of Muslim Mental Health*, *3*(1), 99–116. https://doi.org/10.1080/15564900802035268

Haque, A., Khan, F., Keshavarzi, H., & Rothman, A. E. (2016). Integrating Islamic traditions in modern psychology: research trends in the last ten years. *Journal of Muslim Mental Health*, *10*(1), 1556–4908. https://doi.org/10.3998/jmmh.10381607.0010.107

Hodge, D. R. (2011). Alcohol treatment and cognitive-behavioral therapy: enhancing effectiveness, 21–31. https://doi.org/https://doi.org/10.1093/sw/56.1.21

Husain, A., & Hodge, D. R. (2016). Islamically modified cognitive behavioral therapy: Enhancing outcomes by increasing the cultural congruence of cognitive behavioral therapy self-statements. *International Social Work*, *59*(3), 393–405. https://doi.org/10.1177/0020872816629193

Inayat, Q. (2007). Islamophobia and the therapeutic dialogue: Some reflections. *Counseling Psychology Quarterly*, *20*(3), 287–293. https://doi.org/10.1080/09515070701567804

Jongsma, A. E., Peterson, M. L., & Bruce, T. J. (Eds.). (2014). *The Complete Adult Psychotherapy Treatment Planner* (5th ed.). New Jersey: Wiley.

Khan, R. (2016). *Islamic Cognitive Behavior Therapy*. Malaysia.

King, M; Davidson, O; Taylor, F; Haines, A; Sharp, D; Turner, R (2002) Effectiveness of teaching general practitioners' skills in brief cognitive behavior therapy to treat patients with depression: randomized controlled trial. BMJ, 324 (7343). pp. 947–950. ISSN 1468-5833 DOI: https://doi.org/10.1136/bmj.324.7343.947

Kring, A., Johnson, S. L., Neale, J. M., & Davison, G. C. (2013). *Abnormal psychology* (12th ed.). New Jersey: Wiley.

Manafe, D. (2018). Kesehatan Jiwa di Indonesia Masih Terabaikan [Mental Health in Indonesia Still Neglected]. *Berita Satu*. Retrieved from http://www.beritasatu.com/nasional/502826-kesehatan-jiwa-di-indonesia-masih-terabaikan.html

Meganck, R., Inslegers, R., Krivzov, J., & Notaerts, L. (2017). Beyond clinical case studies in psychoanalysis: A review of psychoanalytic empirical single case studies published in ISI-ranked journals. *Frontiers in Psychology, 8,* Article 1749. https://doi.org/10.3389/fpsyg.2017.01749

Mehraby, N. (2003). Psychotherapy with islamic clients facing loss and grief. *Psychotherapy in Australia, 9*(2). Retrieved from http://www.startts.org.au/media/Research-Doc-Psychotherapy-with-Islamic.pdf

National Institute of Mental Health. (2016). *Depression Basics*. NIH Publication.

Rehm, L. P. (2015). *Cognitive and behavioral theories of depression* (e-book). International Psychotherapy Institute.

Rosenberg, R., & Kosslyn, S. (2011). *Abnormal psychology. Harvard University.* New York: Worth Publisher.

Sotelo, J. L., & Nemeroff, C. B. (2017). Depression as a systemic disease. *Personalized Medicine in Psychiatry,* 11–25. https://doi.org/10.1016/j.pmip.2016.11.002

Statistik, B. P. (2018). *Statistical Yearbook of Indonesia. BPS-Statistics Indonesia.*

Siti Fauziah & Suryanto

Islamic Parenting Strategy: Introducing Islamic Parenting for Young Parents

Abstract: This research aimed to describe the implementation of Islamic Parenting Class for parents and to examine the impact on the child. Islamic parenting is a parenting style that incorporates religious elements in its implementation, which includes examples that are both integrated (*qudwah hasanah*), habituation (*al aadah*), effective advice (*al mauidzah*), care and open control (*al mulahadzah*) and proportional consequence with reward and punishment (*uqubah wa ujarah*). This research is a qualitative narrative approach with phenomenology design. Data collection is done by observation, interview, and documentation. Data validity was assured using source triangulation. The results show that: 1) Active parents who follow Islamic parenting show better parenting behavior. 2) There are behavior changes from students whose parents follow Islamic parenting 3) The parents' presence still becomes an obstacle for the smoothness of Islamic parenting activities. The best suggestion for parents is that they should be actively involved in the parenting process, so that with their understanding of Islamic nurturing patterns and patterns of child development they could do better in raising and educating their children.

Keyword: Islamic Parenting, early age parents, parenting style

1. Introduction

The responsibility of parents in educating children is not easy, because through parenting applied, the character and personality of the child is formed. The childcare process is an important phase that requires a learning process, especially for families of young couples who have young children to raise. For young families with young children, parenting is often carried out through a process of trial and error. In addition, each parent has a different experience in how they had been raised by their own parents. It is often taken as the parenting norm in how they raise their young children. The practice of caregiving is often influenced by how these parents had been raised and cared for. According to Jalaluddin (2002), religious children are not formed instantly. They need guidance and continuous coaching, and this becomes the responsibility of their parents.

The researcher was interested in examining Islamic parenting strategies for young parents who have children under five years old. Young couples, in their process of parenting, often experience trial and error. The question in this study was how would parents perceive the principles of Islamic parenting strategy for children under five years old? The specific questions are (1) What was the form of Islamic parenting strategy? (2) What is meaning of Islamic parenting? (3) How did the parents apply Islamic parenting in early childhood?

2. Theoretical Review

2.1 Parenting

Parenting is the way parents raise their children by fulfilling the children's needs, providing protection, educating children, and influencing children's behavior in daily life (Baumrind, 1991). In line with previous definition, Brooks (1991) says parenting is a process in which there are elements of maintaining, protecting, and directing children during their developmental period. Martin and Colbert (1997) defined parenting as a process related to adults who gave birth, maintained, nurtured, and directed the children. Based on the explanation above, the definition of parenting used in this study is a process of interaction between parents and children, which includes activities such as maintaining, protecting, and directing the behavior of children during the child's development phase.

In Islam, parenting has begun since choosing a partner for marriage. It is from marriage that the foundation of the household is built. As stated in the hadith (life examples) of Muhammad, in choosing a partner:

> "Women are usually married for four things: because of their wealth, because of their position, because of their nature and because of their religion. Then you must choose a woman who is good in religion (Islam). If not, you will be at loss." (Narrated by Bukhari-Muslim).

After marriage, parenting is already started during the fetus was in the womb. In the education concept, the pregnancy period is an important phase to start giving education. After birth, the next upbringing is parenting when the child is at an early age. According to Montessori (Hurlock & Elizabeth, 1978) children aged 3–6 years are children who are in a critical period in which certain functions need to be stimulated and directed so that its development is not hampered.

2.2 Islamic Parenting Style

Islamic parenting refers to the principles taken from the Qur'an and Al-Hadith (examples from Prophet Muhammad peace be upon him). One source from Islamic educators is the main reference in developing the sessions. Ulwan (2014) explained in his book "*Tarbiyatul Aulad fil Islam*" or Children Education in Islam that there were four parts of educating children in Islam, which includes: giving a good example (Qudwah Hasanah), habituation

(Al 'Aadah), effective advisory (Al Mauidzah), open care and control (Al Mulahadzah) and proportional consequences through reward and punishment (Uqubah wa Ujurah).

3. Method

3.1 Sample

The criteria for participants in this study were (1) parents who have children in one of the kindergartens in Surabaya (2) Participants of Islamic parenting skills session . There were five parents who participated in this session. The research sampling technique used purposive sampling with data collected from parents who had participated in the Islamic Parenting Class (Sugiyono, 2014).

3.2 Design

This research is qualitative research. The paradigm used by researchers is the paradigm of narrative analysis. Creswell (2015).The paradigm of narrative analysis is used to tell stories of individual experiences in expressing their identities or other identities known by using a recording device to store the results of interviews.

3.3 Procedure

In this research, the main data from the participants was based on unstructured interviews and completed with additional data from observation and documentation. The data validity was assured by using source triangulation. The interview is non structured (Sugiyono, 2014) in which the researcher did not use interview guidelines that had been systematically arranged and completed for the data collection.

3.4 Analytical Technique

The qualitative data analysis technique used in this study is based on model theory (Miles & Huberman, in Husna, 2016) through three stages namely data reduction, data display, and conclusion & verification of results.

4. Results

4.1 The Form of Islamic Parenting Strategy

Islamic parenting strategy was an approach in parenting to equalize the vision of Muslim parents through parenting skills activity. The Islamic parenting session was held at Al Falah Kindergarten in Surabaya. This activity was done routinely by inviting parents to attend and study together about parenting based on the Qur'an and Sunnah by experienced trainers.

All participants who became the source of data for this research were parents of kindergarten pupils who had joined the Islamic Parenting class in their school. There were 5 participants with 3 women and 2 men.

> "I regularly attend parenting skill activities because I felt there were many mistakes that I applied in nurturing my children. They were easy to be angry and liked screaming when they wanted something" (Mrs. N).

4.2 Islamic Parenting Pattern

The source of the knowledge of Islamic parenting pattern was derived from the education expert, Ulwan (2014), who stated in the book of "Tarbiyatul Aulad fil Islam" (Educating Children in Islam), that parenting in Islam involves giving good examples, habituation, effective advisory, open care and control, proportional reward and punishment. Thus the material presented and the activities designed for the parenting skill class includes the following session that aims to help parents to understand Islamic upbringing in children's: giving a good example (Qudwah Hasanah), habituation (Al 'Aadah), effective advisory (Al Mauidzah), open care and control (Al Mulahadzah) and proportional consequences with reward and punishment (Uqubah wa Ujurah).

4.2.1 Qudwah hasanah

Qudwah hasanah, is a parenting principle that promotes a good example so that children follow what is taught by parents. This is also exemplified by the Prophet Muhammad, as the word of Allah SWT:

> "Indeed, there is already in himself the Messenger of Allah who is a good example for you, that is, for those who hope for the mercy of Allah and the coming of the Day of Judgment…." (Al Ahzab: 21).

The parenting method by giving modeling is in harmony with social cognitive or social learning theory. The main point of this theory is that humans learn through observations that they see in the behavior of others, as stated in

Behavior Learning theory by Bandura (1969). Yet this is not an easy thing to practice among parents:

> "The most difficult way to educate children is to give an example. I admit that I often fail in giving examples of the behavior that I ordered my child to do. But I do believe that giving an example is the right way to care for my child "(Mr. F).

4.2.2 *Al 'aadah*

Al 'aadah, is an approach to parenting by using a habituation approach. This pattern has been conveyed by the Prophet Muhammad through a hadith:

> "*The* practice that is most loved by Allah the Exalted is the practice that is continuous even though it's a small act – (Al Hadith) .

In psychology, this habitual parenting style is in accordance with the law of exercise, namely the more frequent behavior is repeated / trained (used), the more powerful the association will be.

> "Indeed, I have to train continuously so that children get used to do the good habits, for example, my child, now he is used to Maghrib prayer at home when he hears the Maghrib (evening) call to prayer (adzan) " (Mrs. R)

The habituation principle is in line with psychological theory called law of exercise, namely the connection between conditions (which are stimuli) and actions will be stronger because of the exercises but will be weakened if the connection between the two is not continued or stopped. The psychologists usually recognize the habitual or behavioral theory proposed by Ivan Pavlov and Skinner. They were famous for their theory of Classical Conditioning (Ivan Pavlov) and Operant Conditioning (B. Skinner).

4.2.3 *Al Mauidzah*

Al Mauidzah is an approach in parenting which focuses on providing good advice . For this approach, parents need to choose a polite and understandable language for their children. In the Qur'an, Allah SWT says: "Call upon the path of your Lord with good wisdom and teaching and help them in a good way. Verily, your Lord, He knows better who is strayed from His way, and He knows better who gets guidance " (An Nahl 125). The statement from the participant showed that giving good advice is not always easy:

> "Because they were still children, sometimes I was also tired of advising children, it felt like they needed to be told many times so they could understand. But if they were not advised they also didn't know right and wrong behavior "(Mr Q)

Advice is a word that comes from the same root as "An Nush-hu" meaning to purify, cleanse, and improve. Advice is an idea (the parents, in this regard) that is conveyed to other parties (the children, in this case) and is recommended to be implemented because it is beneficial (Latipun, 2006).

4.2.4 Al Mulahadzah

Al Mulahadzah means supervision. Parents do supervision on their children to ensure that they are well behaved, and to give attention when needed for their children. This form of supervision was also mentioned in the word of God in surah At Tahrim, verse 6: "O believers! protect yourself and your family from a fire whose fuel is people and stones. Overseen by formidable and severe angels, who never disobey whatever Allah orders -always doing as commanded" One participating parent said the following:

> "I have to make sure that my children carry out the rules that we have agreed to, because they are still children, so supervision is still very much needed in daily activities" (Mrs. W)

The function of parenting by supervising and controlling are also intended to bring the intimate relationship between parents and children.

4.2.5 Uqubah wa Ujarah

Uqubah wa ujarah is a parenting principle that refers to providing behavioral proportional consequences with reward and punishment for children. This concept refers to the hadith of Prophet Muhammad BUH: "Ask your children to pray when they are seven years old .." and to be firm with them in this matter (A Hadist narrated by Ahmad).

In psychology, this approach refers to the law of effect, that is the relationship of stimulus and responses tends to be strengthened if the consequences are pleasant and tend to be weakened if the consequences are not satisfactory. As one participant stated:

> "For me, giving consequences is important to my child, he became aware of good behavior to do, and the bad behavior not to do" (Mrs. N)

This approach was also similar to the principle of operant conditioning: a process of behavior positive and negative reinforcement, and as a result good behavior are repeated and negative behavior are diminished depending on the consequences.

4.3 The Way Parents Apply Islamic Parenting to Early Childhood

There are five approaches that are applied in Islamic parenting proposed by Ulwan (2014). He presented varied treatments to the children, according to the level of ability that participants had. One parent gave the testimony that:

> "I felt the advantage from this parenting skill activity. I have applied the one that has the proportional consequences given. When they are good mannered, I would give them reward, and when they did not behave, certainly I would give them punishment. It was a habitual pattern that had the most effect on my children"(Mr. Q)

5. Conclusion

From the results of observations and interviews conducted on the application of Islamic parenting it can be concluded that parenting skill activities provide and broaden parenting insight to the participants to do better effort in parenting for their children in early childhood. The results of the study show that: 1) parents who actively participate in Islamic parenting class showed better parenting behavior. 2) there was a change in behavior of students whose parents followed Islamic parenting class, 3) the presence of parents gave a positive contribution for the success of Islamic parenting class.

6. References

Al- Qur'an Karim & Translation. (2009). Ministry of Religion of the Republic of Indonesia

Bandura, A. (1969). Social learning of moral judgments. *Journal of Personality and Social Psychology, 11*(3), 275–279. https://doi.org/10.1037/h0026998

Baumrind, D. (1991). The influence of parenting style on adolescent competence and substance use. *The Journal of Early Adolescence, 11*(1), 56–95.

Brooks, J. B. (1991). *The Process of parenting.* California: Mayfield Publishing Company.

Creswell, J. W. (2015). *Qualitative research & research design: Choosing between five approaches.* Yogyakarta: Student Library.

Hurlock., & Elizabeth, B. (1978). *Child Development,*(6th ed). New York: Mcgraw Hill, Inc.

Husna, N. (2016). Analisis pengaruh kinerja keuangan terhadap harga saham pada perusahaan perbankan [Analysis of the influence of financial performance on stock prices in banking companies]. e-Jurnal Apresiasi Ekonomi. Vol 4(2), 151–156. DOI: 10.31846/jae.v4i2.158

Jalaluddin. (2002). *Preparing the Virtuous Child.* Jakarta: Srigunting.

Latipun. (2006). *Experimental Psychology.* Malang: UMM Press.

Martin, C.A., & Colbert, K.K. (1997). *Parenting a Life Span Perspective.* New York: McGraw-Hill.

Sugiyono. (2014). *Qualitative quantitative research methodology and r & d*, Bandung: Alfabeta.

Ulwan, A. N. (2014). *Tarbiyatul Aulad fii Islam.* (Translation: Arif, RH). Solo: Insan Kamil.

Ricky Firmansyah & Anne Octavia

Islamic Psychotherapy Model Based on al-Ghazali's Minhajul Abidin

Abstract: What makes the Islamic perspective different in providing psychological assistance is the inclusion of awareness of the hope of the goodness of life in the world and in the hereafter in every intervention. In addition to getting healed, a person also gets a heavenly reward for his piety. Al-Ghazali who was born in 1082 AD, before the end of his life, compiled the book *Minhajul 'Abidin* containing the stages of worship purification and the way of conducting psychological intervention with a religious approach to help people solve their problems. According to al-Ghazali, if we conducted a therapy, it was not enough for us to only use the rational method, but we also need to use the healing process in accordance with the *shari'a*. This study aimed at constructing a model of Islamic psychotherapy interventions by contextualizing al-Ghazali's thinking and presenting them in a systematic and structured model of Islamic psychotherapy. This study analyzed al-Ghazali's thinking about psychology described in the book *Minhajul 'Abidin* and compared it with the models and methods of today's modern psychotherapy.

Keywords: Al-Ghazali, Islamic Intervention, Islamic psychotherapy, *Minhajul 'Abidin*.

1. Introduction

Islam considers that spirituality and religion cannot be separated in daily life. Referring to the Qur'an, Muslims believe that the purpose of human creation is to worship God/Allah, and according to Al-Ghazali the purpose of worship is to heal and free the soul from various heart diseases, to keep the soul alive and make the soul stay healthy and better in order to achieve happiness in the hereafter. The purposes generate *taqwa* (piety), which is the nature and state of the heart, not the nature and state of the body (Al-Ghazali, 2012). By changing the nature and behavior of the heart, the nature and behavior of the body will follow.

According to the survey conducted by the World Gallup Poll (Crabtree and Pelham, 2009), the proportion of the world population had significant religious beliefs and practices that were important for everyday life. For example, from the data of sampled population of 143 countries (n = 140,000), it was found that 92 % of people in 32 developing countries consider religion as an important part of their everyday life. Koenig (2012) also had a review of more than 3,300 studies analyzing the correlation between religious-spiritual problems and mental and physical health, health behavior and outcomes. The review presented a theoretical model describing that religious spirituality affects mental and physical health. Quantitative research studies analyzed the correlation between the spiritual-religious involvement and the depression symptoms or disorders during the last 50 years (1962 to 2011). At least there were 444 studies that quantitatively analyzed this correlation. Of the amount, more than 60 % reported less depression and faster recovery from the depression cases of people experiencing spiritual-religious intervention or decreasing depression severity in response to religious-spiritual intervention (Rosmarin, et al. 2013).

A classical Islamic thinker like al-Ghazali has developed psychological interventions that were systematic, structured, and more holistic since they consider humans as not only bodies but also as spiritual-religious beings. The intervention theories that were independent and established based on the Qur'an and hadith. Al-Ghazali has also developed therapeutic techniques that also exist in modern psychotherapy (Firmansyah, 2018), among others: *Imagery technique, paradoxical behavior technique, homework technique, cognitive technique.* Based on the background, Al-Ghazali was rich in psychological concepts. We can model the interventions carried out by Al-Ghazali as Islamic, psychotherapeutic models and contextualize them into the current development in psychology. Among his works, the one mentioning the meaning of psychological intervention was the book *Minhajul 'Abidin.*

2. Theoretical Review

2.1 The Book *Minhajul 'Abidin and* Psychotherapy

Minhajul 'Abidin is the ultimate and complete *tasawwuf* book of Al-Ghazali (1058 -1111 M) before he died. *Minhajul 'Abidin* provides a basic guide of meaning for Islamic worshipers. Not many of Al-Ghazali students directly studied this book, except his special friends. This work invites people to reflect on the nature of worship and various stages to achieve the purity of worship. The stages are the stage of knowledge (*'ilm*), the stage of repentance (*al-tawbah*), the stage of facing the obstacles of worship (*al-'awa'iq*), the stage of facing obstruction of worship (*al-'awaridh*), the stage of inducement or motivation to worship (*al-bawa'its*), the stage of worship impairment (*al-qawadih*), the stage of praise and gratitude (*al-hamd wa al-shukr*).

The stages of worship purification are a process of change, in which the process of change is the basic element in psychotherapy. The change process is identified as the way in which a person tries to change with or without therapy. In the trans-theoretical model, the behavior change is conceptualized as a process carried out over time and involves development through six stages, namely pre-contemplation, contemplation, preparation, action, maintenance, termination. This model has proven useful in conceptualizing and guiding changes that occur in psychotherapy (Petrocelli, 2002).

The following is a comparative study of trans-theoretical stages and the stages of worship purification in the book of *Minhajul 'abidin* by Firmansyah (2018), referring to the stages of trans-theoretical change, the stages in *minhajul' abidin* can be categorized as follows: in the precontemplation stage, in which individuals do not understand their behavior causing problems and do not want to change. In *minhajul 'abidin,* this stage is equivalent to *'ilm* (knowledge), in which individuals have not aware of their heart diseases, and individuals are given *ma'rifa* insight on monotheism (*tawhid*), *tasawwuf*, and Shari'a sciences. In the contemplation stage, individuals begin to think about the existence of their behavior leading to problems and proceed to the Preparation stage when the individuals intend and commit to change their behavior in the near future. This stage is in line with the *tawbah stage* (repentance), intending to improve the dimensions of the future by not repeating it. In the current dimension, the individuals acknowledge their mistakes and invoke the forgiveness of Allah, and in the past dimensions, the individuals seek to improve the relationship they have neglected (*qada*). This is the action stage where individuals begin to change their behavior to overcome problems. This stage is in line with the stage of facing the obstacles of worship (*al-'awaiq*), the stage of facing the obstruction of worship (*al-'awaridh*). Next is the Maintenance stage, this stage aims to maintain the change of behavior from the possibility of returning to the abandoned behavior, in this case, related to the stage of worship inducement or motivation (*al-bawa'its*), the stage of worship impairment (*al-qawadih*). While the last stage is to stop committing blameworthy behaviors that consequently they will not be repeated. The individuals feel confident that they will not commit their previous behaviors. The last stage is the praise and gratitude stage *(al-hamd wa al-shukr)*. After the individuals have passed this last stage, their intent and goal will be achieved. After that, the individuals will find conveniences by always remembering Him.

3. Method

This study was carried out using Literature Study which was a series of activities relevant to the method of collecting literature data, reading, and recording and processing the research materials (Zed. 2008). Sources of data in this study were the primary and secondary data sources. The primary data source of this literature study was the work of al-Ghazali, namely the bilingual book *Minhajul*

'Abidin, printed in Arabic and Indonesian, published by Pustaka Mampir (2010). The secondary data sources of this literature study were in the form of books, journals and other scientific works, which were used for supporting the primary data. The data analysis method that the writers used was content analysis and comparison.

4. Results

4.1 Knowledge Stage (*'Ilm*)

Al-Ghazali emphasized the importance of science in changing behavior. The first stage consists of knowledge and *ma'rifa* stage, which includes observation, search for evidence and teaching.

In the strategy of cognitive psychotherapy (Szymanska & Palmer, 2010), the way an individual feels or behaves is largely determined by an individual's assessment of psychological incidents and problems perpetuated because of retaining wrong way of thinking and worthless schemes. In the beginning of cognitive therapy, individuals are invited to realize which belief is not useful and then modify their beliefs.

Likewise, according to al-Ghazali, troubled individuals were invited to conduct good research and look for evidence, maturing their mind, also learning, and questioning of what they have done and providing new insights or reminding them of the three sciences that must be understood by individuals. Those three sciences were the *tawhid,* the *sharia*, and the *tasawwuf.* The *tawhid* is an invitation to acknowledge from their heart that they have The One Almighty God. The Sharia would re-establish the obligatory services and perfecting again the procedures. The *tasawwuf* is the knowledge of the nature of the heart *(qalb)* that is commendable and its prohibitions, as well as various threats that can spoil the heart *(qalb).*

Al Ghazali (2010) suggested that the heart disease is not enough to be treated only with *aql* (rational), heart disease cannot be cured except by using the provisions taken from the religious sharia, such as religious duties and practices compiled by the prophets for heart restoration. This is what distinguishes the model of Islamic psychotherapy with the Western psychotherapy. Islamic psychotherapy is not only focusing on the goodness of the world, but also incorporating the goodness in the afterlife. According to al-Ghazali behavior starts from one's knowledge *('ilm)*, then it will bring up the state of heart/*qalb (hal),* and the state of heart/*qalb (hal)* will bring out the behavior *(amal),* as well as behavior *(amal)* that someone does can influence the state of heart/*qalb (hal).*

4.2 Repentance Stage (*al-Tawbah*)

After gaining insight and knowledge, someone who is troubled will realize his mistakes, that is the time when troubled people enter the next stage, repentance (al-Ghazali, 2010).There are three phases for the therapy at this repentance stage (al-Ghazali, 2012) namely, the knowledge phase, inviting people to know the cause and seriousness of self-impairment resulting in the emergence of a *hal* phase, arousing the will and intention to change. It leads to *'amal* phase, a strong desire to correct mistakes in three dimensions-the dimension that will come in the form of a strong will not to do the mistake again, the current dimension in the form of invoking Allah's apology for all mistakes and sins, and the dimension of the past, namely repairing the lost relationship at that time (*qada*) . In positive psychology, these three dimensions are also used to achieve happiness, such as being satisfied with the past, enjoying the present, and enthusiasm in facing the future.

4.3 Obstacle Stage (*al-'Awa'iq*)

After passing through the repentance stage, subsequently, individuals will realize and understand the various obstacles often approaching him. To understand the forms of obstacles, al-Ghazali classified obstacles into four types; two types are in the external environment namely, the world and human beings, while the other two are in the internal environment, within oneself, namely, passions and devil. Passions and the devil work on us in the form of *khatir* (automatic mind). According to al-Ghazali, it is *khatir* that whispers and raises bad behaviors. In cognitive behavioral literature, there is a working principle that is similar to *khatir*, it is automatic thought. Automatic thought is a self-detrimental belief, so called because the mind appears very quickly and can be realistic in the owner's mind and can also appear in the form of images or figures (Neenan, 2010).

In Rational Emotive Behavior Therapy (REBT) technique for facing the automatic thoughts in a constructive way, individuals are taught to examine evidence that support and oppose their irrational belief using the three main criteria-logic, realism, and usefulness. Al-Ghazali used the three-comparison method to know whether a behavior is good or bad, such as: collating *the khatir* and sharia, comparing it with the practice of righteous people, and comparing it with passion.

4.4 Obstruction Stage (*al – 'awa'rid*)

After being able to manage his mind and encouragement from the four sources, the troubled individuals are invited to recognize various obstructions, which are his main problems, preventing him from the mind to achieve the intended goal. According to al-Ghazali (2010), there were four categories of obstruction forms and human problems, the sustenance, anxiety, distress and disaster, and the destiny or decree of God. The sustenance is something that is always demanded by someone. Anxiety toward those feared and expected as well as those desired and hated. As a result, it is possible for someone to fall into an abyss and be damaged. Distress and disaster are the great bitterness that someone has experienced. The destiny or decree of God is the acceptance of the destiny of both the sweet and bitter ones. Passions often drive anger and spread slander. To pass these four obstacles of worship, one needs to follow through four therapies; those are *tawakal, tafwid, patience (sabr) and contentment (rida).*

4.5 Inducement Stage (*al-Bawa'its*)

After passing the fourth stage, someone is encouraged to do good deeds as before, someone needs a "driver" who is expected to be able to encourage him to do good deeds and obedience, and stimulate himself to be more intensive in worshiping, and "deterrent", which can prevent him from doing evil and disobedience/immorality. The "driver" and "deterrent" are hope (*ar-raja'*) and fear *(al-khauf)*. People are motivated to approach beyond pleasure and avoid pain (Higgins, 2012) and the Muslims want it to be effective in their life pursuits to get rewards and punishment from God. Hope is a great reward driver from God which includes a variety of glory promised by God. Yet, fear is a deterrent from suffering from the pain of God's punishment as well as difficulties and insults. Precisely, these two things are the deterrents of being able to avoid and to restrain the person from doing immoral or violating God's law and to keep them from committing sins (Al-Ghazali, 2010).

4.6 Impairment Stage (*al-qawadih*)

This is the stage of examining the destroyer of worship (*qawadih*), recognizing everything that can spoil and cause heart disease such as ostentation (*riya'*) and conceit (*ujb*). Sometimes in behaving, individuals show their obedience to humans that consequently, the attitude damages the obedience itself. Sometimes, someone tries to prevent *riya'*, but what emerges is the attitude of conceit. Both attitudes remove the rewards of worship, damaging and even destroying them. To pass this stage someone goes through sincerity therapy (*ikhlas* therapy), remembers His gifts, so that Allah accepts the good deeds he does (al-Ghazali, 2010).

4.7 Gratitude Stage (*al-shukr*)

The stage of praise (*al-hamd*) and gratitude (*al-shukr*). In this stage, people who have problems are invited to praise God and be grateful for all His blessings. When someone completely passes this stage, the purpose and goal will be achieved. After that someone will find ease from Him, the desert of longings of Him, and the expanse of His love (al-Ghazali, 2010).

5. Conclusion

Islamic psychotherapy is not only focusing on the goodness of the world, but also incorporating the goodness in the afterlife. Therefore al-Ghazali's Islamic intervention model in conceptualizing and guiding changes in individuals' behaviors consists of seven stages-knowledge (*'ilm*), the stage of repentance (*al-tawbah*), the stage of facing the obstacles of worship (*al-'awa'iq*), the stage of facing obstruction of worship (*al-'awaridh*), the stage of inducement or motivation to worship (*al-bawa'its*), the stage of worship impairment (*al-qawadih*), the stage of praise and gratitude (*al-hamd wa al-shukr*). *First, the cognitive aspect,* emphasizes the importance of science, especially the concept of *Tawhid* which is a basic belief about divine natures, Shari'a which is a standard of values in behavior, and *Tasawwuf* which is the knowledge of knowing the heart and its magic and competence in carrying out strategy coping against stress. *Second, the behavior aspect,* the importance of controlling bad behaviors and practicing good behaviors. *Third, the religious aspect includes* the religious values contained in the Qur'an and hadith that relate to the cognitive and behavior aspects. Behavior starts from one's knowledge *('ilm),* then it will bring up the state of heart/*qalb (hal),* and the state of heart/*qalb (hal)* will bring out the behavior *(amal),* as well as behavior *(amal)* that someone does can influence the state of heart/*qalb (hal).* So according to al-Ghazali, the target of change is to change the conditions of heart/*qalb (hal),* by intervening the knowledge *('ilm),* and adjusting that knowledge to the tawheed, sharia and tasawwuf, or by modifying behavior *(amal)* by accustoming good behavior and avoiding bad behavior. The heart will be cured by using rational *(aql)* and the provisions taken from the religious sharia, such as religious duties and practices compiled by the prophets for heart restoration.

6. References

Al-Ghazali, I. (2010). *Minhajul 'Abidin* (Zainal Arifin Yahya, translator). Jakarta: Pustaka Mampir.

Al-Ghazali, I. (2012). *Ihya 'ulumuddin* (Ibnu Ibrahim Ba'adilah, translator). Jakarta: Republika.

Crabtree, Steve and Pelham, Brett. (2009). World Gallup Poll: Religion Provides Emotional Boost to World's Poor, The Gallup Poll. November 27, 2018. http://www.gallup.com/poll/116449/Religion-Provides-Emotional-Boost-World-Poor.aspx.

Firmansyah, R. (2018). Relevansi psikoterapi sufistik dalam minhajul 'abidin ditinjau dari psikoterapi modern rational emotive behavior therapy (REBT) [The relevance of sufistic psychotherapy in minhajul 'abidin in terms of modern rational emotive behavior therapy (REBT)]. In Zulfan, Taufik., Angraini, Dewi (ed). *Proceeding International seminars on imam al-ghazali's sufism the role and contribution of imam al-ghazali on peace and harmonious world.* (pp. 163–183). Jakarta: Al-Kamil Institute for Research and Islamic Studies.

Higgins, E. Tory. (2012) *Beyond pleasure and pain: how motivation works.* New York: Oxford University Press.

Koenig, H. G. (2012) *Religion, spirituality, and health: The research and clinical implications.* ISRN Psychiatry. November 27, 2018. http://www.hindawi.com/journals/isrn/2012/278730/abs/

Neenan, M. (2010). Rational emotive behavior therapy. In Palmer, Stephen (ed). *Introduction to counseling and psychotherapy the essential guide.* (pp. 99–524), Sage Publication Ltd.

Petrocelli, John V. (2002). Processes and stage of change: counseling with the transtheoretical model of change. *Journal of Counseling & Development,* Vol. 80.

Rosmarin, D. H., Bigda-Peyton, J. S., Kertz, S. J., Smith, N., Rauch, S. L., & Björgvinsson, T. (2013) A Test Of Faith In God And Treatment: The Relationship Of Belief In God To Psychiatric Treatment Outcomes. *Journal of Affective Disorders.* 146, 441–446. November 27, 2018. http://dx.doi.org/10.1016/j.jad.2012.08.030

Szymanska, K., & Palmer, S. (2010). Cognitive counselling and psychotherapy. In Palmer, Stephen (ed). *Introduction to counseling and psychotherapy the essential guide.* (pp. 99–121), Sage Publication Ltd.

Zed, Mestika. (2008). Metode penelitian kepustakaan [Library research methods]. Jakarta: Yayasan Obor Jakarta.

Rias Pratiwi Safitri, Fitri Romadonika & Baiq Nurul Hidayati

Psychosocial Conditions in the Aftermath of an Earthquake Disaster among Children in North Lombok – Indonesia

Abstract: A few studies have explored anxiety and symptoms of psychological problems in children. This study aims to identify anxiety and psychological symptoms in the aftermath of an earthquake among children in the Lombok region. The design used in this study is descriptive with a sample of 298 respondents from 13 villages in North Lombok Regency, the sample was determined by convenient sampling technique. The data were collected by using psychosocial assessment questionnaires for children, and some qualitative in-depth interviews with parents in refugee shelters. The results showed that most of the children respondents indicated the urgency for treatment because it showed that 56.7 % of them experienced psychological and emotional problems. The results of the qualitative study show that the earthquake caused changes in the psychosocial condition of some children, which were manifested in daily life both at home and at school. Future research is expected to focus and confirm on the appropriate therapy for children affected by disasters so that the psychological impact they experience can be reduced.

Keywords: *Psychosocial Conditions, Early Childhood, Earthquake Disaster*

1. Introduction

Indonesia is the meeting point between the three major plates of the world, namely the Pacific Plate, the Eurasia Plate, and the Indian-Australian Plate which is commonly called the Triple Junction. The movement of the Indian-Australian Plate annually is about 7 cm to the north and the Pacific Plate is about 12 cm annually towards the southwest. The impact of the movement of the triple junction plate causes the Indonesian archipelago to have high earthquake level so that it is prone to tectonic earthquakes. One of the earthquakes that caused severe damage was an earthquake measuring 7 on the Richter Scale (SR) that struck North Lombok, West Nusa Tenggara (NTB) on Sunday (5/8/2018) at 18.46 WIB. Lombok, an area that originally seemed very safe, peaceful, and dynamic, in an instant became ruins. All lines and sectors of life starting from the education, social, religious, and cultural sectors experienced total paralysis, (Jakandar, 2018).

It was recorded that 483 people were lost due to this natural disaster, the number of refugees was reported to reach 417,529 people. Material losses in the form of damaged houses around 71962 units, educational facilities around 671 units consisting of 124 children, 341 SD, 145 SMP, 55 SMA, 50 SMK, 6 LSB, and 128 places of worship reportedly damaged with details of 115 mosques, 10 Temples or Pura, and 3 Pelinggih (religious congregation place?). In addition, the public facilities that were damaged include: 6 damaged bridges, 52 health facility units in the form of 1 hospital, 11 community clinics, 35 supporting public clinics, and 4 Polindes (community maternity clinic), 1 pharmacy, and around 20 collapsed office buildings (Humaira. Isnaini & Ilham, 2018).

Earthquakes that have occurred consecutively in Lombok since July 29th 2018, have had a tremendous impact on various aspects of the lives of disaster survivors, both physical, social and psychological aspects. Earthquake survivors not only experience emergency problems such as physical damage, but also psychological problems, such as: anxiety, stress, depression (moodiness), and trauma (Ramirez & Peek-Asa, 2005). Earthquakes have consistently been shown to be associated with problems with psychosocial conditions such as depression and post-traumatic stress disorder, a survey showed that after a catastrophic event, around 15–20 % of the population will experience mild or moderate mental disorders which refer to post-traumatic stress disorder (PTSD), while 3–4 % will experience severe disorders such as psychosis, major depression and high anxiety (Surendra, Samuel, Marahatta, Anwar, Van Ommeren, & Ofrin, 2017).

Disasters have the greatest influence on the most vulnerable groups, especially children (Nakamura, 2005). This is because children directly experience, feel, and witness the impact, and they are vulnerable because at a young age psychological maturity has not yet occurred. Early childhood is children who are in the age range of 0–8 years according to NAEYC (National Association for The Education of Young Children). At the age of 0–8 years, the child's brain can develop up to 80 %, this is known as the golden age. The child's brain is composed of billions of neurons that are interconnected to produce synapses that arise because of stimuli from the environment that are picked up by the five senses. Some connected neurons are stored, and some are discarded. The discarded neurons are neurons that come from synapses that are rarely used while synapses that are unique, repetitive, and memorable will last in the brain. A natural disaster can be a very memorable event for a child, so that things related to it are kept and remembered strongly in the child's mind (Taliningtyas, 2017). This conclusion is supported by the results of interviews with and observations on informants in 5 villages that were worst affected by the disaster in North Lombok district. From this early assessment, it was found that the refugees had been cared for physically, psychologically, and socially. The fulfillment of physical needs includes meeting the needs for food, clothing, shelter, health services, clean water, and facilities. The earthquake disaster in North Lombok regency which became the national spotlight had taken many victims, and the handling of child survivors had not become the main concern of the government. The location of the disaster, which is quite accessible to researchers, encouraged researchers of the current study to find out more about the description of the psychosocial and physical conditions of the children after the earthquake disaster in KLU, and the intervention methods that can be used to overcome the experienced disruptions.

2. Theoretical Review

According to Ihrom (Semiun, 2006), psychosocial conditions are the realization of personal integrity, in harmony with identity, growth towards self-realization, and towards healthy relationships with others. Psychosocial condition is a condition that tells the level of 'mental well-being' where individuals can function adequately, can enjoy their life in a balanced manner and are able to adapt to life's challenges and be able to contribute to socio-cultural and religious life. Psychosocial condition is the foundation of achieving individual well-being and effective functioning in the community. Schneiders (Semiun, 2006) suggests several criteria that are very important and can be used to assess psychosocial conditions. These criteria can be described as follows according to Schneiders (in Semiun, 2006): Mental efficiency, control and integration of thought and behavior, integration of motives and control of conflict and frustration, positive and healthy feelings, and emotions, calm or peace of mind, healthy attitudes, healthy self-concept, adequate ego identity and adequate relationship with reality.

Disasters are events that cause traumatic experiences for those who experience them. When a person experiences a disaster, he will feel confused, panicked, restless and stressed. For both children and adults, the impact of a disaster varies from short-term to long-term. The traumatic event does not affect a person in the same way. Socio-economic status, gender, age, health status, education, or occupation or race and ethnicity are factors that can influence the extent to which a person is vulnerable to the impact of a disaster (Laluyan, 2007). Those included in vulnerable groups include the poor, women, ethnic minorities, people with disabilities or mental health, the elderly and children. Early childhood is included in the vulnerable group who are prone to injury, damage, loss, suffering and death due to disasters. Given that early childhood is more difficult in dealing with traumatic events because of their limitations in terms of life experience, problem solving skills and limitations in expressing their feelings and needs, the right understanding of their psychosocial condition is important in order to provide the appropriate support in the extraordinary situation.

Kenardy (2011) explained in a book entitled Childhood Trauma Reaction: A Guide For Teachers from Preschool to Year 12 that there are several types of reactions that children generally show due to traumatic events such as natural disasters, including: a) Asking many questions about upcoming events; b) Avoiding talking about what happened (traumatic events); c) Wanting to help people affected by a traumatic event; d) Crying, feeling weak; e) Nightmare; f) Fear of being separated from loved ones; g) Sleep disturbance; h) Physical or health problems (for example: heart palpitations, abdominal pain, headaches); i) Irritability; j) Difficulty in concentrating; k) Difficulty in studying at school; l) Agitation; m) Difficulty in interacting with peers and adults; n) Playing, drawing, reliving trauma parts; o) Difficulty with daily functions (eg, not doing homework, forgetting to pack); p) Grief and sorrow.

3. Method

3.1 Sample

The design used in this study is a descriptive study with a cross sectional approach, which is to collect data with a questionnaire to determine the psychosocial condition of children affected by the disaster in 13 villages in North Lombok Regency. The population used in the study were children living in refugee camps in 13 villages in North Lombok Regency using incidental sampling, with a sample 298 of children from that village.

3.2 Measurement Tools

Research variables according to Suyanto and Salamah (2009) are characteristics or measures inherent in the object of research, either physical (real) or psychological (not real). The variable in this study is the child's psychosocial condition. The data collection tool used in this study was a psychological observation sheet for children.

3.2.1 Characteristics of Common Problems

In general, the problems in the affected areas are divided into 4 aspects, namely no problems, physical health problems, psychological and emotional problems, social and behavioral problems. Based on these 4 aspects, the frequency distribution of problems experienced in the 20 disaster-affected villages is described below:

Table 1. Distribution of general problems in post-disaster children

No	Characteristics of common problems in children	f	%
1	None	71	23.8
2	Physical health	26	8.7
3	Psychological and emotional	169	56.7
4	Social and behavior	32	10.7
	Total	298	100.0

Based on Table 8 above, it can be seen that the psychological and emotional aspects of children show the urgency to be given treatment because it shows 56.7 % of children experience psychological and emotional problems.

3.2.2 Description of Children's Physical Problems

Table 2. Distribution of changes in general physical condition of children after the disaster

No	Change in general physical condition	n	%
1	Healthy	162	54.4
2	Prone to sickness	136	45.6
	Total	298	100.0

Table 3. Distribution of changes in sleep patterns of children after the disaster

No	*Characteristics of sleep patterns*	f	%
1	No Change	50	16.8
2	Lack Of Sleep	82	27.5
3	Difficulty Sleeping	100	33.6
4	Get More Sleep	40	13.4
5	Difficulty getting awake	5	1.7
6	Trouble Staying Awake	21	7.0
	Total	298	100.0

Table 4. Distribution of changes in appetite for children after the disaster

No	*Characteristics of change in appetite*	f	%
1	Normal	48	16.1
2	Decreased	49	50
3	Increased	101	33.9
	Total	298	100.0

Based on Tables 2, 3, and 4 physical problems that require special attention related to children who experience problems with decreased appetite by up to 50 % and difficulty sleeping reaches 33.6 %.

3.2.3 *Psychological Problems*

Table 5. Distribution of post-disaster children's anxiety levels

No	*Change in anxiety*	f	%
1	No Change	155	52
2	There is anxiety	85	28.5
3	Anxiety increased	58	19.5
	Total	298	100.0

Table 6. Distribution of changes in the emotional condition (mood) of children after the disaster

No	*Mood change*	f	%
1	No Change	186	62.4
2	Decreased	71	23.8
3	Increase	28	9.4
4	Capable	13	4.4
	Total	298	100.0

Based on Tables 5 and 6, psychological problems show that there is no anxiety by 52 % and there is no change in emotional condition by 62.4 %.

3.2.4 *Social*

Table 7. Distribution of post-disaster children's behavior changes

No	*Characteristics of change in behavior*	f	%
1	No Change	181	60.7
2	Positive behavior	12	4
3	Negative behavior	105	35.2
	Total	298	100.0

3.2.5 Education

Table 8. Distribution of children's concentrations during post-disaster activities

No	*Concentration of children during activity*	f	%
1	Normal	48	16.1
2	Decreased	149	50
3	Increase	101	33.9
	Total	298	100.0

4. Results

The results of the early detection of psychological symptoms in earthquake survivors in the Lombok region show that the psychological and emotional aspects of the child show the urgency for treatment. The responses show that 56.7 % of children experience psychological and emotional problems. Although many disaster survivors in the age group of children show some type of psychological reaction after a disaster, clinical research shows that these symptoms also depend on age. Previous research has shown that age is a key factor in children's understanding of disasters. Age as an index of children's development skills in reflecting the ability to understand a disaster or event. Their still undeveloped skills can cause trauma. Research related to disasters in the school age group empirically states that school-age children show a more comprehensive psychological distress (Purnamasari, 2016). These statements are supported by the evidence of the psychological impact on children due to the earthquake in the Lombok region, which indicate that there are psychological problems in the form of clinical anxiety and behaviour changes. As for the problems found among respondents after the earthquake in Lombok, they were: changes in attitude such as children becoming more sensitive, crying easily, irritable, when they heard something rumbling they immediately panicked and cried, often worried about entering the house and disturbances of sleep patterns, and children who are more silent and withdrawn with a high dependence on their parents.

The results of previous studies also focused on variations in the reactions of school age children after an earthquake, which can vary according to gender or age. The psychological impact felt by survivors, especially among most of the children population, is related to very serious mental trauma. Children show behavioral symptoms such as difficulty sleeping, excessive fear, fear of entering the house, not wanting to sleep in the house, being overwhelmed by anxiety and withdrawal (Astuti, 2006).

This is also in line with the results of Bedriye's research disaster impact on school-age children in Turkey. This study showed the form of children's reactions after an earthquake, namely: avoidance, becoming angry, self-deprecating, and behavioral changes such as dreams about earthquakes, fear of staying indoors, disturbed by sudden sounds and noises, sleep difficulties, reluctance to go to school and to join games (Bedriye, 2014).

5. Conclusion

In conclusion, the earthquake experienced by the people of Lombok region of West Nusa Tenggara province not only had an impact on physical and environmental conditions, but also on the psychological condition of children who were survivors of the earthquake. Children show symptoms such as normal anxiety and clinical anxiety that led to PTSD, as indicated by changes in children's behavior. These symptoms are felt by children at home and at school and thus will require further handling through post-disaster health services which should include mental health service provisions targeted towards children.

6. References

Astuti, B. (2006). Layanan bimbingan dan konseling bagi korban gempa bumi di Yogyakarta [Guidance and counseling services for earthquake victims in Yogyakarta]. Makalah. Jurusan Psikologi Pendidikan dan Bimbingan, Fakultas Ilmu Pendidikan, Universitas Negeri Yogyakarta.

Bedriye, A. K. (2014). Determination and evaluation of the effect of earthquake on school age children (6–12 years old) behaviors. Procedia-Social and Behavioural Science, 152, 845–851. doi: 10.1016/j.sbspro.2014.09.332

Humaira., Isnaini., Ilham. 2018. Psikososial Sebagai Bentuk Trauma Healing Untuk Anak-Anak Terdampak Gempa Di Dusun Tanjung, KLU NTB [Psychosocial as a Form of Trauma Healing for Children Affected by the Earthquake in Dusun Tanjung, KLU NTB]. Sinergi Jurnal Pengabdian Universitas Muhammadiyah Mataram, Volume 1, Nomor 1 Desember 2018. e-ISSN: 2656-4661. Download. http://journal.ummat.ac.id/index.php/JSPU/article/view/686/570

Jakandar,L.I.E. 2018. Dampak Gempa Bumi Lombok Terhadap Kondisi Sosial Ekonomi Masyarakat di Desa Kekait Kecamatan Gunung Sari Kabupaten Lombok Barat [The Impact of the Lombok Earthquake on the Socio-Economic Condition of the Community in Kekait Village, Gunung Sari District, West Lombok Regency]. Jurnal Sosial, Politik, Kajian Islam dan Tafsir, Volume 1, No. 2. ISSN 2656-1220. Kontekstualisasi Pemikiran Keislaman dalam

Realitas Modern. Download. October, 14. http://sophist.or.id/index.php/js/article/view/18/11

Kenardy, J. (2011). Childhood Trauma Reactions: A Guide for Teachers from Preschool to Year 12. Australia: Queensland Government Natural Disaster Response

Laluyan, T (2007). Pemulihan trauma: Panduan praktis pemulihan trauma akibat bencana alam [Trauma Recovery: A Practical Guide to Trauma Recovery from Natural Disasters]. Jakarta: Lembaga Pengembangan Sarana

Nakamura, Y. (2005). Public health impact of disaster on children. *Japan Medical Association Journal, 48*(7), 377–384.

Purnamasari, I. (2016). Perbedaan reaksi anak dan remaja pasca bencana [Differences in the reactions of children and adolescents after a disaster]. *Jurnal Penelitian dan Pengabdian kepada Masyarakat, 3*(1), 49–55. Doi: 10.32699/ppkm.v3i1.336

Ramirez, M., & Peek-Asa, C. (2005). Epidemiology of traumatic injuries from earthquakes. (online) Diperoleh dari http://epirev.oxfordjournals.org/cont

Semiun, Y. (2006). *Kesehatan Mental 2* [Mental Health 2]. Yogyakarta: Kanisius

Semiun, Y. (2006). *Teori kepribadian dan psikoanalitik freud* [Freud's Theory of Personality and Psychoanalytic]. Yogyakarta: Kanisius.

Surendra S., Samuel, R., Marahatta, K, Anwar, N., Van Ommeren, M. H., & Ofrin, R.. (2017). Post-disaster mental health and psychosocial support: Experience from the 2015 Nepal earthquake. *WHO South-East Asia Journal of Public Health, 6*(1), 22–29. Doi: 10.4103/2224- 3151.20616

Suyanto & Salamah. (2009). Riset Kebidanan: Metodologi dan Aplikasi [Midwifery Research: Methodology and Application]. Yogyakarta: Mitra Cendikia Press

Taliningtyas. (2017). Pemulihan Trauma Terhadap Perilaku Emosi Anak Usia Dini Pasca Bencana Tanah Longsor di Dusun Jemblung Desa Sampang Kecamatan Karangkobar Kabupaten Banjarnegara [Trauma Recovery Against Early Childhood Emotional Behavior Post Landslide Disaster In Jemblung Hamlet, Sampang Village, Karangkobar District, Banjarnegara Regency]. Download. http://lib.unnes.ac.id/29824/1/1601410029.pdf

Dinie Ratri Desiningrum, Seger Handoyo, Rahkman Ardi,
Dewi Retno Suminar & Endang Retno Surjaningrum

Literature Review for Theory of Compassionate Parenting and Islamic Parenting

Abstract: Compassionate parenting is in line with Islamic psychology approach on Islamic parenting. The purpose of this study was to compare the literature on the theory of compassionate parenting and literature from Islamic psychology regarding parenting. PRISMA extraction form was applied in this literature review for articles published after January 1, 2008, and the search was conducted from October 10–19, 2018. The search was limited to research articles in the following database: Science Direct, PsycINFO, ProQuest, and IPI by filtering the result based on several keywords. From a total of 502 found articles, only 18 articles, which consist of 11 articles on compassionate parenting and 7 articles on Islamic parenting met the inclusion criteria. Compassionate parenting is a way of caring for children by recognizing the emotional and cognitive needs of children. It is in line with research findings on parenting in Islamic psychology, emphasizing the teachings of the Prophet and the Sahaba in the implementation of compassionate parenting. The practices and teachings on performing the role as parents have been around since the beginning of Islamic history and are listed in the Qur'an and Al-Hadith.

Keywords: compassionate parenting, islamic parenting, concept, theory.

1. Introduction

Parents face various challenges with lifelong parenting commitments while preparing for the future of children. The process affects the mental health of mothers and the quality of parenting (Alexander, 2018; Cachia et al., 2016; Walter & Smith, 2016). Works of literatures on parents' wellbeing expose that, for some parents, parenting can be stressful and full of negative emotions (Doss et al., 2009; Garfield et al., 2014; Paulson et al., 2010), while for others, parenting can improve wellbeing and meaning in life (Nelson et al., 2013).

The experience of having children helps parents to focus on parenting towards empathy and compassion, and lead to meaning and personal satisfaction in their lives (Brodey, 2007, Bazzano et al., 2015). The goal of parenting may be important for parents to successfully deal with the stress of parenting. The purpose of compassionate parenting emphasizes understanding, respecting, and fulfilling the unique needs of children. Compassionate parenting underlines respect for children's possession, passion, and skills as well as recognizes the needs of children as individuals (Blanchette, 2010; Chierchia & Singer, 2016).

According to Berscheid, (2006; 2010) research on compassion and compassionate love is relatively new, as well as the examination on their correlation to religiosity and spirituality. Underwood, (2002) examined the role of compassionate love in Trappist monks and observed that compassionate love is an important part of their way of life. Love, described as compassionate, altruistic, and nurturing, has been established as the basis for several religious traditions and spiritual practices (Gillath et al., 2005). In Buddhism for example, the common practice is to meditate on the experience of receiving selfless love from a person who is bound to channel love to others.

In Christianity, love is proven in the Golden Rule, loving the enemy, and brotherly love. Similarly, Sprecher & Fehr, (2005) observed positive relationships between religion and spirituality with compassionate love for people who have close relations and for strangers/human relations. Those who possess a high level of religiosity/spirituality show bigger compassionate love (Sprecher & Fehr, 2005). There is evidence that compassion has a greater influence on the prosocial behavior of nonreligious individuals than religious individuals (Saslow et al., 2013).

In the perspective of Islamic psychology, parenting has been exemplified by Prophet Muhammad, peace be upon him, and his Sahaba (companions). Islam considers that family has an important role in education, both in the Islamic and non-Islamic communities (Miharso, 2004). Family is the first place for children to grow, to interact with all family members, in every important and critical period in their development, to obtain an education, and to be nurtured by parents (Adhim, 2006). As stated by the Prophet Mohammad SAW: الأم مدرسة الأولى which means: *Mother is the first school* (Yust, 2006) for their children.

In families, parents have roles and responsibilities for children so that children can grow and develop according to their age, be able to socialize, and become righteous children. According to Jalaluddin (in Yusuf, 2008), children are born in good and holy nature. In their development, starting in their early childhood, he/ she is then influenced by the environment, which will shape him/her to become a good individual or vice versa. So, they need purposeful, planned, and regular guidance and counseling from the environment, especially from both parents. Parental guidance contains three principles, that is: 1) theological principle; 2) philosophical principle; and 3) pedagogical principle, which is integrated as responsibilities for children. Similarly, guiding children focus on three efforts (Mujib & Mudzakir, 2001), namely: a) providing examples, b) nurturing, and c) developing good habits based on religious principles.

After several studies reviewing compassionate parenting from the point of view of Buddhism and Christianity, the purpose of this study was to conduct a literature study of articles related to the basic concept of compassionate parenting, compared to articles related to the basic concept of Islamic parenting.

2. Theoretical Review

Compassion is the readiness to provide assistance and reduce the difficulties or distress experienced by others and to provide what they need (Batson et al., 2002; Goetz et al., 2010). Compassion can be seen as emotions facilitating closeness with others (Nussbaum, 1996; Shiota et al., 2006). Parents who apply compassion in parenting will be able to take possible action that overcomes the difficulties faced by children, by applying some values such as sympathetic, empathetic, full of affection, pressure on distress, and non-judgmental. By developing compassion, the psychological wellbeing of parents will increase and support the progression of child development (Catarino et al., 2014; Neff & Faso, 2015; Sheldon & Cooper, 2008).

Islamic parenting is a unified whole of behavior and treatment of children in educating, fostering, familiarizing, and guiding children optimally based on Islamic teachings. According to Hamid, attitudes in Islamic parenting are compassion, fairness, and the installment of religious education (Innayati, 2012).

3. Method

3.1 Criteria for Inclusion and Exclusion of Articles for the Review

The literature review focused on compassionate parenting and Islamic parenting. The research articles and literature studies that are included in the analysis should comprise the following criteria: (1) It contains the basic concepts of compassionate parenting and Islamic parenting, (2) It mentions factors affecting compassionate parenting and Islamic parenting. (3). Currencies: In this study, the search was limited to studies published in English and Bahasa Indonesia after January 1, 2008.

3.2 Procedures to Identify Relevant Studies

Systematic database search was based on the following criteria: studies were published after January 1, 2008, and the search was conducted from October 10, 2018, to October 19, 2018. The search was only limited to research articles containing the key words: *"compassionate parenting"*, *"pengasuhan compassion"*;

"Islamic parenting", and "pengasuhan islami". Pengasuhan is the Indonesian word for parenting. The keywords were applied to the following databases: Science Direct, PsycINFO, Proquest, and IPI (*Portal Garuda*).

3.3 Data Extraction

Details of eligible studies were extracted using PRISMA extraction form (Moher, Liberati, Tetzlaff, & Altman, 2009) in Excel document format.

4. Results

4.1 Database Search

Database search resulted in 502 articles based on the keyword "pengasuhan/parenting" (science direct: 375; ProQuest: 75; PsycINFO: 24; IPI: 28). All articles were reexamined and duplicates were deleted, resulting in 488 articles. After that, the articles were checked for the author's clear citation, resulting in 309 articles. The next search result using keywords "compassion" and "pengasuhan islami / pola asuh islami/ pendidikan keluarga islami" (Islamic Parenting in Indonesian) in titles showed 72 relevant studies. In the next stage, a filter is applied to search for the articles containing "gaya/cara pengasuhan/ parenting style/type" or their synonyms written in the abstracts, resulting in 18 relevant studies which met inclusion criteria and thus were included in the reviews.

4.2 Article Finding

Analysis was carried out on 18 articles, 11 articles on compassionate parenting and 7 articles on Islamic parenting. All articles were reviewed one by one using descriptive narrative analysis method. The stages of the review process are: (1) reading articles related to the construct of compassion and parenting; (2) classifying articles that have similar concepts; and (3) mapping themes according to the study's objectives of the literature review. The results found several basic concepts, theories, and definitions of parenting.

4.3. Discussion

Compassion includes empathy (appreciating family attention) and sympathy (feeling family emotion) which were combined to act when faced to suffering of others and to alleviate suffering. In parenting, the aspects of compassion include affiliation, two-way communication, and compassionate relationship. Affiliation fulfills the needs to maintain family interactions and requires bonding attachment between parents and children (Altimier, 2015). Bonding attachment as part of compassionate parenting is attached to a mother's figure. In Islam, the position of mother is greatly glorified, so Islamic parenting is mainly represented in the affection of a mother for her children. A study stated that there is a pattern of Islamic motherhood as a parenting pattern that prioritizes children's Islamic nature, by considering spiritual, emotional, rational, social, natural, and physical potentials in children (Rahayu, 2008).

Compassion describes the act of recognizing the suffering of others, and the motivation to alleviate that suffering, thus, compassion can be directed into self-compassion, to others, or received from others. Compassion is also defined as self-kindness vs. self-judgment; common humanity vs. isolation; mindfulness vs. over-identification (Gilbert, 2009; Neff, in Ahmed & Hussain, 2016; Edward, 2017; Kelly & Dupasquier, 2016; Mitchell et al., 2018; Neff & Faso, 2015; Moreira et al., 2018). In Islamic psychology, Islamic parenting seeks to create a quality and righteous generation. Parents help their children to respect their mother and father, show courtesy, have empathy for weak people, be responsible for upholding truth and justice, and avoid all things that cause harm to oneself or to the community (Usmadi, 2016). Another study emphasized parenting based on the method of the Prophet, like mingle with children, calling children with a good attitude, treat them well, be gentle and wise, explore children's potential, support children to pursue fields of expertise based on their talents, teach noble character, and pray for the good of the children (Shofiah & Asra, 2006).

In a family that prioritizes caring, children develop an internal working model, deserve parental care and love, and foster affection to connect with themselves and others. This positive experience cultivates a positive emotional memory, a feeling of being protected and taken care of, allowing individuals to handle their emotions based on love, warmth, and attention when needed, and in parenting, the essential thing is to teach children to love and respect others and show mindfulness (Moreira et al., 2015; Volling et al., 2009). A study that examined the practices of the Prophet shows that parenting which prioritizes child wellbeing and affection, helps children to be courteous, helpful, and respectful towards human dignity (Usmadi, 2016). Another research reveals the importance of Islamic parenting which emphasizes: *tarbiyah*, *akhlakul karimah*, exemplary, and communication. This competence in children includes guiding how to learn while playing at the age 0–7 years old; teaching courtesy and discipline at the age of 7–14 years old; and exchanging ideas at the age level of 14–21 years, to build their sense of independence. Before the implementation, it is important to make sure that: (1) parents master their knowledge before applying the knowledge,

(2) *tarahum*, or parents show love and pray for the good of the children (Alinaksi & Sari, 2015; Yani, 2017).

Goetz et al., (2010) define compassion as an emotion that arises when witnessing the suffering of others and that emotion motivates the desire to help. Furthermore, it is mentioned that compassion is a four-component construct which includes cognitive (awareness of suffering); affective (emotionally moved by suffering); intention (desire to alleviate suffering); and motivation (readiness to help alleviate suffering), in parenting is to get a comprehensive point of view from the perspective of children indicates that parents recognize children's needs, interests and abilities which must be respected (Conti, 2015; Prabhakar, 2018). Research on Islamic parenting stated that the materials to be included in parental teaching are (1) *aqeedah*, shown by feeling ashamed of being disgraceful, being trustworthy and brave in defending the truth, and (2) social ability, shown by loving behaviors, respecting others, offering help, and showing empathy; parents should respect the abilities and needs of children. Parents can develop their parenting skills so that their children develop according to their stages, as independent individuals, especially in spiritual, cognitive, linguistic, social-emotional, and physical motor aspects. (Alinaksi & Sari, 2015; Hadi, 2017; Innayati, 2012)

5. Conclusion

Compassion is the awareness of others' needs and suffering, which is emotionally and cognitively stimulated, and a willingness to provide any assistance. Characteristics of early parenting contribute to the long-term effects of compassion development in adulthood, and compassionate parenting also affects a child's wellbeing as well as parent wellbeing. In Islamic parenting, parents are expected to imitate the method of the Prophet Mohammad (peace and blessing be upon him) in parenting, which is based on compassion, full of gentleness and firmness in upholding Islamic law to shape Islamic character and personality adapted to the ages and stages of the child's development. Islam has the principle of parenting that share some similarities with compassionate parenting, yet it touches the responsibility to stand firm for truth and justice, as well as avoiding harm for oneself and the community. Islamic Parenting also emphasizes on the parents to be knowledgeable about the right childrearing practices and to pray for the children for their good development and destiny. There are principles that Islamic parenting covers as established in the Holy Quran and Al Hadeeth that are not discussed in compassionate parenting.

6. References

Adhim, M. F. (2006). *Positive parenting: Cara-cara islami mengembangkan karakter positif pada anak anda*. PT Mizan Publika.

Ahmed, N., & Hussain, B. Z. (2016). Relationship between parenting styles and self compassion in young adults. *Pakistan Journal of Psychological Research, 31*(2), 441–451.

Alexander, K. (2018). Integrative review of the relationship between Mindfulness-Based Parenting interventions and depression symptoms in parents. *JOGNN - Journal of Obstetric, Gynecologic, and Neonatal Nursing, 47*(2), 184–190. November, 25. https://doi.org/10.1016/j.jogn.2017.11.013

Alinaksi, A. N., & Sari, E. P. (2015). Dinamika kompetensi pengasuhan islami [The dynamics of Islamic parenting competence]. *Psikologika, 20*(2). http://journal.uii.ac.id/Psikologika/article/view/7732

Altimier, L. (2015). Compassionate family care framework: A new collaborative compassionate care model for NICU families and caregivers. *Newborn and Infant Nursing Reviews, 15*(1), 33–41. https://doi.org/10.1053/j.nainr.2015.01.005

Batson, C. D., Ahmad, N., Lishner, D. A., & Tsang, J. A. (2002). Empathy and altruism. In *Handbook of positive psychology* (C. R. Snyd, pp. 485–498). Oxford University Press.

Bazzano, A., Wolfe, C., Zylowska, L., Wang, S., Schuster, E., Barrett, C., & Lehrer, D. (2015). Mindfulness based stress reduction (MBSR) for parents and caregivers of individuals with developmental disabilities: A community-based approach. *Journal of Child and Family Studies, 24*(2), 298–308. https://doi.org/10.1007/s10826-013-9836-9

Berscheid, E. (2006). Searching for the meaning of "love" In R. J. Sternberg & K. Weis (Eds.). In *The new psychology of love* (pp. 171–183). Yale University Press.

Berscheid, E. (2010). Love in the fourth dimension. *Ssrn*. https://doi.org/10.1146/annurev.psych.093008.100318

Blanchette, J. A. (2010). Compassion fatigue, forgiveness, and empathy in foster parents. In *ProQuest LLC* (Vol. 9, Issue 1).

Brodey, D. (2007). *Elephant in the playroom: Ordinary parents write intimately and honestly about the extraordinary highs and heartbreaking lows of raising kids with special needs*. Hudson Street Press.

Cachia, R. L., Anderson, A., & Moore, D. W. (2016). Mindfulness, stress, and well-being in parents of children with autism spectrum disorder: A systematic review. *Journal of Child and Family Studies, 25*(1), 1–14. https://doi.org/10.1007/s10826-015-0193-8

Catarino, F., Gilbert, P., McEwan, K., & Baião, R. (2014). Compassion motivations: Distinguishing submissive compassion from genuine compassion and its association with shame, submissive behavior, depression, anxiety, and stress. *Journal of Social and Clinical Psychology*, *33*(5), 399–412. https://doi.org/10.1521/jscp.2014.33.5.399

Chierchia, G., & Singer, T. (2016). The neuroscience of compassion and empathy and their link to prosocial motivation and behavior. In *Decision Neuroscience: An Integrative Perspective*. Elsevier Inc. https://doi.org/10.1016/B978-0-12-805308-9.00020-8

Conti, R. (2015). Compassionate parenting as a key to satisfaction, efficacy and meaning among mothers of children with autism. *Journal of Autism and Developmental Disorders*, *45*(7), 2008–2018. https://doi.org/10.1007/s10803-015-2360-6

Doss, B. D., Rhoades, G. K., Stanley, S. M., & Markman, H. J. (2009). The effect of the transition to parenthood on relationship quality: An 8-year prospective study. *Journal of Personality and Social Psychology*, *96*(3), 601–619. https://doi.org/10.1037/a0013969

Edward, C. (2017). *Parental attachment and child adjustment: The role of parenting stress and self-compassion* (Issue July).

Garfield, C. F., Duncan, G., Rutsohn, J., McDade, T. W., Adam, E. K., Coley, R. L., & Chase-Lansdale, P. L. (2014). A longitudinal study of paternal mental health during transition to fatherhood as young adults. *Pediatrics*, *133*(5), 836–843. https://doi.org/10.1542/peds.2013-3262

Gilbert, P. (2009). An Introduction to compassion focused therapy. *Advances in Psychiatric Treatment*, *15*(2), 199–208. https://doi.org/10.1521/ijct.2010.3.2.97

Gillath, O., Bunge, S. A., Shaver, P. R., Wendelken, C., & Mikulincer, M. (2005). Attachment-style differences in the ability to suppress negative thoughts: Exploring the neural correlates. *NeuroImage*, *28*(4), 835–847. https://doi.org/10.1016/j.neuroimage.2005.06.048

Goetz, J. L., Keltner, D., & Simon-Thomas, E. (2010). Compassion: An evolutionary analysis and empirical review. *Psychological Bulletin*, *136*(3), 351–374. https://doi.org/10.1037/a0018807

Hadi, S. (2017). Pola Pengasuhan Islami dalam Pendidikan Keluarga [Islamic parenting pattern within family education]. *Tadris*, *12*(1), 117–133.

Innayati, E. M. (2012). Hubungan antara pengasuhan islami dengan identitas diri pada remaja di kota Yogyakarta [The relationship between Islamic parenting and self-identity among adolescents in Yogyakarta city]. *Jurnal Hisbah: Jurnal Bimbingan Konseling dan Dakwah Islam*, *9*(1), 1–17.

Kelly, A. C., & Dupasquier, J. (2016). Social safeness mediates the relationship between recalled parental warmth and the capacity for self-compassion and receiving compassion. *Personality and Individual Differences, 89*, 157–161. https://doi.org/10.1016/j.paid.2015.10.017

Miharso, M. (2004). *Pendidikan keluarga Qur'ani* [Education of Quranic family]. Safiria Insania Press.

Mitchell, A. E., Whittingham, K., Steindl, S., & Kirby, J. (2018). Feasibility and acceptability of a brief online self-compassion intervention for mothers of infants. *Archives of Women's Mental Health, 21*(5), 553–561. https://doi.org/10.1007/s00737-018-0829-y

Moher, D., Liberati, A., Tetzlaff, J., Altman, D. G., & Prisma Group. (2009). Preferred reporting items for systematic reviews and meta-analyses: the PRISMA statement. *PLoS medicine, 6*(7), e1000097.

Moreira, H., Gouveia, M. J., & Canavarro, M. C. (2018). Is mindful parenting associated with adolescents' well-being in early and middle/late adolescence? The mediating role of adolescents' attachment representations, self-compassion and mindfulness. *Journal of Youth and Adolescence, 47*(8), 1771–1788. https://doi.org/10.1007/s10964-018-0808-7

Moreira, H., Gouveia, M. J., Carona, C., Silva, N., & Canavarro, M. C. (2015). Maternal attachment and children's quality of life: The mediating role of self-compassion and parenting stress. *Journal of Child and Family Studies, 24*(8), 2332–2344. https://doi.org/10.1007/s10826-014-0036-z

Mujib, A., & Mudzakir, J. (2001). *Nuansa-nuansa Psikologi Islam* [Nuances of Islamic Psychology]. Raja Wali Press.

Neff, K. D., & Faso, D. J. (2015). Self-compassion and well-being in parents of children with autism. *Mindfulness, 6*(4), 938–947. https://doi.org/10.1007/s12671-014-0359-2

Nelson, S. K., Kushlev, K., Dunn, E. W., & Lyubomirsky, S. (2013). Parents are slightly happier than nonparents, but causality still cannot be inferred. *Psychological Science, 25*(1), 303–304. https://doi.org/10.1177/0956797613508561

Nussbaum, M. C. (1996). Compassion: The basic social emotion. *Social Philosophy and Policy, 13*, 27–58.

Paulson, J. F., Bazemore, S. D., Prevalence, H. E., & Fac, R. (2010). Clinician's corner prenatal and postpartum depression in fathers and its association with maternal depression: A meta-analysis. *JAMA, 303*(19), 1961–1969.

Prabhakar, A. S. (2018). Interventions I develop through the rest of my dissertation. *CHI*, 1–4.

Rahayu, I. T. (2008). *Pola pengasuhan islami sebagai awal pendidikan kecerdasan emosional* [Islamic parenting style as a beginning of educating emotional intelligence].

Saslow, L. R., Willer, R., Feinberg, M., Piff, P. K., Clark, K., Keltner, D., & Saturn, S. R. (2013). My brother's keeper? Compassion predicts generosity more among less religious individuals. *Social Psychological and Personality Science*, *4*(1), 31–38. https://doi.org/10.1177/1948550612444137

Sheldon, K. M., & Cooper, M. L. (2008). Goal striving within agentic and communal roles: Separate but functionally similar pathways to enhanced well-being. *Journal of Personality*, *76*, 415–447.

Shiota, M. N., Keltner, D., & John, O. P. (2006). Positive emotion dispositions differentially associated with Big Five personality and attachment style. *Journal of Positive Psychology*, *1*(2), 61–71. https://doi.org/10.1080/17439760500510833

Shofiah, V., & Asra, Y. K. (2006). Efektivitas islamic parenting training untuk meningkatkan harga diri orangtua yang memiliki anak retardasi mental [Effectiveness of islamic parenting training in improving self-esteem of parents of children with mental retardation]. *Jurnal Psikologi*, *12*(1), 53–58.

Sprecher, S., & Fehr, B. (2005). Compassionate love for close others and humanity. *Journal of Social and Personal Relationships*, *22*(5), 629–651. https://doi.org/10.1177/0265407505056439

Underwood, L. G. (2002). The human experience of love: Conceptual mapping and data from selected studies. In *Altruism and altruistic love: Science, philosophy, and religion in dialogue* (S. G. Post, pp. 72–88). Oxford University Press.

Usmadi. (2016). Pendidikan berbasis nilai-nilai islami dalam pola pengasuhan keluarga [Education based on Islamic values within family parenting style]. *AULADUNA: Jurnal Pendidikan Dasar Islam*, *3*(1), 25–36.

Volling, B. L., Kolak, A. M., & Kennedy, D. E. (2009). Empathy and compassionate love in early childhood: Development and family influence. *The Science of Compassionate Love: Theory, Research, and Applications*, 161–200. https://doi.org/10.1002/9781444303070.ch6

Walter, S. M., & Smith, M. J. (2016). Mothering a child with autism. *Archives of Psychiatric Nursing*, *30*(5), 600–601. https://doi.org/10.1016/j.apnu.2016.01.016

Yani, A. (2017). Implementasi islamic parenting dalam membentuk karakter anak usia dini di RA At-Taqwa kota Cirebon [Implementation of Islamic parenting in shaping the character of early childhood in RA At-Taqwa, Cirebon city]. *AWLADY. Jurnal Pendidikan Anak*, *3*(1). http://syekhnurjati.ac.id/jurnal/index.php/awlady/article/view/1464

Yust, K.-M. (2006). *Nurturing child and adolescent spirituality: Perspectives from the world's religious traditions.* Rowman & Littlefield.

Yusuf, S. (2008). *Psikologi perkembangan anak & remaja* [Developmental Psychology: Childhood and adolescence]. Remaja Rosdakarya.

Nabila Ayu Gumilang & Ike Agustina

Talent Management and Commitment of Generation Y Employees: A Preliminary Study

Abstract: This study aims to determine the relationship between talent management and the commitment of generation Y employees. Subjects were 49 employees (34 men, 15 women) from two coal mining companies in South Kalimantan, Indonesia. Data collection was carried out by using the employee commitment scale and the talent management scale developed from the concept of talent management. Data analysis showed that there is a positive relationship between talent management and employee commitment with a correlation coefficient of 0.702 ($p < 0.05$). Also, talent management provides an effective contribution of 49.3 % towards employees' commitment to their organization.

Keywords: talent management, employee commitment, generation Y

1. Introduction

Commitment is one of the most important parts of progress and development to achieve organization goals. According to Robbins (2001), commitment is a work attitude because it reflects a person's feelings (like or dislike) towards the organization where the individual works. Commitment is defined as an individual orientation towards the organization which includes loyalty, identification, and involvement.

Employee commitment is more than just a formal attachment because it includes the attitude of employees who like the organization and a willingness to put in the maximum effort for the achievement of organizational goals. Employee commitment to the organization is more than passive loyalty, it is an active loyalty. Employees with a high commitment to the company will give their best of their efforts, put the interests of the organization above their self interests, improve the quality of work both in quantity and quality, are productive and thus their work attitude will result in good performance for the organization. While employees with a low level of commitment could give the following impact to the organization: high turnover rates, absenteeism, unproductivity, lack of initiative, poor quality and quantity of work.

According to Mathis and Jackson (2011), employee commitment reflects the level of trust and acceptance of employees towards organizational goals and a desire to remain in the organization, which is ultimately reflected in the low levels of tardiness, absence, and turnover of employees. The determinants of employee commitment to the company can come from internal factors and external factors. Luthans (2011) stated that the determinants of employee commitment are age, tenure, and the tendency of positive or negative affect, or internal and external controls, job design, values, support, and supervisor's leadership style.

In recent years, the coal mining industry has experienced problems. One of them is the increasing turnover rate from year to year. The sustainability report of one main coal company in Borneo showed that from 2012 to 2016 the employee turnover rate increased by 85 % from 2012. Another major national company also experienced an increase in turnover rate, in 2011 it reached 5 %. High turnover rates adversely affect the organization. One of them is the reduced sense of loyalty of other employees due to the large number of turnovers. This situation creates a sense of concern for other employees and creates instability in employees' working climate.

This high turnover phenomenon has become increasingly prevalent when generation Y begins to dominate many industrial sectors. A survey conducted by The Boston Consulting Group in 2014 resulted in 60 % of Y generation employees changing jobs in the first three years. Based on research conducted by Krajcsak, Jonas, and Finna (2014), it was found that generation Y had the lowest level of professional commitment compared to generation X.

Generation Y are tech-literate. They were born when technology was available, so they prefer playing with gadgets (cellphones, laptops, software, and applications) than previous generations. According to Alexander and Sysko (2012), generation Y tends to be more selfish, impatient, narcissistic, hedonistic, has a high work ethic, and is willing to work hard and extra for direct rewards and praise. Generation Y is also considered to have high self-confidence, independence, creativity, and are goal oriented. Generation Y is considered to be disloyal to the companies they work for and tends to move from one company to another because of their high self-esteem and narcissism (Twenge & Campbell, 2008). They have no problem moving from one organization to another that will give them the offer they want (Meler, Stephen & Crokcker, 2010). So, organizations need to understand the characteristics of generation Y.

The existing conditions show that management often has difficulties in motivating generation Y employees and keeping them loyal to the organization (Myers & Sadaghiani, 2010), especially in managing their super keeper. The super keeper is a small group of employees. Employees who are superkeeper can show superior performance and their superior performance can motivate other employees to achieve superior performance as well (Berger & Berger, 2007).

Superkeepers need to be selected and well prepared as future leaders in the organization. Since there are many radical differences in work attitudes between generation Y and the previous generations, especially for the super keepers, then the management should implement a certain strategy to maintain them.

Talent management is a systematic activity to attract and retain superior employees who are competent, contribute, and able to commit to the organization. Talent management includes placing the right people in the right position to increase the company's competitiveness (Karuri & Nahashon, 2015). Several research studies show that organizations that manage their employees actively and appropriately are more successful than companies that don't pay attention to this (Seleim, Ashour & Bontis, 2007; Dooley, 2000; Bontis & Fitzenz, 2002).

Based on the description above, the researchers are interested in finding out whether there is a relationship between talent management and the commitment of generation Y employees.

2. Theoretical Review

Changing working conditions due to the dominance of generation Y employees have not been followed by changes in human resource management practices in several organizations. This has resulted in an increase in the turnover rate (Davidson, McPhail & Barry, 2011). The increase in turnover rate must be taken seriously by the organization because it indicates the low commitment of employees to their organization. Commitment is a condition in which an employee or individual considers the extent to which his personal values and goals are following values and goals of the organization, and the extent to which the employee's desire to maintain membership in the organization (Allen & Meyer, 1990). Employee commitment is another term for organizational commitment. Employee commitment to the organization is defined as a strong desire to remain as a member of the organization, the desire to try hard according to the wishes of the organization, and certain beliefs, and acceptance of the organization's values and goals (Luthans, 2006). Simply, Mohsan, et.al (2004) considered employee commitment as the employee's effort to achieve organizational objectives.

Meyer and Allen (1990) suggested that there are three aspects of organizational commitment: (1) Affective commitment, the willingness to stay as a member of the organization because of emotional attachment and involvement in the organization, this happens because the employees themselves want to stay in the organization. One of the reasons is because they found a value match between the values that employees believe in and the values that exist in the organization;

(2) Continuance commitment, the desire to stay in the organization because they have a fear of leaving the organization, this happens when employees stay in the organization because they feel the need to stay put or in other words they have no other choice to be disloyal to the organization. They feel they must stay in the organization because they have a fear of leaving their job because of salary, career satisfaction, and age factors; and (3) normative commitment, the desire to stay in an organization because they feel that staying an employee in the organization is a must and a responsibility, this occurs when employees feel that they must stay in the organization because they feel obliged to do so.

Meanwhile, talent management is a series of integrated activities in an organization to ensure that the organization can attract, retain, motivate, and develop talented individuals in the organization for the needs of the organization today and in the future (Amstrong, 2006). To fulfil these targets, there are several aspects that the organization needs to pay attention to, namely: the resourcing strategy, attraction and retention policies, talent audit, role development, the relationship management, performance management, total reward, learning and development and career management.

3. Method

3.1 Sample

The respondents of this study were 49 employees (34 men; 15 women) from two coal mining companies in South Kalimantan, Indonesia. They are generation Y (range of age between 25 years to 35 years), considered to be the talents in their organization and having worked in their organization for approximately 2 years.

3.2 Measurement Tools

In this study, the researchers used two questionnaires in which respondents were asked to respond to several statements as they relate to their experience at work. The questionnaire used in this study is the employee commitment scale adapted from the theory of Allen and Meyer (1990) and the talent management scale developed from the theory of Armstrong (2006).

3.2.1 Talent Management Scale

The talent management scale was developed by researchers based on the aspects of talent management proposed by Armstrong (2006): resourcing strategy, attraction and retention policies, talent audit, role development, relationship management, performance management, total rewards, learning and development, and career management. This scale consists of 63 items with a Cronbach alpha reliability coefficient of 0.964 and item discrimination indexes are from 0.312 to 0.783.

3.2.2 Employee Commitment Scale

The scale used to measure employee commitment based on the theory of organizational commitment proposed by Meyer and Allen (1990) consists of 17 items that reflect three aspects: affective commitment, continuance commitment, and normative commitment. The Cronbach alpha reliability coefficient is 0.869 and item discrimination indexes are from 0.342 to 0.692.

Table 1 below shows the distribution of the number of items from the two measurement tools.

Table 1. Blueprint of talent management scale and employee commitment scale

Variable	Aspect	Number of Item
Talent management	Resourcing strategy	6
	Attraction and retention policies and programs	6
	Talent audit	7
	Role development	7
	Relationship management	8
	Performance management	8
	Total reward	7
	Learning and development	6
	Career management	8
Employee commitment	Affective commitment	6
	Continuance commitment	6
	Normative commitment	5

4. Results

Table 2 below indicates that both scores of talent management and employee commitment were in the moderate level.

Table 2. Respondents' score of talent management and employee commitment

Categorization of Score	Talent Management	Employee Commitment
Very Low	0 (0 %)	1 (2 %)
Low	8 (16 %)	12 (24.5 %)
Moderate	23 (47 %)	23 (47 %)
High	17 (35 %)	12 (24.5 %)
Very High	1 (2 %)	1 (2 %)

The results of the hypothesis testing show $r = 0.702$ with $p = 0.000$ ($p < 0.05$). Based on the results of this correlation, it can be concluded that there is a significant positive relationship between talent management and employee commitment, so the proposed hypothesis is supported. The coefficient of determination (r^2) is 0.493, it indicates that talent management influences the employee commitment as much as 49.3 %, while the remaining 50.7 % is influenced by other variables.

Table 3. Result of hypothesis testing

Variable	R	P	r^2	Sig
Talent management * employee commitment	0.702	0.000	0.493	Significant

This study aims to determine the relationship between talent management and employee commitment of the generation Y employees in the coal mining industry. Generation Y is a generation with the lowest level of commitment compared to previous generations. Generation Y tends to move frequently from one company to another. As said by Wee (2013), current generation Y already fulfill 40 % of the total employees in the organization, so they will become leaders in the future.

The result shows that there is a positive relationship between talent management and employee commitment. The high value of *r* coefficient indicates a strong relationship between the two variables (Sarwono, 2006). Furthermore, the result of this study indicates that the better and more effective the organization is in providing talent management programs, the better the commitment that employees have to their organization. Conversely, if the talent programs provided are not good and effective, the commitment of employees will tend to be low as well.

This finding is similar to the study conducted by Nobarieidishe, Chamanifard, and Nikpour (2014) which stated that there is a positive relationship between talent management and employee commitment in Tejarat Bank. According to Nobarieidishe, Chamanifard, and Nikpour (2014), talent management is one of the most important activities to achieve success in organization. Another research conducted by Suharmono (2016) also found that there is a positive and significant relationship between talent management and employee commitment to the organization.

Similar research was conducted by Kheirkhah, Akbarpouran, and Haqhani (2016). This research was conducted because researchers were aware of the minimum level of commitment of employees, especially employee commitment in the service sector. Talent management is the newest method that is considered to have a different positive effect on the low level of commitment of employees. Based on research conducted by researchers, there is a positive and significant relationship between talent management and employee commitment.

This research also found that the categorization of employee commitment of the respondents is in the medium/ moderate category (47 %). In this case, it means that the subject has an average commitment value. Whereas, the categorization of talent management, employees' perceptions of the talent management program are in the medium category (47 %). Based on these results, it can be ascertained that the talent management program is carried out on average. The coefficient of determination (r^2) = 0.493 which means that the variable talent management affects employee commitment by 49.3 %. This suggests that talent management is a factor that affects the commitment of generation Y employees and affects employee commitment to generation Y employees. As we all know that generation Y employees are employees who tend to have a low level of commitment to the organization and are easily bored with something. Therefore, it is very challenging to manage the talents of generation Y.

The findings of this research highlight the critical role of talent management on employee commitment. The practical implication of the results is that organizations need to actively improve their talent management process so that employees would achieve their higher level of commitment. The number of respondents obtained in this study is rather small and only from the coal mining industry. Since this study is a preliminary study, the next future research must involve a larger population from the various industries so a more comprehensive description about the commitment of Y generation employees can be obtained. .

6. References

Alexander, C. S., & Sysko, J. M. (2012). A study of the cognitive determinants of generation Y's entitlement mentality. *Academy of Educational Leadership Journal, 6*(2), 63–68.

Allen, N. J., & Meyer, J. P. (1990). The measurement and antecedents of affective, continuance and normative commitment to the organization. *Journal of Occupational and Organizational Psychology, 63*(1), 1–18.

Armstrong, M. (2006). *Human Resource Management Practice.* London: Kogan page.

Berger, L. A., & Berger, R. D. (2007). *Best Practice on Talent Management.* Jakarta: Penerbit PPM.

Bontis, N. & Fitzenz, J. (2002). Intellectual capital ROI: A current map to human capital antecedents and consequences. *Journal of Intellectual Capital, 3*(3), 223–247.

Davidson, M. C. G., McPhail, R., & Barry, S. (2011). Hospitality HRM: past, present and the future. *International Journal of Contemporary Hospitality Management, 23*(4), 498–516.

Dooley, E. (2000). Intellectual capital in the software industry: An empirical test. *PhD dissertation.* College of Business Administration, University of Washington, Tacoma, WA.

Karuri, M., & Nahashon, L. (2015). Effect of talent management on employee outcomes: A case study of the central bank of Kenya. *The Strategic Journal of Business & Change Management, 2*(43), 882–899.

Kheirkhah, M., Akbarpouran, V., & Haqhani, H. (2016). Relationship between talent management and organizational commitment in midwives working in Iran university of medical sciences. *Journal of Client-Centered Nursing Care, 2*(3), 145–152.

Krajcsak, Z., Jonas, T., & Finna, H. (2014). An analysis of commitment factors depending on generation and part-time working in selected groups of employees. In Hungary. (E. Knichnicka, & A. Mercik, Eds.). *Argumenta Economica, 33*(2), 115–143.

Luthans, F. (2006). *Perilaku Organisasi.* Yogyakarta: PT. Andi Offset.

Luthans, F. (2011). *Organizational Behavior: An Evidence-Based Approach (12th ed.).* Singapore: McGraw Hill.

Mathis, R. L., & Jackson, J. H. (2001). *Manajemen Sumber Daya Manusia* [Human Resource Management]. Jakarta: Salemba Empat.

Meler, J., Stephen, F., & Crokcker, M. (2010). Generation y in the workforce: Managerial challenges. *The Journal of Human Resource and Adult Learning, 6*(1), 68–78.

Mohsan, F., Nawaz, M. M., Khan, M., Shaukat, Z., & Aslam, N. (2004). Are employee motivation, commitment and job involvement inter-related: Evidence from the banking sector of Pakistan. *International Journal of Business and Social Science, 2*(17), 226–233.

Myers, K. K., & Sadaghiani, K. (2010). Millennials in the workplace: A communication perspective on millennials' organizational relationships and performance. *Journal of Business Psychology, 25,* 225–238.

Nobarieidishe, S., Chamanifard, R., & Nikpour, A. (2014). The relationship between talent management and organizational. *European Online Journal of Natural and Social Sciences, 3*(4), 1116–1123.

Robbins S. P. (2001). *Perilaku Organisasi* [Organizational behavior] *(Jilid 2).* Jakarta: PT. Prenhallindo.

Sarwono, J. (2006). *Metode Penelitian Kuantitatif dan Kualitatif.* Yogyakarta: Graha Ilmu

Seleim, A., Ashour, A., & Bontis, N. (2007). Human capital and organizational performance: A study of Egyptian software companies. *Management Decision. 45*(4), 789–801.

Suharmono, A. K. (2016). Analisis pengaruh manajemen talenta dan global mindset terhadap kinerja karyawan dan turnover intention dengan komitmen organisasi sebagai variabel intervening [Analysis of the influence of talent management and global mindset on employee performance and turnover intention with organizational commitment as an intervening variable]. *Diponegoro Journal of Management, 5*(3), 1–15.

Twenge, J. M., & Campbell, S. M. (2008). Generational differences in psychological traits and their impact on the workplace. *Journal of Managerial Psychology, 23,* 862–877.

Wee, T. C. (2013). Talent retention: The pressures in Malaysia SMEs. *American Journal of Economics,3*(5),35–40.

Resnia Novitasari, Dian Sari Utami, Libbie Annatagia, Wanadya Ayu Krishna Dewi, Muhammad Novvaliant Filsuf Tasaufi, Nur Widiasmara & Marcus Stueck

Parent–Child Emotional Communication Strategy: A Pilot Study in Indonesia

Abstract: Emotional communication among parent and child is essential in developing emotional quotient, as a healthy coping strategy for the children, and to build a psychologically healthy family. This research objective is to study the difference in the strategy of communicating emotions between parents (the fathers and the mothers) towards their child, and to compare the strategy based on the child's gender. This study involved 72 parents (M_{age} = 35.458; *SD* = 3.307) with children between 3–12 years. A 24-item questionnaire of Parent-child Conversations about Emotions were administered. Independent sample t-test was performed in the data analysis to find the differences of emotions communication strategy in the family based on gender, among parents and children. The study results show there are significant differences in the conversations of emotions as seen from parents' gender ($p = .021$; $t = -2.356$) and child's gender ($p = .035$; $t = -2.154$). Thus, it can be concluded that mothers and girls have more frequent talks on emotions with each other than fathers and boys. These results strengthen the previous findings that mothers' emotion related conversation occurred more spontaneously with their female child, which will give impacts to their children's emotion regulation and their ability to use adaptive emotion regulation behavior to enhance their affective mental health.

Keywords: emotional communication, parent-child conversations, mental health, Indonesia

1. Introduction

Emotional communication between parents and children is important for enhancing emotional intelligence in children. Emotional understanding has grown from preschool age and rises to middle childhood and reaches its peak in adolescence (Kårstad, Wichstrøm, Reinfjell, Belsky, Berg-Nielsen, 2015. Widen, Pochedly, & Russell, 2015). However, preliminary research from Qudsyi, Trimulyaningsih, Novitasari, and Stueck (2018) found that children in Indonesia (aged 9–12 years) who were involved as research respondents tended to have limited emotional vocabulary in only a few types of basic emotions. Whereas mastery of emotional vocabulary is the initial bridge of the ability to express and regulate emotions (Santiago-Poventud et al., 2015).

The impact of children's inability to understand their emotions will lead to low social adjustment and their ability of social cognition (Mazzone, Roskam, Mikolajczak, & Nader-Grosbois, 2017). In addition, other impacts can also occur such as a decrease in academic ability in schools (Eisenberg, Sadovsky, & Spinrad, 2005), as well as the presence of developmental psychopathology, for example internalizing and externalizing behavioral problems (Southam-Gerow & Kendall, 2002). Based on this explanation, it can be concluded that low understanding of emotions can have a negative effect on children's mental health.

One of the efforts to foster this ability is through emotional conversation strategies between parents and children (Fivush & Wang, 2005; Morris, Silk, Steinberg, Myers, & Robinson, 2007). The role of parents in providing sufficient understanding of emotions has been studied in recent times. The role of parents in the social and emotional development of children appears through the following means: the intergenerational transmission through the explanation of emotions, rules and limitations on children, and the cultural beliefs and practices of showing appropriate emotional expression (von Salisch, 2001). This is confirmed by the results of research from Dinallo (2016) who conducted community intervention to improve children's emotional understanding. The result is the enhancement of parental skills related to emotional regulation, modeling, and affirmation of knowledge in children. Increasing these skills will eventually increase self-efficacy in parents when communicating emotions with children. On the other hand, emotional conversation also help children to strengthen children's constructive coping (Gentzler, Contreras-Grau, & Kerns, 2005) and even children's coping to traumatic events (van Delft, Finkenauer, De Schipper, & Lamers-Winkelman, 2018). Thus, the strategy has a positive impact on parent-child interactions.

Based on previous research, there are differences in emotional conversation styles between fathers and mothers and their children (Aznar & Tenenbaum, 2013; Chaplin, Cole, Zahn-Waxler, 2005). Meanwhile, the level of children's age that is correlated with cognitive, social, and language abilities is also claimed to influence the strategies used (Bariola, Hughes, & Gullone, 2012). On the other hand, gender differences in children also play an important role. Differences in emotions can be divided into emotional understanding (cognitive level) and emotional expression (affective and behavioral level). Evidently, there are differences in understanding emotions in girls and boys in terms of understanding emotions that are different from belief or mental domain (Fidalgo, Tenenbaum, & Aznar, 2018). In terms of emotional expression, meta-analysis research from Chaplin and Aldao (2013), found that there are differences in emotional expression styles between girls and boys. Girls were more likely to show positive emotions and less visible emotions (such as sadness). Meanwhile, boys were more open in showing negative emotions, such as anger.

Based on this explanation, this study aims to examine the differences in parenting strategy as it relates to emotional communication between fathers and mothers as well as the comparison of the strategy based on children's gender.

2. Theoretical Review

Emotional competence is an important aspect of child development. There are several emotional competencies developed in childhood according to Denham (2007), namely awareness of various emotional experiences, understanding of emotions experienced by oneself and others, use of emotion-related vocabulary, the ability to empathize with other people's emotions, regulating oneself when negative emotions arise, understanding that internal emotions with emotional expression can be different, and understanding that social relationships are also bridged by understanding emotions. This shows the diversity in emotional competence which includes internal and external parties.

Emotion is also part of mental understanding in children (Ruffman, Slade, & Crowe, 2002). The understanding of emotions is influenced by many things, especially from social interactions. One of them is the use of mental state language by parents through conversation (Harris, 2005; Ontai & Thompson, 2008; Ruffman, Slade, & Crowe, 2002). A statement conveyed clearly by the mother shows the meaningful conversation related to mental state language between a parent and a child that leads to the vocabulary in mental processes such as cognition, desire, belief, preference, and emotional condition (Ruffman, Slade, & Crowe, 2002).

Socialization about emotions is a concept related to efforts to foster understanding, emotional expression, and regulation of emotions in a social context (Kitzmann, 2012). According to Eisenberg, Cumberland, and Spinrad (1998), there are several strategies for parents to socialize emotions to their children. These strategies are the response of parents to their children's emotions, emotional discussions between parents and children, and parents' emotional expressions. Based on the results of the study, parents differentiate how to explain the types of emotions in early childhood (Knothe & Walle, 2017). Parents tend to describe images of sad emotions longer than happy emotions (Knothe & Walle, 2017). Thus, this strategy varies depending on the social context within the family.

3. Method

3.1 Subjects

This study involved 72 Indonesian parents of 3–12 years-old children. There were 54 mothers (M_{age} = 35.227; *SD* = 2.723) and 18 fathers (M_{age} = 36.153; *SD* = 2.536). Most of the subjects (97 %) were living in Java, Indonesia and coming from Javanese (83 %) and using Bahasa Indonesia (Indonesian) in daily conversation (71 %).

3.2 Measurement Tools

We used online questionnaires to gain the data. Subjects filled out the demographics data (including name, gender, age, origin, ethnicity, children's gender, children's age and children's birth order) and administered a 24-item Questionnaire of Parent-child Conversations about Emotions. This original scale has a very good consistency of the total score ($\alpha = 0.910$) (Mazzone, et al., 2017). However, after we conducted the reliability analysis using Cronbach's alpha, three items were excluded (i.e., item number 16, 17, and 22) and 21 items retained with a very good consistency as well ($\alpha = 0.950$).

3.3 Data Analysis

Independent sample t-test was performed in the data analysis to find the differences of parent-child conversations about emotions in the family based on the child's gender.

4. Results

This study aims to understand (1) the difference of parental emotional communication strategy between fathers and mothers and (2) the difference of parental emotional communication strategy between parents and children based on the child's gender (boys and girls).

Test of normal distribution was conducted using non-parametric analysis Kolmogorov-Smirnov. The scores of the samples in this study show a normal distribution ($Z = 1.103$; $p > .05$), which means that the mean scores and the standard deviation are equal with the set of scores in the particular population.

The first results of independent samples t-test analysis in Table 1 show that the parental emotional communication between fathers and mothers are significantly different ($t = -2.214$, $p < 0.05$) and the equal variances are assumed.

Table 1. Results of the parental emotional communication between fathers and mothers

		Levene's Test for Equality of Variances		**t-test for Equality of Means**						
		F	***p***	***t***	***df***	***p* (2-tailed)**	**M Difference**	**SE Difference**	**95 % Confidence Interval of the Difference**	
									Lower	**Upper**
TotalQPCCE_rel	Equal variances assumed	2.363	.129	-2.214	70	.030	-7.703	3.479	-14.643	-.764
	Equal variances not assumed			-2.527	37.841	.016	-7.703	3.048	-13.876	-1.530

Table 2. Descriptive statistic of parental emotional communication between fathers and mothers

Parents	*N*	*M*	*SD*	SE Mean
father	18	48.22	10.33	2.43
mother	54	55.92	13.47	1.83

Depicted from Table 2 above, mothers have higher mean on the parental emotional communication strategy (M = 55.92; SD = 13.47) compared with fathers (M = 48.22; SD = 10.33). This portrays that the intentions of mothers using emotional communication strategy towards their children are higher rather than fathers.

Table 3. Results of parental emotional communication strategy in terms of the child's gender

		Levene's Test for Equality of Variances		t-test for Equality of Means						
		F	*p*	*t*	*df*	*p* (2-tailed)	Mean Difference	Std. Error Difference	95 % Confidence Interval of the Difference	
									Lower	Upper
Total QPCCE_rel	Equal variances assumed	4.021	.049	-2.102	70	.039	-6.377	3.033	-12.427	-.327
	Equal variances not assumed			-2.064	60.959	.043	-6.377	3.090	-12.557	-.197

Table 4. Descriptive statistic of parental emotional communication based on the child's gender

Group Statistics					
	Child's Gender	*N*	*M*	*SD*	*SE Mean*
TotalQPCCE_rel	boys	39	51.076	11.434	1.831
	girls	33	57.454	14.302	2.489

Second results of this study as depicted in Table 3 show that there is a significant difference in parental emotional communication strategy based on the child's gender (t = -2.102, $p < .05$). This means that parents use a different emotional communication strategy towards their male or female children. Statistically, it is shown in Table 4 that female children (girls) have a higher score of parental emotional communication (M = 57.454; SD = 14.302) rather than male children (boys) (M = 51.076; SD = 11.434).

Therefore, based on the results above, we may conclude that parents have a different emotional communication strategy. Statistically, mothers have a higher score when using emotional communication strategy on their children rather than fathers. Meanwhile, there is also a difference in emotional communication strategy used by parents towards their daughter or sons. Parents have a higher score when using emotional communication strategies towards their female children rather than male children.

Communication is one of the main activities carried out by humans with various purposes. Especially in the context of the family, where communication is the core of the expressive process and an important factor in building a relationship (Day, 2003). As each individual has uniqueness, each family member has their own way of communicating and preference over the topics deemed as appropriate to be communicated with their members.

The results in this study indicate that there is a significant difference between the role of the father and the role of the mother based on the gender of children when parent-child communication about several things related to emotions take place. This study is in line with the research of Chaplin et al. (2005) which showed that there are gender differences in expressing emotions, especially at the beginning of pre-school age and are influenced by how fathers and mothers respond to communication with children. This can occur because the family context is an important part of children's emotional regulation. Children learn through observation, modelling emotional expressions shown by fathers and mothers, and from the emotional climate that is built in the family (Morris, et al, 2007).

In terms of gender differences, girls are receiving communication with emotional contents more intensively than boys. This is in line with some studies that revealed that girls show higher family communication than boys, especially with their mothers (Cava, Buelga, & Musitu, 2014). Also, for some children in middle childhood, they are more closely related to the emotion regulation of their mother than their father (Bariola, Hughes, & Gullone, 2012). Fivush and Wang (2005) emphasized that there is a link between a mother's emotional experiences and children's gender. The experience of mother-child interaction is also shown from the use of words that describe emotions for certain events. This is also in line with the findings of Bariola, et al. (2012) which show that mothers emphasize emotions more in communication with children than fathers. It can be concluded that mothers and daughters have more frequency when communicating about emotions than fathers and sons.

5. Conclusion

Fathers and mothers show a significant difference in their strategy of emotional communication to their children. Mothers use emotional communication more intensively than fathers. Moreover, girls received more emotional communication from parents rather than boys.

These results will give an implication about the relationship and interaction of father-child and mother-child in particular. This finding implies that in parenting practices or early childhood education, it is necessary to apply emotional communication regardless of children's genders. The impact on parent-child relationships between mothers and fathers to their children is providing an insight into family communication and emotional intelligence within family members. Adequate information, such as training, might be necessary to strengthen the parental strategy to communicate emotions properly.

Nevertheless, there are several limitations in this study that are necessary to be mentioned. The range of children's age that was assessed by parents was too wide. Thus, the form of parental emotional communication strategy with regard to the child's gender is presumably different between early and middle childhood. The specific strategy used by parents to communicate emotions was not examined thoroughly. Moreover, this study was using only gender to assess the difference of emotion communication strategy. There are other factors that could be added to understand deeper the differences of parental emotion communication strategy to their children.

Future research should consider other variables as determinant factors of the difference of emotional communication strategy and its impacts with other behavioral aspects. Also, it is necessary to develop an intervention program based on the findings.

6. References

Aznar, A., & Tenenbaum, H. R. (2013). Spanish parents' emotion talk and their children's understanding of emotion. *Frontiers in Psychology*, *4*, 670. Doi:10.3389/fpsyg.2013.00670

Bariola, E., Hughes, E.K., & Gullone, E. (2012). Relationships between parent and child emotion regulation strategy use: A brief report. *Journal of Child and Family Studies, 21*, 443–448. Doi: https://doi.org/10.1007/s10826-011-9497-5

Cava, M., Buelga, S., & Musitu, G. (2014). Parental communication and life satisfaction in adolescence. *Spanish Journal of Psychology, 7*, 1–8. DOI: https://doi.org/10.1017/sjp.2014.107

Chaplin, T. M., & Aldao, A. (2013). Gender differences in emotion expression in children: A meta-analytic review. *Psychological Bulletin, 139*(4), 735–765. DOI: 10.1037/a0030737

Chaplin, T. M., Cole, P. M., & Zahn-Waxler, C. (2005). Parental socialization of emotion expression: gender differences and relations to child adjustment. *Emotion, 5*(1), 80–88. doi: http://dx.doi.org/10.1037/1528-3542.5.1.80

Day, R.D. (2003). *Introduction to family processes*. New Jersey: Lawrence Erlbaum Associates Publisher.

Denham, S. A. (2007). Dealing with feelings: How children negotiate the worlds of emotions and social relationships. *Cognition, Brain, and Behavior, 11*(1), 1–48

Dinallo, A. M. (2016). Social and emotional learning with families. *Journal of Education and Learning, 5*(4), 147–158.

Eisenberg, N., Cumberland, A., & Spinrad, T. L. (1998). Parental socialization of emotion. *Psychological Inquiry, 9*(4), 241–273.

Eisenberg, N., Sadovsky, A., & Spinrad, T. L. (2005). Associations of emotion-related regulation with language skills, emotion knowledge, and academic outcomes. *New directions for child and adolescent development*, (109), 109–118.

Fidalgo, A. M., Tenenbaum, H. R., & Aznar, A. (2018). Are there gender differences in emotion comprehension? Analysis of the Test of Emotion Comprehension. *Journal of Child and Family Studies, 27*(4), 1065–1074. https://doi.org/10.1007/s10826-017-0956-5

Fivush, R., & Wang, Q. (2005). Emotion talk in mother-child conversations of the shared past: The effects of culture, gender, and event valence. *Journal of Cognition and Development, 6*(4), 489–506. doi: https://doi.org/10.1207/s15327647jcd0604_3

Gentzler, A. L., Contreras-Grau, J. M., & Kerns, K. A. (2005). Parent–child emotional communication and children's coping in middle childhood. *Social Development, 14*(4), 591–612.

Harris, P. L. (2005). Conversation, pretense, and theory of mind. *Why Language Matters for Theory of Mind*. Editors: Janet Wilde Astington & Jodie A. Baird. Oxford: Oxford University Press, Inc.

Kårstad, S.B., Wichstrøm, L., Reinfjell, T,, Belsky, J., Berg-Nielsen,T. S.(2015). What enhances the development of emotion understanding in young children? A longitudinal study of interpersonal predictors. *British Journal of Developmental Psychology, 33*(3), 340–354. doi: 10.1111/bjdp.12095.

Kitzmann, K. M. (2012). Learning about emotion: Cultural and family contexts of emotion socialization. *Global Studies of Childhood, 2*(2), 82–84.

Knothe, J. M., & Walle, E. A. (2017). Parental communication about emotional contexts: Differences across discrete categories of emotion. *Social Development*, 1–15. DOI: 10.1111/sode.12276

Mazzone, S., Roskam, I., Mikolajczak, M., & Nader- Grosbois, N. (2017). Do Parents Talk about Emotions with Their Children? The Questionnaire of Parent – Child Conversations about Emotions (QPCCE). Psychology, 8, 987–1007. https://doi.org/10.4236/psych.2017.87065

Morris, A. S., Silk, J. S., Steinberg, L., Myers, S. S., & Robinson, L. R. (2007). The role of the family context in the development of emotion regulation. *Social Development (Oxford, England), 16*(2), 361–388. doi: 10.1111/j.1467-9507.2007.00389.x

Ontai, L. L., & Thompson, R. A. (2008). Attachment, parent–child discourse and theory-of-mind development. *Social Development, 17(1),* 47–60.

Qudsyi, H., Trimulyaningsih, N., Novitasari, R., & Stueck, M. (2018). Developing a module of nonviolent communication among children in Yogyakarta. *Proceedings of the International Conference On Child-Friendly Education, Universitas Muhammadiyah Surakarta,* 149–160.

Ruffman, T., Slade, L., & Crowe, E. (2002). The relation between children's and mothers' mental state language and theory-of-mind understanding. *Child Development, 73,* 734–751.

Santiago-Poventud, L., Corbett, N. L., Daunic, A. P., Aydin, B., Lane, H., & Smith, S. W. (2015). Developing social-emotional vocabulary to support self-regulation for young children at risk for emotional and behavioral problems. *International Journal of School and Cognitive Psychology, 2*(3), 1–9. doi: 10.4172/2469-9837.1000143

Southam-Gerow, M. A. & Kendall, P. C. (2002). Emotion regulation and understanding implications for child psychopathology and therapy. *Clinical Psychology Review, 22,* 189–222

Van Delft, I., Finkenauer, C., De Schipper, J. C., & Lamers-Winkelman, F. (2018). Talking about feelings: Mother–child emotion dialogues among sexually abused children. *Journal of Interpersonal Violence, 0*(00), 1–23, DOI: 10.1177/0886260518795176.

Von Salisch, M. (2001). Children's emotional development: Challenges in their relationships to parents, peers, and friends. *International Journal of Behavioral Development, 25*(4), 310–319.

Widen, S. C., Pochedly, J. T., & Russell, J. A. (2015). The development of emotion concepts: A story superiority effect in older children and adolescents. *Journal of Experimental Child Psychology, 131*, 186–192

Nailul Fauziah, Arina Dina Rusyda, Dinie Ratri Desiningrum,
Anggun Resdasari Prasetyo & Erin Ratna Kustanti

Family Support for Mothers of Children with Autism Spectrum Disorder

Abstract: Autism spectrum disorder (ASD) is a developmental disorder that hinders the growth and development of children. Autism requires complex management and the active role of parents in various therapy-related matters. Generally, the care of autistic children is done by mothers. The special needs of children with ASD occasionally lead parents, especially mothers, to experience stress. Therefore, social support is required from various parties, especially family members. The purpose of this research is to explore the dynamics of family support for mothers of children with ASD. This research used the purposive sampling technique to select respondents of the study. Respondents were mothers of children with ASD who attended rhythm therapy at one music studio. A descriptive qualitative approach was used in this study, with the data collection conducted via interviews. Data analysis involved three phases, namely data reduction, data display, and conclusion. Findings show that four out of five respondents received the most significant support from their spouses in the form of instrumental support. The fifth respondent received the most support from her brother-in-law in the form of informational support. In addition, findings show that at first, respondents' parents and parents-in-law tend to reject the child's condition though they begin to accept it eventually.

Keywords: children with autism spectrum disorder, family support, mothers

1. Introduction

Autism is a term used to describe a type of pervasive developmental disorder that results in cognitive, language, behavior, communication and social impairment or delay in children (Desiningrum, 2016). The prevalence of Autism Spectrum Disorder (ASD) children according to the Data Center of Disease Control (CDC) in America in March 2014 was 1 in 68 children. In Indonesia, 1 out of 42 boys and 1 out of 189 girls are diagnosed with ASD (Departemen Kesehatan [Depkes.go.id], 2016). According to research reported by the Kompas daily, there are an estimated 475,000 children with symptoms of ASD in Indonesia. However, there is no specific data on the prevalence of ASD (Widodo, as cited in Wardani, 2009).

Parents of children with ASD face many challenges, including struggles of attaining diagnoses, finding treatment and appropriate educational programs, and funding the required services (Ekas, Lickenbrock, & Whitman, 2010). The presence of children with special needs in a family can change the family's routine (Mangunsong, 2011). General reactions that occur in parents whose children are diagnosed with a special need include sadness, disappointment, guilt, rejection, or anger before finally accepting the child's condition. Parents who have children with special needs go through various stages, including phases of shock and disruption, stress, sadness, anxiety and fear, anger until they eventually adjust to the situation (Mangunsong, 2011).

Mothers of children with ASD children have moderate scores on the Beck Depression Inventory (Weiss, 2002). In addition, mothers of children with ASD experience more anxiety and somatic symptoms compared to mothers of children with mental retardation or typically developing children. Mothers of children with ASD children also experience more burnout than mothers of children with mental retardation or typically developing children (Weiss, 2002). Mothers of children with ASD experience high levels of parenting stress, with managing demanding behaviors and upset feelings, discipline, and managing behavior in public places being the highest sources of stress (Phetrasuwan &Miles, 2009).

Research by Maswati (2004) which was conducted in Jakarta found that parents who have children with ASD in their middle childhood years, use social support as a strategy to cope with stress and better manage their children's developmental problems. In addition, parents of children with ASD are reported to need more professional support to work with children and their families (Siklos and Kerns, 2006).

2. Theoretical Review

The essential features of autism spectrum disorder include persistent impairment in reciprocal social communication and social interaction, as well as restricted and repetitive patterns of behavior, interests, or activity. These symptoms are present from early childhood and limit everyday functioning (American Psychiatric Association, 2013).

Parenting is a task related to guiding children to be physically and psychologically independent later in their adult life (Andayani & Koentjoro, 2004). There is a reciprocal relationship between them that could affect the child's condition until adolescence. Parenting can also be defined as the implementation of a series of decisions regarding children's socialization (Berns, 2013).

Parenting stress is described as a feeling of anxiety and tension that transcends boundaries of the parent's emotion and is specifically related to the role of parents and interactions between parents and children (Abidin as cited in Ahern, 2004). Deater-Deckard (2004) argues that parenting stress is a process that involves unwelcome psychological conditions and physiological reactions that arise as an effort to adapt to the demands of the role of parents. Whereas according to Lestari (2014), parenting stress can be understood as a stressful situation that occurs when carrying out childcare duties.

According to Safaria (2005), parents pass the following stages before finally being able to accept the child's condition:

a. Denial: doubt expert diagnosis, disconcerted about the diagnosis, unsure of what to do, and perplexed about the cause of the problem.
b. Anger: easily angered and sensitive to small problems.
c. Bargaining: attempt to comfort yourself by stating, for example, "maybe if we wait things will turn out well on its own".
d. Depression: the beginning of despair and loss of hope, occasionally resulting in guilt, especially on the part of the mother.
e. Acceptance: the beginning of acceptance toward a child's condition, thereby resulting in a chance of expectation adjusted to the child's capacity.

Social support refers to comfort, attention, appreciation, or assistance given by other people or groups to an individual. There are two classifications of social support, namely, received social support and perceived social support (Sarafino & Smith, 2011). Received social support is measured based on the form or amount of social support provided by others. At the same time, perceived social support is measured based on individual perceptions about the comfort, attention, assistance and help that is received from others.

Sarafino and Smith (2011) distinguish social support based on the form of support received by individuals:

a. Emotional and esteem support: take the form of expressions of empathy, attention, concern, and positive appreciation for the individual concerned.
b. Intangible/instrumental support: take the form of direct assistance.
c. Informational support: take the form of advice, direction, feedback, or input on the individual's behavior.
d. Network companionship: take the form of people's willingness to spend time together or provide a feeling of membership in a group that has the same hobby.

Social support can come from partners, family members, friends, social contacts, peer groups, religious communities, coworkers, and the community in general. According to Sarafino and Smith (2011), social support can be classified into several resources groups, including:

a. Significant others, such as non-professionals who surround the individuals, such as family, close friends, or colleagues
b. Professionals such as psychologists or doctors
c. Social support groups

3. Methods

3.1 Research Design

The approach used in this study is descriptive qualitative. Bogdan and Taylor (as cited in Moleong, 2011) suggest that qualitative research is "a research procedure that produces descriptive data in the form of written or oral words from people and observable behavior". Qualitative research relies on natural settings to draw a holistic picture of the phenomena or problem, positions humans as research tools, conducts data analysis inductively, and is more concerned with the research process than the results, which are agreed upon by the researchers and research subjects. The descriptive method was chosen because the research topic is an ongoing phenomenon. Nazir (2011) describes the descriptive method as "a method of examining the status of a group, a subject, a set of conditions, a system of thought or even a class of events that occur in the present. The purpose of this descriptive study is to make a systematic description, depiction or illustration of the phenomena investigated". Sugiyono (2015) describes qualitative research as "a research method based on the philosophy of positivism, used to examine objects in their natural settings, in which researchers are key instruments (as opposed to experiments), sampling is done using purposive and snowball techniques, merging the techniques through triangulation, is inductive/qualitative, and the results emphasizing meaning rather than a generalization (of the phenomenon)".

3.2 Sample

The research subjects were five selected using a purposive sampling technique based on the following criteria: a) Mothers of children with ASD; b) Children with ASD aged 6–15 years old; c) Children who attend rhythm therapy at *Gilang Ramadhan Studio Band.*

3.3 Instruments

Data collection was conducted via interviews. Data analysis was done in several phases, including data reduction, data display, and conclusion.

4. Results

The interview resulted in a description regarding the role of family support in the wellbeing of mothers of children with ASD. Various reactions upon knowing one's child is diagnosed with autism include confusion, surprise, baffled, and denial. Rejection is typically a temporary form of self-defense to avoid excessive anxiety (Mangunsong, 2011). Mrs. S's first reaction when her child was diagnosed with ASD was confusion and failure to grasp the situation. Mrs. H experienced similar reactions and was confused, shocked, and struggled to understand the condition and diagnosis of her child.

Initially, Mrs. S's spouse was not accepting of the child's condition as autism is stigmatized as 'different', subsequently leading to reluctance to interact with the child. After being reassigned to work in the same city as Mrs. S, the husband had more interaction increasingly with the child. However, until the time of data collection, the husband continued to show rejection, implying that he had not entirely accepted the child's condition.

Similarly, Mrs. M's husband also initially rejected the diagnosis. After the child reached the age of four, Mrs. M's husband began the attempt at better understanding his child's condition, expressing his desire to share the responsibility of taking care of his child who has ASD. For example, if Mrs. M cares for their child in the early evening, then Mrs. M's husband takes over from evening tonight. Mrs. M obtained information about ASD solely from internet search engine results without the help of her husband. Meanwhile, Mrs. V's husband tends to be lax in responding to his child's diagnosis of ASD. However, he also did not seek further information about ASD or forms of treatment that may be needed or required.

Mrs. H's husband responded to his child's diagnosis of ASD by asking Mrs. H to resign from her job and focus on caring for their child as Mrs. H's husband lives in a different city. Mrs. H's husband visits his wife and children once a month, or if he is busy, then Mrs. H and the children will visit him instead.

Mrs. S's parents and parents-in-law reside in a different city; thus, Mrs. S has not entirely felt supported. In contrast, Mrs. M's mother-in-law, who resides with the family, has not accepted that her grandson has been diagnosed with autism. Mrs. M's mothers-in-law questions her grandson's diagnosis of ASD and why it should be treated. Acceptance of her grandson's condition has not developed even after the child turns four years old. Meanwhile, Mrs. H's parents and parents-in-law neither rejected nor accepted their grandson's ASD diagnosis, because they felt that their offspring was perfectly fine.

Mrs. S's brother-in-law has been more supportive than her husband in the development of her child with ASD. The brother-in-law had prior knowledge on ASD thus knows there are differences between children with ASD and typically developing children and has helped find further information about ASD and necessary treatments for the condition. Mrs. S's brother-in-law also helped communicate the condition of the child to her husband. According to Sarafino & Smith (2011), advice, direction, and feedback regarding an individual's behavior is a form of informational support.

The four other mothers received the most support from their husbands. Mrs. V and Mrs. M received adequate financial support from their husbands yet lacked emotional support. Also, Mrs. V and Mrs. M's spouse lacked interaction with the children. Meanwhile, Mrs. H's husband provides her with all the facilities needed – including a house and a car – for the child to receive appropriate treatment. The support provided by Mrs. H's husband is classified as instrumental support (Sarafino & Smith, 2011).

In the case of Mrs. N, her husband not only provided material support but also helped care for and educate their child with ASD. Together, Mrs.N and her husband seek information about ASD, and the appropriate treatments needed, as well as accompany the child to undergo treatment. Both parents are open about their child's condition to their neighbors. However, because Mrs lives in a remote area, limited knowledge about ASD results in a lack of support from surrounding neighbors.

Family support does not always mean that the support always originates from family members. It is not so crucial to whom mothers receive social support. Rather, the concern is on acquiring the needed support. Support in this context is not in material form, but emotional and social support from core family members (e.g., husband) or otherwise. Social support from other people provides strength for mothers to take action and hold their children in various ways. With excellent social support, mothers are empowered and have better self-esteem to take necessary actions that help their children. Thus, social support may be seen as the source of a mother's strength.

The wide range of family stressors associated with having a child with ASD includes financial burden, social isolation, and a negative impact on siblings (Dillenburger, Keenan, Doherty, Byrne, & Gallagher, 2010). Families of children with ASD report higher levels of a burden compared to families of children with other developmental disabilities, mental health conditions, or comorbid developmental disabilities (Vohra et al., 2014). Subjective family burden, defined as parent and family problems, has been suggested as a more comprehensive and appropriate measure of family impact within Latinx families than an individual subjective burden (Magaña, Schwartz, Rubert, & Szapocznik, 2006). Family burden emphasizes the overall impact on the family unit.

Passive optimism is described as the lack of action or help-seeking while maintaining a positive outlook (Sloper & Turner, 1992). Carver and Scheier (1993) highlight that passive optimists believe they can wait for positive things to happen without trying. In contrast, active optimists confront challenges with effort (Carver & Scheier, 1993). Thus, optimists who engage in active coping are more likely to have fewer unmet service needs as they actively seek services (Lopez, Reed, & Magaña, 2019).

From social support, mothers build optimism which will help children to be more independent. Adaptive coping strategies, informal social support sources, and beliefs about the efficacy of the interventions were associated with lower reported stress (Hastings & Johnson, 2001).

Supporting people with ASD, as well as their families, has become an urgent priority for service providers and government organizations (Brookman-Frazee, Drahota, Stadnick, & Palinkas, 2012). Family and couple relationship strain has been explored in research addressing families with children of varying disabilities which may provide some insight into couple and marital dynamics of parents of children with ASD specifically. A meta-analysis by Risdal and Singer (2004) found that between 2.9 % and 6.7 % more marriages end in divorce among parents of children with disabilities, compared with parents of children with no disabilities. Another study found that among couples with satisfying relationships, the challenges of dealing with a child's disability can serve to strengthen and enrich relationships (Scorgie & Sobsey, 2000). Sabbeth and Leventhal (1984) reviewed 34 studies and found no increased risk of divorce rates in such families but did find higher rates of marital distress and lower marital satisfaction for parents with children with ASD compared to parents of children with other disabilities. So, family social support is considered crucial for mothers, as caregivers for children with autism spectrum disorder.

On the other hand, Islam, as the primary way of life for the majority of Indonesian people teaches us to help other people who have problems. The concept of lending a hand is called *Taawun* (help each other). The result of this research shows that four of the five mothers acquire social support from their husband (father of the child); the fifth mother has not received much support from her spouse. The first time their children were diagnosed with autism spectrum disorder, the parents experienced shock and denial; this was especially the case for the fathers who would then need more time to accept their children's condition. Holy Al-Qur'an states in At Tahrim verse 6: "*O you who believe, protect yourself and your family from the fires of hell whose fuel is man and stone;*

guardian angels who are rough, hard, and do not disobey God for what He has commanded them and always do what they are commanded".

Thus, parents must care for and love their children unconditionally, as proof of human's reverence for God. Thus, parents can work as a team to take care of and parent their children. It is considered a big sin if they cannot accept their children's condition. Life is full of an ordeal to test people's faith in *Allah* the almighty. Human beings must be patient and believe in God to create a better life.

5. Conclusion

The results of the study showed that four out of five research subjects who are mothers of children with ASD received the most support from their spouse in the form of intellectual support. The fifth subject received the most support from her brother-in-law in the form of informational support.

6. References

Ahern, S. L. (2004). *Psychometric Properties of The Parenting Stress Index-Short Form.* Thesis. Raleigh: Faculty of Psychology North Carolina State University.

American Psychiatric Association. (2013). *Diagnostic and statistical manual of mental disorder* (5th ed.). Arlington, VA: American Psychiatric Association.

Andayani, B. & Koentjoro. (2004). Psikologi keluarga: Peran ayah menuju Co-parenting [Family psychology: The role of fathers towards Co-parenting]. Surabaya: Citra Media.

Berns, R. M. (2013). *Child, family, school, community: Socialization and support* (9th ed.). Belmont, CA: Wadsworth, Cengage Learning.

Brookman-Frazee, Drahota, Stadnick, & Palinkas. (2012). Therapist perspectives on community mental health services for children with autism spectrum disorders. Administration and Policy in Mental Health and Mental Health Services Research, 39(5) 365–73

Carver, C. S., & Scheier, M. F. (1993). *On the power of positive thinking: the benefits of being optimistic.* American Psychology Society.

Deater-Deckard, K. (2004).*Parenting stress.* New Haven: Yale University Press. Depkes.go.id.(2016).http://www.depkes.go.id/article/view/16041300001/2016/kenali-dan-deteksi-dini-individu-dengan-spektrum-autisme-melalui-pendekatan-keluarga-untuk-tingkatka.html

Desiningrum, D. R. (2016).*Psikologi anak berkebutuhan khusus.* Yogyakarta: Psikosain.

Dillenburger, K., Keenan, M., Doherty, A., Byrne, T., & Gallagher, S. (2010). *Meeting the needs of families living with children diagnosed with autism spectrum disorder.* Coleraine: University of Ulster Published.

Ekas, N. V, Lickenbrock, D. M., & Whitman, T. L. (2010). Optimism, social support, and well-being in mothers of children with autism spectrum disorder. *Journal Autism Developmental Disorder, 40*, 1274–1284. October, 15. http://doi.org/10.1007/s10803-010-0986-y

Hastings, R. P., & Johnson, E. (2001). Stress in families conducting intensive home-based behavioral intervention for their young child with autism. *Journal of Autism and Developmental Disorders, 31*(3), 327–336

Lestari, S. (2014).*Psikologi Keluarga*. Jakarta: Kencana.

Lopez, K., Reed, J., & Magaña, S. (2019). Associations among family burden, optimism, services received and unmet need within families of children with ASD. *Children and Youth Services Review, 98*, 105–112. doi.org/10.1016/j.childyouth.2018.12.027.

Magaña, S., Schwartz, S J., Rubert, M P., & Szapocznik, J. (2006). Hispanic caregivers of adults with mental retardation: Importance of family functioning. *American Journal On Mental Retardation, 111*(4), 250–262. https://doi.org/10.1352/0895-8017(2006)111[250:hcoawm]2.0.co;2

Mangunsong, F. (2011). Psikologi dan Pendidikan anak berkebutuhan khusus [Psychology and Education of children with special needs]. Jakarta: LPP3.

Maswati, R. (2004). Stress dan strategi coping pada orang tua dengan anak spektrum autistik yang berada di Sekolah Dasar [Stress and coping strategy for parents with primary schoolchildren with autism spectrum]. *Thesis.* Jakarta: Pasca sarjana Fakultas Psikologi Universitas Indonesia.

Moleong, L. J. (2011). *Metodologi penelitian kualitatif edisi revisi* [Qualitative Research Method Revised Edition]. Bandung: PT. Remaja Rosdakarya.

Nazir, Moh. (2011). Metode penelitian [Research method]. Bogor: Ghalia Indonesia.

Phetrasuwan, S., & Miles, M. S. (2009). Parenting stress in mothers of children with autism spectrum disorder. *JSPN, 14*(3), 157–165.

Risdal, D., & Singer, G. H. S. (2004). Marital Adjustment in Parents of Children with Disabilities: A Historical Review and Meta-Analysis. *Research & Practice for Persons with Severe Disabilities, 29*, 95–103. http://dx.doi.org/10.2511/rpsd.29.2.95

Sabbeth, B. F. & Leventhal, J. M. (1984). Marital adjustment to chronic childhood illness: a critique of the literature. *Pediatrics, 73*(6), 762–768

Safaria, T. (2005). *Autisme: Pemahaman baru untuk hidup bermakna bagi orang tua* [Autism: A new understanding for meaningful life for parents]. Yogyakarta: Penerbit Graha Ilmu.

Sarafino, E. P., & Smith, T. W. (2011). *Health Psychology: Biopsychosocial Interactions* (7th ed.). New Jersey, NJ: John Wiley & Sons, Inc.

Scorgie, K., & Sobsey, D. (2000). Transformational outcomes associated with parenting children who have disabilities. *Mental Retardation, 38*(3), 195–206. https://doi.org/10.1352/0047-6765(2000)038%3C0195:toawpc%3E2.0.co;2

Siklos, S., & Kerns, K.A. (2006). Assessing Need for Social Support in Parents of Children with Autism and Down Syndrome. *Journal of Autism Development Disorder,* 36, 921–933. doi: https://doi.org/10.1007/s10803-006-0129-7.

Sloper, P. Turner, S. (1992). Service needs of families of children with severe physical disability. *Agris.*

Sugiyono. (2015). Metode penelitian kuantitatif, kualitatif, dan R&D [Research method quantitative, qualitative, and R&D]. Bandung: Alfabeta.

Vohra, et.al. (2014). Access to services, quality of care, and family impact for children with autism, other developmental disabilities, and other mental health conditions. *Autism, 18*(7), 815–826.

Wardani, D. S. (2009). Strategi coping orangtua menghadapi anak autis [Parental coping strategies for autistic children]. *Indigenous, 11*(1), 26–35.

Weiss, M. J. (2002). Hardiness and social support as predictors of stress in mothers of typical children, children with autism, and children with mental retardation. *Autism, 6*(1), 115–130. http://doi.org/10.1177/1362361302006001009

Olga Pavlova

Ideas about the Inner World of a Person and the Concept of Soul (Nafs) in the Qur'an and Hadith*

Abstract: This paper attempts to describe the concept of Nafs (Soul), which is very important in understanding Islamic Psychology from the holy book of Islam (the Quran) and Hadith (narrations of Prophet Muhammad). The belief of religious Muslims accommodates both life in this world and the hereafter, and to maintain the purity of one soul is deemed critical for the secure and blessed life in both worlds. Other than that, the centrality of God in the life of the religious Muslims is important in understanding their psychological issues. Often the secular modern Psychology are not familiar with such belief, although many research findings show the critical role that religiousness plays in people's wellbeing. The writing of the article is critical within the context of Russian Muslims, as it serves as the ground for the Muslim Psychologists in Russia in developing knowledge and understanding of Psychology that relate to the worldview of the Muslim communities who adhere to the religion of Islam in the nation.

Consideration of the psychological aspects of Islamic theology must begin with the study of the primary sources of Islam, the Qur'an (the Holy Book) and Hadiths (the collection of the sayings and examples shown by Prophet Muhammad- Peace be upon him, during his life), as well as the works of Muslim scholars: theologians, philosophers, who actively developed ideas about the inner world of man in their works.

The psychological aspects related to the perception of the word of Allah are set forth in the Qur'an and Sunnah of the Prophet: "It is the grace of Allah that you were gentle towards them. If you were rude and hard-hearted, they would certainly leave you" (Qur'an, 3: 159). This position is detailed in the hadiths: one cannot even begin a sermon without understanding whether the listeners are ready to psychologically accept the sermon and the instructions, whether it will

* This paper is part of a chapter (Chapter 1) of the Monograph on Psychology in Islam, written by Dr. Olga Pavlova and published in the network of the Association for the Psychological Assistance for Muslims of Russia, 2020.

bore them, or cause rejection. "Do not bring the matter to the point of boring people with the Qur'an, and do not approach them if you see that they are busy with their conversations. If you start telling them, you will get bored. But listen: if they ask you, then tell me – it means they want to listen".

One of the first Qadis (Judges) in Iraq, Ibn Masud, in response to a request to read sermons to people every day, noted:"Truly, I do not do this just because I do not want to make you bored. For this reason, I appeal to you with admonitions following the example of the Messenger of Allah, who admonished and instructed us at different times, fearing to bore us" (Al-Bukhari in Gainutdin, 2014). Indeed, the Prophet urged believers: "Teach, ease and do not create difficulties, and if any of you get angry, let him close his mouth" (al-Bukhari)". And more: "Talk to people about what they admit, and do not touch on what they have a negative attitude towards. Or do you want Allah and His Messenger to be rejected?" (Al-Bukhari in Gainutdin, 2014).

The Companions of the Messenger of Allah tried to follow this example, which is why they said: "Hearts tend to desire and perceive, but also be lethargic and reject. So address them when they desire and perceive, and do not touch them when they become lethargic and reject "(Ibn Mas'ud in Gaitnudin, 2014). In these examples, we see that the issue of communicating the words of Allah and the instructions of His Prophet to people is decided based on knowledge of the laws of psychology. And without knowledge of these laws, it is forbidden to start preaching.

The central psychological aspect of Islamic theology is certainly the concept of the soul. The Arabic phrase ilm al-nafs ("knowledge of the soul") is identical in meaning to the term "psychology" derived from the Greek words psyche – soul and logos – teaching. First, it is necessary to analyze what is known about the soul from the Qur'an and hadith.

The term النفس (an-nafs) occurs 292 times (Kostylev & Babintsev, 2018) in the Qur'an and is very ambiguous: it is used in the following cases:

- To indicate a person's personality **(Surah 12: verse 54)**
  "The ruler said: " Bring him to me! I'll take it to myself." And when he spoke to him, he said: "Truly, today with us you have become respected, reliable." (Almaty, 2019)
- In relation to Allah **(3:28)**
  "Believers should not take unbelievers as companions instead of believers. And if someone does this, he has nothing in common with Allah, except when you fear them. And Allah warns you against Himself, and there is a return to Allah". In six verses (3:28; 3:30; 5: 116; 6:12; 6:54; 20:41).

- Concerning the gods whom people worshiped **(23: 5)**
  "They took instead of themselves other gods who are not capable of creating anything, and they themselves were created. They have no power to harm or benefit even themselves. They have no power over death, over life, or over resurrection ".
- Acquiring the host of jinn and people **(6: 130)**
  "Oh, host of jinn and people! Didn't come to you the messengers of you who have told you My signs and announced to you about meeting this day of yours? They will say: "We testify against ourselves." Seduced them near life and they testified against themselves, that they were unfaithful " (Sabdin, 2019).
- To denote a human soul **(6:93)**

  "Who is more unjust than the one who invented a lie against Allah or who said: A revelation has been sent down to me, although nothing was sent down to him" or than the one who said "I will send down like that which Allah sent down?" If you could see how the lawless will remain in the agony of death, and the angels stretch out their hands (and say to them): "Bring out your souls! Today you will be rewarded with humiliating torment for the fact that you raised falsehood against Allah and exalted yourself over His signs!" (Sabdin, 2019).

Explaining in detail the use of the term Nafs in the Qur'an, Kostylev and Babintsev (2018) distinguishes the following characteristics of Nafs:

1) Nafs is a repository of mental activity: memories, intentions, beliefs, inner speech, conscience, doubts (Mukhetdinov, 2015).
2) Nafs is a repository of sensations, emotions, desires, a source of dreams. (Mukhetdinov, 2015).
3) Nafs encourages evil, is a source of sin and disaster, stingy (in relation to spending in the name of Allah), not telling the truth. (Mukhetdinov, 2015)

In the Qur'an, in the context of the concept of "soul", there is a description of the several types of Nafs.

1. Nafs أمارة (amaara), which is translated literally as "orders pushing", "nudging", "inclined", " timely", `` passionate". This is a soul "prone to evil, and if not tested and controlled, it leads to spiritual destruction." We read about this in Surah Yusuf **(12:53)**. Here are several versions of the translation of the meanings of this verse:

   "And I do not justify [the passions] of my soul, truly [the passions] of the soul – really commanding to evil, unless my Lord has mercy. Verily, my Lord is Forgiving, Merciful" (Yusuf, 2018)

> "I do not justify myself (from condemnation), because the soul (of a person) commands evil, unless my Lord shows mercy to her. Indeed, my Lord is Forgiving, Merciful." (Quran in Mukhetdinov, 2015)
> "I do not justify myself, because the soul commands over evil, unless my Lord has mercy. Indeed, my Lord is Forgiving, Merciful".

This is the lowest level of nafs development, which encourages a person to do bad, pushes to evil. "The passions of the soul always induce a person to commit atrocities," writes Sheikh Muhammad Sadyk Muhammad Yusuf in the tafsir of the Qur'an (Sabdin, 2019)

2. Nafs لوامة (lawama) literally translates as "reproaching, condemning, hesitating" and is mentioned in surah Al-Qiyama **(75: 2)**:

> "I swear by the reproaching soul".
> "I swear by the reproaching soul".

Based on the meaning of the word "hesitant", scientists explain the meaning of this level of development of Nafs as fluctuating between good and evil. Such a person sometimes sins, then repents. On the other hand, if you pay attention to another meaning of this word – "reproaching", it means that such a Nafs pushes a person to sin, but later reproaches him for committing a sin. This is a soul that "is sensitive to evil and rejects it, asks for the mercy and forgiveness of Allah after repentance and strives for improvement, hoping for salvation." (Mukhetdinov, 2015). This state can be compared to conscience.

3. Nafs مطمئنة (mutmainnah), as stated in the surah Al-Fajr **(89:27)**:

> "O soul that has found peace!"
> "(The righteous soul will be told): O soul that has found peace!"

Nafs mutmainnah is the highest level of development of nafs, the level of the highest fear of God and piety. The serene Nafs is a person who has achieved happiness and found peace. This is "the highest state when complete peace and satisfaction is achieved."

The Qur'an clearly traces the idea of reward for one's own deeds (2: 281) as explained in the following verses, extracted by Sabdin (2019):

> "Fear the Day when you will be returned to Allah. And every soul will be rewarded in full for what it has acquired, and they will not be treated unjustly "
> "And leave those who accept their religion as play and fun and who have been seduced by worldly life. And remind with it that the soul will be doomed to perish for what it has gained. Apart from Allah, she has no protector and intercessor. If she offers any kind of replacement, she will not be accepted from her. They are the ones who have doomed

themselves to destruction by what they have acquired. For them it is drinking from boiling water and a painful punishment for not believing "[6:70].

The most important reminder of a person's responsibility for their actions and the inevitability of reward is ayah 79 of the Surah An-Nisa **(4:79)**:

"The good that befell you is from Allah. And the bad thing that befell you is from yourself. We sent you as a Messenger to people. It is enough that Allah is a Witness".

It is very difficult to achieve this state, which is why the Prophet Muhammad called the fight against the Nafs a great jihad, the education of the inner world. Jihad al-nafs is a struggle against one's vices and passions. This idea is based on hadith, which tells about the moment when the Prophet Muhammad returning to Medina from a difficult battle, said: "From the small jihad we returned to the great jihad. "The participants of the battle, who were very exhausted in the battle, who listened to him, were surprised, and the Prophet continued: "The Great Jihad is a struggle with what is in our souls" (al-Bayhaqi in Khairetdinov, 2014)."A true Mujahid (martyr) is one who leads jihad with his nafs" (at-Tirmidhi). And although this hadith cannot be considered reliable, its meaning is correct. This is confirmed by many reliable hadiths dedicated to the good disposition of a Muslim (see, for example, "Islamic Ethics" edited by Sh.A. Pshikhachev (2018); "Morality of a Muslim" by M. al-Ghazali in the translated work by Rustamov (2011), and many other works on this topic.

Fighting with your inner enemy, with your Nafs, with Syaitan, jihad (to seriously struggle) with passions – "is accustoming yourself to obeying the Almighty and disobeying Syaitan, the first enemy of man, and the peculiarities of such a jihad are its continuity, constancy and personal responsibility" (Sabdin, 2019). All scholars who analyze this type of jihad agree that this is the most difficult kind of zeal on the path to the Almighty.

Many hadiths in various collections are devoted to curbing the bad temper of the believer: Ibn Mas'ud noted that the Prophet said: " A believer is not abusive, cursing, foul-mouthed and mean "(at-Tirmidhi in Pshikhachev, 2018). The hadiths are devoted to both general ideas about the character of a Muslim and the fight against certain vices. Among the vices are, for example, the following:

- Anger: "From Abu Hurayra, the Prophet said:" He is not strong,who conquers others. Strong is the one who is able to fight his own anger" (al-Bukhari, Muslim in Sabdin, 2019);
- Drunkenness: From Ibn Abbas, "Said the Messenger of Allah: Avoid wine, because it truly is the key to forbidden deeds " (Tabarani in Sabdin 2019);

- Arrogance: Said the Messenger of Allah " The one who has at least a speck of arrogance in his heart, that Allah pushes his face into the fire" (Ahmad in Sabdin, 2019)
- Envy: It is reported from the words of Abu Huraira that the Messenger Allah said: "Beware of envy, for verily, envy devours good deeds just as fire devours wood (or: grass)!" (Abu Daud in Sabdin, 2019).

A lot of similar hadiths were aimed at fighting human vices. The Qur'an in Sura al-Shams in the first ten verses says:

> "I swear by the sun and its radiance! I swear by the moon when I follow him! I swear by the day when he brings it out! I swear at night when hiding it! I swear by heaven and by the One who raised it! I swear by the earth and by those who spread it! I swear by my soul and by the One who gave it proportionality and inspired her with her sinfulness and fear of God! Indeed, he who purified her succeeded. Truly, the one who concealed (defamed) her suffered a loss. "

Allah Almighty in the Holy Qur'an in no other case, except for the question of the reputation of the soul, swears seven times in succession (Sabdin, 2019) . Truly, this is enough to clarify the degree of importance and indisputable necessity of the education of the soul for the salvation of man. Curbing bad temper and maintaining virtue returns a person to fitra (the true nature-eds) – the natural faith, or religiousness of people.

References

Al-Ghazali, M. (2011). Morality of a Muslim. Translated from Arabic by Rustakov, A.I. Baku: Shams. p 364 .

Gainutdin, S. R. (2014). Introduction to Sharia. Retrieved 20.02.2020 from http://www.idmedina.ru/minbare/?5526 (date of access: 20.02.2020).

Kostylev, P.N. Babintsev, E.O.(2018) *Quranic Anthropology: Main Aspects:* Monograph in Mukhetdinova D.V (Ed). Publishing House "Medina", p. 17.

Mukhtedinov, D.V. (2015.) *Holy Qur'an: Semantic Translation with comment.* Medina: Publishing House.

Khairetdinov (2014). Jihad through the prism of the modern era. Mukhetdinova. (ed). Publishing House "Medina", p. 62.

Pshikhachev (2018). Islamic ethics: 50 moral qualities. ANO SPC "Al-Vasatyya – moderation" p. 240Krachovsky, I.Yu. (1986). *Quran: Translation and comments* . Academy of Sciences of the USSR, Institute of Oriental Studies. Nauka. p. 129.

Sabdin., A. (2019). *Semantic translation of the Holy Quran.* Almaty: NurMubarak,

Yusuf, M. S. M. (2018). Tafsir Hilal. Tashkent: Hilol-Nashr

Ratna Azkia Rakhmandari & Fuad Nashori

The Effectiveness of Murottal Listening Therapy in Reducing Stress Level on Informal Caregivers of Schizophrenia

Abstract: This study is aimed to see the effectiveness of murottal listening therapy either with giving its meaning or not to reduce stress level among informal caregivers for people with schizophrenia. There were 10 participants in this study who were informal caregivers for people with schizophrenia (PWS). Participants in this study were divided into two groups, namely treatment group 1(given with meaning) and treatment group 2 (given without meaning), each of which consisted of five people. The design in this study used an experimental design with measurements before, after training, and follow-up that were carried out two weeks after the training was completed. Participants' stress levels were measured by using the DASS stress subscale which consists of 14 statement items. This research was guided by the module modified by the researcher for the Al-Qur'an Surah Ar-Rahman Murottal Therapy Module which has been compiled by Hidayati and Nashori (2017). The results showed that murottal listening therapy can reduce stress level in informal caregivers of schizophrenia, both murottal listening therapies with meaning or without meaning. Through this, it was also obtained that murottal listening therapy with meaning did not have a greater effect than without meaning in the informal caregivers of people with schizophrenia ($p > 0.05$). Therefore, there is no significant difference in the effectiveness between the provision of murottal listening therapy which is done with meaning or without meaning.

Keywords: Murottal listening therapy, stress, informal caregiver, people with schizophrenia

1. Introduction

Schizophrenia, in general, can interfere with work functions which make the sufferer unproductive. The World Health Organization (Riset Kesehatan Dasar, 2018) explained that schizophrenia is a serious mental disorder characterized by distortions in thinking, perception, language, emotions, and behavior. People with Schizophrenia (PWS) cannot do things independently and thus need support from others (Afriyeni & Sartana, 2016).

The limited ability they have causes schizophrenics to need someone caring for them and helping them in carrying out daily activities (Mueser & Jeste, 2008), especially families as people who care for psychotic sufferers are known as caregivers. Greenberg explained that the type of caregiver is divided into two, namely formal caregiver and informal caregiver (Fitriani & Handayani, 2018). Formal caregiver is a part of a service system that is trained in providing care, such as professionals provided by hospitals, psychiatrists, and paid and voluntary nurses. Meanwhile, an informal caregiver is someone who provides care without prior training and has a relationship with patients such as family members, neighbors, or friends who provide care to patients without getting paid, part time or full time, and live together or separately from the patient.

The informal caregiver has a tough task. In addition to having the responsibility to care for PWS, even though they do not have the knowledge and ability to handle them, informal caregivers are expected to always provide emotional support to the PWS they care for in any situation. It is not surprising that informal caregivers who undergo this situation experience stress and consider it a heavy burden. When these burdens have begun to be felt, they will find it difficult to rest at night or during the day, feel lonely because they do not socialize, feel hopeless, show a lack of enthusiasm in doing activities, are easy to get emotional and cry, especially depression and anxiety. If this condition is ignored, the informal caregivers will become increasingly stressed and their health will worsen.

The impact of stress experienced by the caregiver will indirectly affect the PWS being treated. Caregivers who have uncontrolled and unstable emotions will tend to have excessive emotions in PWS, especially when they are having problems or are in a stressful situation because they must constantly face the symptoms raised by PWS. Excessive emotional expressions that appear continuously can increase the recurrence rate for PWS. This is because when PWS see anger from other people, they will indirectly feel depressed and will eventually have symptoms of schizophrenia (Dewi, 2018).

The stress experienced by the caregiver is due to the lack of adaptability in the caregiver with the symptoms that schizophrenics have (Jansen et al, 2015). The length of time caring for all the problems that must be faced can also trigger a burden for the caregiver. Most of the caregivers feel the burden while providing care for PWS. This opinion is supported by the research results of Fitrikasari et al (2012) which show that there were 89 caregivers out of a total of 100 caregivers felt burdened by the condition of the PWS they are caring for.

2. Theoretical Review

The burden experienced by the caregiver is also inseparable from the coping strategy used. Coping can help individuals reduce, eliminate, regulate, or manage the stress they experience. Coping is a balancing factor for individual efforts to maintain their adjustment during stressful situations (Kholidah & Alsa,

2012). The more positive the coping strategy is, the better the caregiver handles problems and burdens they have (Dewi, 2018). Nashori et al (2020) reveal that an Islamic psychological intervention approach that comes from Islamic teachings such as prayer, listening/reciting/*tadabbur* Qur'an, and other acts of worship can be used to improve positive psychological conditions and reduce negative psychological conditions. This statement is supported by the results of Dewi's (2018) research, in which the coping strategy most used by caregivers is the religious coping strategy. The caregiver leaves all his problems to God (Allah). Islam as the majority religion in Indonesia, has a large chance of finding a Muslim schizophrenic caregiver. The religious coping that can be used to reduce stress levels according to Islamic teachings is listeningQur'anic murottal. God (Allah) says in Qur'an Chapter Al-Anfal verse 2, "*The believers are only those who, when Allah is mentioned, their hearts become fearful, and when His verses are recited to them, it increases them in faith; and upon their Lord they rely.*"

Quran Murottal, according to Salim, is a way of reciting the Qur'an with moderate rhythm, not too slow and not too fast or *tartil* (Wahyuni & Deswita, 2013). The Murottal listening therapy contains several advantages, one of which is for mental health. Nugroho and Kusrohmaniah (2019) research stated that the Qur'an is closely related to one's mental health. Providing Quran murottal listening therapy can bring a sense of calm, tranquility, and comfort for those who listen to it. Al-Qodi also stated that listening to the Qur'an has a relaxing effect on nervous tension and has a positive effect on stress sufferers to 65 % (Fatimah & Noor, 2015).

The study of the Qur'anic murottal listening therapy can provide peace to those who listen to it, It was also found in the research of Abdurahman et al. (2008), who recorded an Electro Encephalo Graphy (EEG) after a Quran Murottal was played. Based on the results of the recording, the EEG is dominated by delta waves in the frontal and central areas on both the right and left sides of the brain, which means being in calm, tranquility, and comfort. Delta waves are the slowest brain waves (0.5–4 Hz) and are often associated with very deep sleep. The delta phase is referred to as the resting phase for the body and mind. This is due to the release of human growth hormone, which is useful in healing. When the delta is in a deep sleep, the body will carry out the self-healing process, repair damaged tissue, and produce new cells.

The research using Quran murottal listening therapy with the informal caregiver of schizophrenia is still highly limited. Therefore, the researcher is increasingly interested in conducting further research. Therefore, the researcher intends to formulate a research objective, namely, to determine the effectiveness of Qur'anic murottal listening therapy to reduce stress level in schizophrenic caregivers.

3. Method

3.1 Sample

The participants in this study involved 10 informal caregivers with schizophrenia. The researcher divided the 10 participants into two groups, with 5 people each in the treatment group 1 and 5 people in the treatment group 2. The criteria for the research participants were as follows: 1) is adult (> 18 years), 2) is male or female, 3) experienced in caring for PWS at least 6 months, 4) is Muslim, 5) minimum attending junior high school or equivalent, 6) having no problems related to hearing, 7) is not currently participating in other psychological interventions, 8) is willing to take part in a series of studies from beginning to end.

3.2 Measurement Tool

This research used observation, interview, and psychological scale measurement methods. Measurement of stress levels in informal caregivers of schizophrenia will be carried out by using the DASS scale by Lovibond and Lovibond (1995) which has been adapted and tested for validity and reliability by Damanik (2006) with a correlation coefficient that moves in the numbers 0.353 – 0.7541. DASS 42 consists of 42 statement items divided into three subscales, namely the depression subscale, the anxiety subscale, and the stress subscale. However, in this study the researcher will only use the stress subscale as a research measurement tool with a total of 14 statement items consisting of 4 aspects, namely difficulty in relaxing, nervous arousal, easily upset or agitation, irritable or over-reactive, and impatient.

3.3 Murottal Listening Therapy

The intervention used in this study wasQur'anic murottal listening therapy, especially Qur'an Chapter Ar-Rahman, which is a form of music therapy by reciting the Qur'an and chanting by a reciter. This research was guided by the module modified by the researcher for Murottal Therapy Module which has been compiled by Hidayati and Nashori (2017). The module used in this research has been assessed by a professional judgment which aims to perfect the concept and basis of research thinking. The stages taken in the implementation of murottal listening therapy include the following: problem formulation, listening to Qur'an Surah Ar-Rahman, interpreting Surah Ar-Rahman (treatment group 1), and sharing experiences. The total duration required to intervene murottal listening therapy for treatment group 1 was 560 minutes while treatment group 2 was 400 minutes. The intervention stage was carried out of 7 sessions in a period of one week, which was carried out with 2 face-to-face meetings and in between the face-to-face meetings, there were 3 days of home assignments.

3.4 Research Design

The experimental research design in this study was by using the pre-test post-test comparison group design. In this design, the subjects were tested three times in each group, namely before the treatment was carried out, after the treatment was given, and two weeks after the treatment was completed.

4. Results

The following is a description of the research participants:

Table 1. Description of research participants (N = 10)*

Group	Name	Sex	Age (years)	Family members who are in care	Duration **	Stress Levels	
						Score	Category
Treat-ment 1	GR	Female	74	Children	26	24	Medium
	HD	Male	75	Children	24	26	Heavy
	GY	Male	49	Wife & younger brother	15	28	Heavy
	KS	Male	22	Mother	10	30	Heavy
	ZB	Female	58	Children	20	21	Medium
Treat-ment 2	YI	Male	55	Older brother	27	27	Heavy
	SJ	Male	65	Children	10	26	Heavy
	SY	Female	54	Younger brother	25	27	Heavy
	PT	Female	48	Mother	2	24	Medium
	TN	Female	55	Children	7	29	Heavy

*The data was collected by the authors (2020)
**Duration of Being Caregiver (years)

Hypothesis testing in this study was carried out by using a nonparametric method. This is because the sample size of participants who took part in this study was relatively small, namely 10 participants. The analytical method used to test the hypothesis in this study was the Mann-Whitney U-test through SPSS 22.0 for Windows. Besides, the researchers also used further tests with the analysis of the Independent Sample T-Test. The results of the analysis can be seen in the following table:

Table 2. Difference test of stress level score between treatment groups 1 & 2

Measurement	Z	*P*
Pre-test	- 0,316	0,752
Post-test	- 0,319	0,750
Followup	- 0, 422	0,673

Table 3. Difference test of stress level score in each group

Measurement	Treatment 1		Treatment 2	
	Z	*P*	Z	P
Pre-test to Post-test	- 2.032	0,042	- 2.023	0,043
Post-test to Follow up	- 1,841	0,066	- 1,618	0,073
Pre-test to Follow-up	- 2,023	0,043	- 2,032	0,042

Based on the results of the hypothesis testing that has been carried out, it can be seen that there are differences in stress level scores on the informal caregivers of schizophrenia after giving the murottal listening therapy, accompanied by its meaning and without its meaning. The results of the analysis show that the first hypothesis in this study is accepted. This can be seen from the results of difference tests carried out on different measurement conditions in each group. In the treatment group 1, there is a significant difference in scores in the pretest to post-test measurement condition ($p = 0.042$; $Z = -2.032$) and in the pre-test to follow-up measurement condition ($p = 0.043$; $Z = -2.023$). However, there is no significant difference from post-test to follow-up ($p = 0.066$; $z = -1.841$).

In the treatment group 2, there is a significant difference in scores in the pre-test to post-test measurement condition ($p = 0.043$; $Z = -2.023$) and in the pre-test to follow-up measurement condition ($p = 0.042$; $Z = -2.032$). However, there is no significant difference from post-test to follow-up ($p = 0.073$; $z = -1.618$). The second hypothesis in this study regarding the difference in the effectiveness of Qur'anic murottal listening therapy between groups with meaning and without meaning is rejected. This is because the value obtained through the results of statistical analysis in the two groups is $p = 0.750$ ($p > 0.05$). It means that there is no significant difference in the effectiveness between the provision of Qur'anic murottal listening therapy which is done with meaning or without meaning.

5. Conclusion

Based on the research results, it is known that the Qur'anic murottal listening therapy that has been carried out provides results and effects for research subjects who are informal caregivers for PWS. These results include Quran murottal listening therapy which show differences in stress scores between subjects in treatment group 1 (with meaning) and between subjects in treatment group 2 (without meaning) although there is no significant difference in effectiveness between the provision of murottal listening therapy which is done with meaning or without meaning. Extraneous variables also have an indirect effect on the results of measuring stress levels in research subjects in the two treatment groups such as PWS conditions, recurrence intensity, the presence of people helping treat the PWS, and daily routines that must be carried out by informal caregivers.

The results of this study are supported by the results of previous research conducted by Shekha et al (2013) that murottal listening therapy can generate negligent waves in the brain that make a person feel calm and relaxed. In addition, reciting Qur'an can also be a medical treatment and affect one's spiritual condition and mental health (Pashib et al, 2014). The results of this study further reinforce that without meaning, murotta*l* listening therapy has good benefits and effects for individuals who listen to or recite it. There are other studies that show the effect of murottal listening therapy to reduce stress levels on abortion patients (Rahmayani et al (2018). These studies show that murottal listening therapy is a therapy that provides benefits for various psychological problems and can be given to various research participants. This study shows that Quran murottal listening therapy can also reduce stress levels and can be applied to informal caregivers of PWS.

Basically, the stress experienced by the participants, among others, is when the individual experiences an increase in adrenaline and excess cortisol which causes the individual to have difficulty sleeping at night, fast heart rate, increased blood pressure, frequent dizzy head, immune system suppression, and increased blood sugar (Alatas, 2017). Meanwhile, psychologically, Brannon et al. (2013) explained that there were three ways that can be used to carry out stress management, namely by practicing relaxation, behavioral cognitive therapy, and disclosing emotions, both positive and negative emotions.

The chanting of the sound that is produced along with the belief in the verses of the Qur'an in chapter Ar-Rahman has a positive effect on those who listen to it. The spiritual experience perceived by the subject further strengthens the therapeutic effect of murottal listening therapy. Almost all subjects felt a change in them. After undergoing the therapeutic process of listening to Qur'an chapter

Ar-Rahman murottal with meaning, the subjects in the treatment group 1 told their experiences about the changes they perceived. Most of the subjects felt that complaints about the trials which had been considered as a real burden were something to be grateful for. Participants realized that there had been many blessings that had not been grateful so far and only complained about the trials given. Participants also expressed that their belief in God's (Allah) help was increasingly perceived so that they felt a sense of hope and felt peaceful.

Listening therapy on the Qur'an chapter Ar-Rahman murottal with meaning also made the participants' hearts calmer and more peaceful so that the body felt relaxed. The calm was caused by the stimulation of the auditory system which increased the formation of endorphins and caused a relaxing effect (Julianto et al, 2016) and raised positive thoughts about life (Julianto & Subandi, 2015).

The same thing even happened to the treatment group 2 who did murottal listening therapy without meaning. Most of the participants experienced changes in a positive direction. The participants explained the power possessed by chapter Ar-Rahman so that it made a feeling of peace and can thrill those who listen to it. The subjects in the treatment group 2 also expected further explanation regarding the content of chapter Ar-Rahman to understand its meaning. The recitation of the Qur'an can also be a medical treatment and affect one's spiritual condition and mental health (Pashib et al, 2014).

The connection to God that results from murottal listening therapy is an important component of murottal listening therapy because through this, the subject can feel calm, feel that his life is prevented from various problems, raise awareness of the self-condition that needs to be improved, and raise hope in God. Murottal listening also has religious and spiritual values from the Qur'an which can overcome the stress and tensions that humans feel. Various studies also support the results of this study. Therefore, the provision of murottal listening therapy is proven to influence changes in stress levels by providing a therapeutic effect in the form of feeling calm, comfortable, and relaxed.

Based on the research of Abdurahman et al (2008), who recorded the Electro Encephalo Graphy (EEG) after the murottal listening therapy was played, it was found that murottal listening therapy could bring out a feeling of calm in those who listened to it. Through the recording results, the EEG is dominated by delta waves in the frontal and central areas on both the right and left sides of the brain, which means being in calm, tranquility and comfort. Delta waves are the slowest brain waves (0.5–4 Hz) and are often associated with very deep sleep. The delta phase is referred to as the resting phase for the body and mind. This is due to the release of human growth hormone which is useful in healing. Basically, the area, which is dominated by delta brain waves, namely the frontal part functions as a general intellectual center and emotional control, while the central area functions as the center for controlling the movements that are carried out. This explanation can describe that murottal listening therapy can make a sense of calm, tranquility, and comfort for those who listen to it (Abdurahman et al., 2008).

6. References

Abdurahman A., Perdana S., & Andhika S. (2008). Murottal al qur'an; alternatif suara baru. *Prosiding Seminar Nasional Sains dan Teknologi – II . Universitas Lampung*. ISBN: 978-979-1165-74-79.

Afriyeni, N. & Sartana. (2016). Gambaran tekanan dan beban yang dialami oleh keluarga sebagai *caregiver* penderita psikotik di RSJ Prof. H.B. Sa'anin Padang [Description of the pressure and burdens experienced by the family as a caregiver for psychotic patients at RSJ Prof. H.B. Sa'anin Padang]. *Jurnal Ecopsy*, *3*(3), 115–120. doi:10.20527/ecopsy.v3i3.2671

Alatas, M. (2020, January 2). Pengaruh terapi *murottal* surat Ar-Rahman terhadap skor pengkajian luka (mungs) dan pengkajian stres (DASS) pada pasien diabetes mellitus di Klinik Kitamura Pontianak [The effect of Murottal Surat Ar-Rahman therapy on the score of wound assessment (mungs) and stress assessment (DASS) in diabetes mellitus patients at the Kitamura Clinic in Pontianak]. *Proners, 3*(1), 1–17. *http://jurnal.untan.ac.id/index.php/jmkeperawatanFK/article/view/22005*

Brannon, L., Feist, J., & Updegraff, J. A. (2013). *Health psychology: An introduction to behavior and health (*8th ed.*)*. USA: Cengage Learning.

Damanik, E.D. (2006). Pengujian reliabilitas, validitas, analisis item dan pembuatan norma Depression Anxiety Stress Scale (DASS): Berdasarkan penelitian pada kelompok sampel Yogyakarta dan Bantul yang mengalami gempa bumi dan kelompok sampel Jakarta dan sekitarnya yang tidak mengalami gempa bumi [Reliability testing, validity, item analysis and norm making of the Depression Anxiety Stress Scale (DASS): Based on research on the Yogyakarta and Bantul sample groups that experienced earthquakes and the Jakarta and surrounding sample groups that did not experience earthquakes]. Fakultas Psikologi Universitas Indonesia, Depok. *Thesis*. Retrieved from: *https//lib.ui.ac.id/file?file=pdf/abstrak-94859.pdf*

Dewi, G,K. (2018). Pengalaman *caregiver* dalam merawat klien skizofrenia di Kota Sungai Penuh [Caregiver experience in caring for schizophrenia clients in Sungai Penuh City]. *Jurnal Endurance*, *3*(1). 200–212. *http://103.111.125.15/index.php/endurance/article/view/2852*

Fatimah, F. S. & Noor, Z. (2015). Efektivitas mendengarkan murottal Al-Qur'an terhadap derajat insomnia pada lansia di selter Dongkelsari Sleman

Yogyakarta [The effectiveness of listening to the murottal Al-Qur'an on the degree of insomnia in the elderly in Dongkelsari Sleman Yogyakarta]. *Jurnal Ners dan Kebidanan Indonesia, 3*(1), 20–25. *http://dx.doi.org/10.21927/jnki.2015.3(1).20-25*

Fitriani, A. & Handayani, A. (2018). Hubungan antara beban subjektif dengan kualitas hidup pendamping (*caregiver*) pasien skizofrenia [The relationship between subjective burden and quality of life of the caregiver in schizophrenic patients]. *Jurnal Proyeksi, 13*(1), 13–24. *http://dx.doi.org/10.30659/jp.13.1.13-24*

Fitrikasari, A., Kadarman, A., & Sarjana, W. (2012). Gambaran beban caregiver penderita skizofrenia di poliklinik rawat jalan RSJ Amino Gondohutomo Semarang [Description the burden of caregiver with schizophrenia in outpatient polyclinic RSJ Amino Gondohutomo Semarang] . *Medica Hospitalia, 1*(2), 118–122 *https://doi.org/10.36408/mhjcm.v1i2.56*

Hidayati, W. & Nashori, H.F. (2017). Efektivitas Terapi mendengarkan murottal Al-Qur'an untuk menurunkan tingkat stres pada ibu hamil trimester III [Therapeutic effectiveness of listening to murottal Al-Qur'an to reduce stress levels in third trimester of pregnant women]. *Thesis*. Fakultas Psikologi dan Ilmu Sosial Budaya. Universitas Islam Indonesia

Jansen, J.E., Haahr, U.,H., Harder, S., Marie, A., & Lyse, T. H. (2015). Caregiver distress in first-episode psychosis: The role of subjective appraisal, over-involvement and symptomatology. *Social Psychiatry and Psychiatric Epidemiology, 50*(3), 371–378. *https://doi.org/10.1007/s00127-014-0935-8*

Julianto, V. & Subandi. (2015). Membaca Al Fatihah reflektif intuitif untuk menurunkan depresi dan meningkatkan imunitas [Read Al Fatihah intuitive reflective to reduce depression and increase immunity]. *Jurnal Psikologi, 42*(1), 34–46. doi: 10.22146/jpsi.6941

Julianto, V., Dzulqaidah, R. P., & Salsabila, S. N. (2016). Pengaruh mendengarkan *murottal* Al Qur'an terhadap peningkatan kemampuan konsentrasi [The effect of listening to the murottal Al Qur'an in increasing concentration abilities]. *Psympathic: Jurnal Ilmiah Psikologi, 1*(2), 120–129. doi: 10.15575/psy.v1i2.473

Kholidah, E., N., & Alsa, A. (2012). Berpikir positif untuk menurunkan stres psikologis [Thinking positive to reduce psychological stress]. *Jurnal Psikologi. 39*(1), 67–75. doi: 10.22146/jpsi.6967

Lovibond,P.F., & Lovibond, S.H. (1995). The structure of negative emotional states: Comparison of The Depression Anxiety Stress Scale (DASS) with the Beck Depression and Anxiety Inventories. *Behaviour Research and Therapy, 33*(3), 335–343. *https://doi.org/10.1016/0005-7967(94)00075-U*

Mueser K.T., & Jeste D.V. (2008). *Clinical handbook of schizophrenia*. New York: Guilford Press.

Nashori, H.F., Diana, R.R. & Hidayat, B. (2020). The trends in Islamic psychology intervention in Indonesia. In Ralph W. Wood Jr and Sariya Cheruvallil-Contractor (eds.), *Research in social scientific study of religion (pp* 162–180*)*. UK: Brill NV

Nugroho, A.Z.W., & Kusrohmaniah, S. (2019). Pengaruh murottal Al-Qur'an terhadap tingkat stres mahasiswa muslim di Yogyakarta [The influence of the murottal Al-Qur'an on the stress level of Muslim students in Yogyakarta]. *Gadjah Mada Journal Of Professional Psychology*, *5*(2), 108–119. doi: 10.22146/gamajpp.50354

Pashib, M., Khaqani, F., Bahrainian, A., & Abedi, A. (2014). Investigation of the effectiveness of Quran recitation and teachings on depression of female students of Torbat-E-Heidariye university. *Journal of Applied Environmental and Biological Science*, *4*(12), 137–140. *https://bit.ly/2VEUbf0*

Rahmayani,M.,P., Rohmatin, E., & Wulandara, Q. (2018). Pengaruh terapi murottal Al-Qur'an terhadap tingkat stres pada pasien abortus di RSUD dr. Soekarno Kota Tasikmalaya Tahun 2018 [The effect of Al-Qur'an murottal therapy on stress levels in abortion patients at dr. Soekarno, Tasikmalaya City in 2018]. *Jurnal Bidan "Midwife Journal"*, *4*(2), 36–41. *http://jurnal.ibijabar.org/pengaruh-terapi-murottal-al-quran-terhadap-tingkat-stres-pada-pasien-abortus-di-rsud-dr-soekardjo-kota-tasikmalaya-tahun-2018/*

Riset Kesehatan Dasar . (2018). *Badan penelitian dan pengembangan kesehatan kementrian RI tahun 2018* . Retrieved from https://www.litbang.kemkes.go.id/laporan-riset-kesehatan-dasar-riskesdas/

Shekha, M. S., Hassan, A. O., Othman, S. A., Hassan, A. O., & Othman, S. A. (2013). Effects of Qur'an listening and music on electroencephalogram brain waves. *The Egyptian Journal of Experimental Biology (Zoology)*, *9*(1), 119–121. *http://www.egyseb.net/fulltext/3-1430521011.pdf*

Wahyuni, R., & Deswita. (2013). Pengaruh terapi murottal terhadap tingkat kecemasan menghadapi persalinan pada ibu hamil di wilayah kerja Puskesmas Andalas [The effect of murottal therapy on the level of anxiety facing childbirth in pregnant women in the work area of the Andalas Health Center]. *NERS Jurnal Keperawatan*, *9*(2), 111–122. *https://doi.org/10.25077/njk.9.2.116-126.2013*

Musa Mugawa

Religious Values and Adolescents Sexual Behaviours among University Students in Uganda

Abstract: Religion plays a significant role in the life of individuals in any society. Its role as a moral builder has been widely known. This study examines the role of religious values in adolescents' valuescent sexual attitudes and behaviors in Uganda. The study was conducted in two national universities in Uganda with a student population. The institutions are located in the eastern and central parts of the country. Data for the study were collected from a sample of university students. Respondents were successfully interviewed but because of the age restriction for adolescents, information from campus-based adolescents aged 19–21 years was analyzed. Logistic regression model was used to do the analysis both at the adjusted and unadjusted levels. Findings are inconsistent with existing literature. The findings revealed a strong negative relationship between religious values and adolescent sexual behaviors, although religious commitment is more important than religious affiliation in affecting adolescent sexual behaviors. The findings suggest a need for another study using longitudinal design so that researchers can establish the relationship between religious values and adolescent sexuality. Since religion affects the sexual lifestyles of university students, university administrators can launch mobilization of university students and engage them into religious activities as these can help in supporting these young adults with accurate information about sexual behaviors and HIV/AIds prevention initiatives in the country.

Key Words: adolescents, religious values, sexuality

1. Introduction

Studies on the characteristics of adolescent sexual behaviour suggest gender differences. And the socio-economic status of having sex with men at a younger age than women, other researchers investigate the role of learning in adolescent sexual behaviour, and adolescent in this age group who advocate schooling in sexual decision making are more likely to be independent (Goddard, 2015).

The role of the family as agents of socialization is investigated. The authors found that modernization and westernization generally weakened the social controls exercised by community elders regarding reproductive and sexuality in young women. By Age 18 and 20, 63 % and about 80 % had sexual intercourse, respectively. Another study, published in 1999, showed that half of the female respondents had sex before age 18. About a quarter had sex begore age 15 (Hans, 2011). Knowledge of sexual behaviours among most adolescents, myths and misconceptions about sexuality, pregnancy, and sexual health are common among adolescents but they often have become significant alternative sources when adolescents are desperate to find accurate and reliable answers about their sexual behaviours (Hensel, et al., 2011).

2. Theoritical Review

Various studies have identified different factors that influence sexual behaviors, which are not detailed in this study conducted by Young and Vazsonyi (2011) using regression analyses to identify six significant predictors of risky sexual practices. These included the number of partners in last six months, religious values, condom attitudes, age at first sex, binging on alcohol, and residential locus (Hunt & Jung, 2009). Additionally, their literature review identified nine factors, which significantly correlated with sexual attitudes and behaviors which included age (sexual practices increase as adolescents' get older), gender (males engage in sexual behaviors at an earlier age than do females), age of first sex, number of sex partners, age of first alcohol use, binging on alcohol (defined as having four or more drinks on a single occasion), and self-esteem (low self-esteem has been found to correlate with risky sexual behaviors (Lefkowitz et al, 2004; Pai, Lee, & Yen, 2012). The developmental need of adolescents for independence and their desire to attain adult status and maturity provide an incentive for them to engage in what they see as adult behaviors. Greater unsupervised time may prematurely grant both independence and emotional emancipation from the family. In contrast, a prolonged supportive environment for adolescents', with gradual steps toward autonomy, appears to enhance healthy behavior.

In the studies by Penhollow et al (2007) and Iskandar et al (2013), with a sample of adolescents aged 19 – 21 years. The measures were a personal data questionnaire; the scale for value-system had 110 items; however, using multi-dimensional analysis of items, 89 items with reliability with$\alpha = .858$, and 118 for sexual self-regulation, 105 items were reliable with $\alpha = 988$. Concerning the relationship between social environment and sexual self-regulation of adolescents, the study revealed that social environment influences one's sexual self-regulation, further analysis was conducted and the analysis indicated ($p < .001$), 36,12 % as an influence from sexual self-regulation and ($p <.000$), 63,68 % as being influence from social environment. Correlation data showed that both variables predict adolescents' sexual behaviors. The purpose of this study is therefore to establish the relationship between religious values and adolescents' sexual behaviors?

3. Method

The data for this study was obtained from a campus- based study of adolescent sexual behavior in two representative tertiary institutions in Uganda. The data were obtained through a self-administered questionnaire across the various faculties and departments in the two universities. Data collection was coordinated in each faculty by a course coordinator, lecturer or professor who had earlier been contacted. The aims and objectives of the study were properly explained to them.

Copies of the questionnaire were handed over to all the coordinators who willingly agreed to coordinate the data collection process. In each department, the purpose of the study was explained and the consent of the students to participate obtained freely. A simple random method was used to select a sample of 40 students among those who agreed to participate.

Those who agreed to participate were then arranged in such a way as to maintain confidentiality and anonymity in their responses. The students, who formed the respondents, were not coerced. Anyone who did not agree to be administered was not compelled to do so. Ethical clearance was obtained from respective heads of departments of selected courses. For example, for the questionnaires to be administered in an economics class, the permission of the head of economics department was sought. A total sample of 1,870 students were interviewed, but for selecting only adolescents between 19 and 24 years of age, the sample size for this analysis was reduced to 1153 adolescents.

Religious affiliation was ascertained by asking the students about the religious groups they belonged to. To measure religiosity, they were asked how often they attended religious services – several times a week, once a week, a few times a month, once a month, or less than once a month.

The importance of religion in the life of the respondents was ascertained by asking them how important religion is to them. The responses were categorized as very important, somewhat important, or not important. Religiosity was defined in four different ways, namely, religious affiliation, which is commonly found in literature; attendance at religious services; value of religion; and religious practices.

Religious affiliation was divided into four categories, namely Orthodox Christianity, Pentecostal Christianity, Islamic religion, and others (unclassified). Attendance at religious services was divided into three categories, namely never, less than once in a month and several times in a month. Value of religion was categorized as "not important", "somewhat important" and "very important".

Religious practices included attending religious programmes frequently, daily reading of the holy book/devotional book, devotional daily prayer, preaching the holy book, tracts distribution and caring about what God thinks of one.

The study expected that those who had experienced sexual intercourse were likely to have radical opinion of premarital sex and were likely to be engaged in current sexual activity. Sexual debut and attitudes to adolescent sexuality were also included in some of the models where relevant. Sexual debut was included in the model's estimating predictors of sexual attitudes and current sexual behaviors; for it was believed that initiation of sex would affect responses to the questions on sexual attitudes. Sexual attitudes are also likely to affect current sexual behaviors.

Regressions were estimated, controlling for the gender of respondents and their religious characteristics. Each of the models was adjusted using backward selection strategy. Only the adjusted results are presented. This was done to identify critical religious variables of influence. The major research questions being explored were: "Will religiosity have a differential effect on adolescent sexuality controlling for gender of respondents?"

4. Results

Descriptions. The respondents were mainly from orthodox religious groups, made up of the Roman Catholics, Anglican, Baptist, Muslims, Presbyterian, and Methodist. The average age of respondents was 20 years, with an age range of 19–21 years. Most of them were from urban areas and were living on campus at the time of the study.

The respondents reported that they came from average income-earning families. Family economic background was measured at several levels, and these included but not limited to rich, average and poor. About one-fifth of the students came from each of the different faculties in the university. Majority of the respondents were third and fourth year, while one third came from the faculty of social sciences.

Table 1. Percentages of distribution of respondent's religious affiliation, attendance, values and practices

	Male	Female	Total
Religious attendance			
Never	2.1	1.9	2.0
A few times a month	17.7	8.3	12.8
Once a week	18.5	19.3	18.9
Several times a week	61.7	67.4	66.3
Importance of religion in life			
Not important	2.6	3.3	3.0
Somewhat important	9.6	5.1	7.3
Very important	87.0	89.5	88.3
Religious practices			
Attend service regularly	67.7	87.2	78.0
Read holy book daily	49.0	67.6	58.8
Devote time to prayer daily	69.3	86.9	78.6
Preach religion	39.1	53.4	46.6
Distribute religious tract	36.5	43.1	40.0
Cares about what God thinks of me	84.6	94.2	89.7

Noted. Significant at 95 %

Table 1 shows that more than two-third of the students attended religious services several times a week and 88 % indicated that religion is very important to them. About seven out of every ten students attended religious services regularly and had devotional daily prayers, more than half of the students studied read their religious books daily, 47 % preached, while 40 % indicated that they evangelized by distributing religious booklets.

Religious values were found to be negatively predictive of adolescent's sexual behaviors in the present study, despite their high feelings, 67 %, knowledge 63 %, effect 50 %, practice 50 % and beliefs 38 %, adolescents aged 19–21 years could not translate their knowledge and feelings into acceptable sexual behaviors, this is attributed to their cognitive stages of development that allows them to question the rationale of their beliefs and their sexual fantasies, adolescents aged 19–21 are rationalistic as opposed to being idealistic as Religious values suggest.

The increasing need for self-discovery among adolescent's aged 19–21 puts teenagers in a desperate position of adopting religious values outside their religious values, they adopt religious values from popular media and the adolescent subculture that allows self-discovery through sexual expression of necking and petting but not intercourse, this is attributed to the fact that adolescents studied attach much importance to their social environment than their religious values that prohibits any form of sexual behaviors through implicit information, this was revealed by the findings of sexual behaviors where it emerged that adolescents studied engage most in petting and necking because these are considered risky free sexual behaviors among adolescents.

Additionally, adolescents aged 19–21 had not yet attained emotional maturity for intercourse, their attitudes reflected 77 % for behavior beliefs and 87 % for outcome evaluation, and these figures imply that adolescents are aware of the problems associated with sexual behaviors of intercourse but not necking and petting. The modern liberal attitudes of adolescents in Uganda; their social environment has become more permissive and promiscuous. The modernists live under the critical misconception that free mixing of sexes is a sign of social progress and symbolizes adolescents' liberation from family and religious values and is not a social evil. Because of the permissive character of modern society, adolescents' sexual behaviors have lost its sanctity and sex outside wedlock is not considered a sin. religious values hold that one's body and figure should be exclusively preserved for one's future partner, this is conflicting to what the research findings indicated, adolescents aged 19–21 at University in Uganda behaviors of necking, petting that include making soft toughs on delicate body parts of the opposite sex, and kissing are done openly. Their figures with all their charms and enchanting beauty are fully exposed to others even before marriage.

The results provide ample evidence that social environments influence religious values and attitudes significantly, related to communication from family environments, emotional support from university environments that emphasize academic achievement, and peers' disapproval of sexual behaviors, these results suggest that this primarily refers to conversations about the morality of adolescent sexual involvement. Beliefs, practices, feelings, affect, and knowledge were found to contribute less towards adolescent's sexual behaviors in all social environments that were studied, these findings are in line with (Young & Vassonyi, 2011) who found that adolescents who associate with defiant peers are more likely to have sexual intercourse before marriage.

Family environments influence adolescent's sexual behaviors through religious values, sexual self-regulation, and attitudes, testing family environments revealed goodness of fit measurement with the available data. Therefore, the hypothesis that family environment influence adolescents' sexual behaviors through religious values, sexual self-regulation and attitudes, results indicates that $x^2 x^2$ = 1,690, df = 300, p value = 0.00; RMSEA =, 049; RMR = .461; GFI = .925; CFI = .940.

This situation of low religious values of adolescents aged 19–21, appears to be more multifaceted. While they are somewhat unsatisfied with family environments that provide them with implicit sexual information, results emerged with a significant relationship between adolescent's sexual regulation and sexual behaviors. However, how adolescents develop these capabilities without being externally supported, remains a question of debate, however, this is not a remote observation because of research findings on how self-regulation develops among adolescents.

Although recent analyses indicate an overall absence of sexual intercourse among teenagers aged 19–21 at university, proportions of necking and petting remain extremely higher among adolescents. Findings indicated that although adolescents were affiliated to institutionalized religious values, they were less likely to comport to the prospects of teachings that prohibit any kind of sexual behaviors before marriage. Additionally, adolescents reported high knowledge, but this could not match their sexual behaviors, this was attributed to cognitive dissonance among adolescents who are more rational than being idealistic.

Family environment was found to influence adolescents' sexual behaviors through religious values and via sexual self-regulation, this is due in part that religion religious values promote self-monitoring through introspective rituals (e.g., prayer, meditation, reflecting on scripture) that encourage adolescents to self-monitor for discrepancies between their goal and their actual behavior. Models of University and peers indicated a significant attitude influence towards adolescent's sexual behaviors but not family, one explanation could be that attitudes are contextual, and adolescents tend to behave in ways that are consistent with their attitudes when they are well informed.

The university environment influences adolescent's sexual behaviors through religious values, sexual self-regulation, and attitudes. Based on testing of the data, the University environment model fits with the data collected that measure adolescent's sexual behaviors as being influenced by the university environment. Therefore, the hypothesis that University environment influence adolescents' sexual behaviors through religious values, sexual self-regulation and attitudes, results indicates that $x^2 x^2$ = 1,963, df = 80, p value = 0.00; RMSEA = .058; RMR = .345; GFI = .929; CFI = .946.

Result. Peers influence adolescent's sexual behaviors through religious values, sexual self-regulation, and attitudes. The testing of peer environment scale revealed goodness of fit measurement with the available data. The data analysis to test that peer's environment influence adolescents sexual behaviors through religious values, sexual self-regulation and attitude indicates that $x^2 x^2$ = 1,778, df = 80, p value = 0.00; RMSEA =, 053; RMR =, 299; GFI = 933; CFI =, 962. This means that available data fit with theoretical constructs of the study.

The result of standardized direct coefficient for peers as a social environment that influence adolescents sexual behaviors through religious values, sexual self-regulation and attitudes; the coefficient between peers environment and religious values is (0.60^2) or 38.44 % of the variance of adolescents religious values are accounted for by peers environment significant ($P< 0.05$), while the remaining 61.56 % of the variance is accounted for by factors outside this study, the coefficient between peers environment and sexual self-regulation is (0.37^2) or 13.69 % of the variance is accounted for by peers environment statistically not significant ($P> 0.05$), while remaining 86.31 % of the variance is accounted for by unique factors, coefficient of peers environment and attitudes is (0.88^2) or 77.44 % of the variance is accounted for by peers environment, statistically significant ($P< 0.05$) while the remaining 22.56 % of the variance is accounted for by other unique factors but not peers environment.

Indirect effect: the study hypothesized that peer environment influences adolescent's sexual behaviors through religious values, sexual self-regulation and attitudes. The result of standardized indirect coefficient for the peers environment, sexual self-regulation towards sexual behaviors is, (0.74^2) or 54.76 % of the variance is indirectly accounted for by peers environment and is statistically significant ($p< 0.05$), the remaining 45.24 % of the variance is accounted for by unique factors, and this was revealed to be statistically significant at ($p< 0.05$), while religious values towards sexual behaviors is (-0.15^2) or -02.25 % of the variance is indirectly accounted for by peers environment while the remaining 102.25 % of the variance is accounted for by unique factors outside this study but not peers environment through religious values, and it was not statistically significant ($p> 0.05$), while attitudes towards sexual behaviors is (0.37^2) or 13.69 % of the variance is the indirect the influence of peers environment while 86.31 % of the variance is the indirect influence from unique factors statistically significant ($p< 0.05$), however, attitudes towards sexual self-regulation is (0.48^2) or 23.04 % of the variance is the indirect influence of peers environment through attitudes and sexual self-regulation, while the remaining 76.96 % of the variance is indirectly accounted for by other factors and this was found to be ($p < 0.05$) statistically significant. It emerged that the hypothesis that peers' environment influences adolescent's sexual behaviors through religious values, sexual self-regulation and attitudes was partially proved. Peers' environment was found to be statistically significantly influencing adolescents' sexual behaviors through attitudes and sexual self-regulation.

Analysis of peer's environment towards religious values and sexual behaviors were similar to those of family and University environment. At University, adolescents experience tensions between secularism, with the attractions associated with deviant behavior and the constraints associated with adhering to religious values. These tensions may be particularly pronounced where adolescents are simultaneously exposed to strong demands and the international youth culture which is permissive to sexual behaviors. The associations between adolescents and their friends with respect to religious values, however, does not appear to be attributable solely to either personal levels sexual behavior or the tendency of adolescents to associate with deviant peers that endorse sexual behaviors as the results indicated. Adolescents who are inclined to religious values may associate with others who are likely to reinforce these tendencies.

5. Conclusion

The findings of the present study demonstrated a negative relationship between religiosity and adolescents' sexual behaviors, this could be due to the fact that the sensitivity and nature of the information concerning adolescent's sexual behaviors, adolescents' have been known to provide inaccurate reports of their sexual behaviors especially when relating to religious issues and attitudes.

The peer environment in the present study assesses the possibility that peers influence friend's sexual behaviors through religious values, sexual self-regulation, and attitudes. Peer influence likely includes both approval and communication, for example, adolescents tend to approve behaviors of friends that are similar to themselves, and socialization processes through communication. Results showed that approval and communication was slightly high towards religious values and attitudes but not sexual self-regulation, this is attributed to traditional norms that hold the views of sexual issues as being taboo and that adolescents are afraid of being promiscuous. Results from the present study provide controversial evidence about peer influence of adolescent's sexual behaviors; religious values of peers were not predictive of sexual behaviors; this relationship was found to be insignificant.

These tensions may be particularly pronounced in Indonesia where adolescents are simultaneously exposed to strong demands and the international youth culture that approve sex before marriage. Peers' exposure to the Western media, alcohol and drugs are widely available. The communication between adolescents and their friends with respect to sexual behaviors, however, does not appear to be attributable solely to either personal levels of problem behavior or the tendency of adolescents to approve of deviant peers as the associations between religious adolescence and that of their friends was found to be insignificant.

The tendency of adolescents to approve friends with those who are similar to themselves in religious values and attitudes may be extremely important for explaining the possible influence of peers on sexual behaviors; adolescents who approve and communicate with peers of similar religious values and attitudes are inclined to refrain from sexual behaviors of intercourse but not necking and petting behaviors. Conversely, less youth may associate with low peers who reinforce less behavior. Thus, adolescents who are either highly or on a trajectory to increase their religiosity are likely to find like minded friends. Within these friendships, adolescents likely influence each other to maintain a high level of consistent practice.

These findings must be interpreted with caution, these are interesting findings, which need further comprehensive research studies to explore how social environment influence adolescents' sexual behaviors in the Ugandan context, the fact that religious values are preserved and taught to adolescents at University, these religious values had negative significant effect on adolescents sexual behaviors as being mediators between social environment and sexual behaviors in all models.

Adolescents aged 19–21 at University in Uganda haven't internalized religious values of sexual behaviors, this was revealed in their relaxed approval of petting and necking as being their behaviors that gives them satisfaction. Taking this analysis further, adolescents fear social consequences from their social environment of family, University, self, and peers in case of intercourse as compared to those consequences assigned by teachings. One reason could be that social consequences as physical, yet religious consequences are ideological of which adolescents aged 19–21 have not attained the formal operational stage of reasoning from an abstract standpoint but their reasoning is based on concrete proof.

To survive as an individual in the modern world, adolescent's religious values remain significant in adapting to increasing focus on individualism and meeting the demands of the globalized world. As such, religious values on sexual self-regulation significantly influence their sexual regulative capacities of sexual behaviors. The results of the present study demonstrated that religious values significantly influence adolescent's sexual self-regulative capacities of self-efficacy towards sexual behaviors of intercourse, but not necking and petting. As was hypothesized, religious values mediated the social environment's influence toward adolescent's sexual behaviors. However, this was not factual for university and peer environments.

Interestingly, higher levels of religious values of knowledge and feelings among adolescents aged 19–21, did not relate to their subsequent behaviors of necking and petting. As identified by Piaget that individuals who have not reached the formal operational stage of thinking abstractly, religious values of adolescents remain important but not sufficient to predict their behaviors relating to the sexual behavior of necking and petting.

Low levels of belief among university students' religious values were insignificant towards sexual self-regulation and sexual behaviors, however, these environments were found to influence adolescent's attitudes and sexual self-regulation towards sexual behaviors. Thus, it is conceivable that in the context of the family environment, religious values act as restrictive forces yet in university and peer environments, it is conservative attitudes that restrict sexual behaviors. In any case, it appears that religious values are contextually relevant to adolescents aged 19–21 as opposed to being consistent in their lives. Thus, it is not surprising that it was associated with conservative sexual behaviors of intercourse but not necking and petting, these results demonstrate that adolescent's sexual behaviors are not majorly predisposed by their liberal religious values, but by their conventional attitudes. These findings are not compatible with those of Iskandar et al (2013) who found that being spiritual, or believing in higher power was linked to positive sexual behaviors of adolescents of avoiding risky behaviors, not likely to engage in early sex, having sex less frequently, and not becoming pregnant, these findings are interesting but misleading for adolescents whose religious values are Religious oriented, behaviors of necking and petting are equally risky but because their punishment are not concrete or practical, adolescents take such behaviors as risky free.

The absence of value influence towards adolescents' sexual behaviors is attributed to their rationalistic forms of thinking, yet religious values are idealistic that calls for absolute belief without question. But contrary to adolescents' cognitive levels of development and increased self-identity, adolescents learn to question the religious values of their beliefs and those of their significant others. This is done by forming their own identities that acknowledge sexual behaviors of necking and petting because these behaviors are considered risky free by adolescents. Yet, given the religious values, such behaviors are considered risky and attract similar punishments, but because these reprimands are not administered to the individual directly, such ideologies remain abstract for adolescents aged 19–21 to acknowledge. The results in the present study demonstrated that adolescents attitudes significantly influence their sexual behaviors, this relationship is attributed to the fact that adolescents aged 19–21 know the risks attributed to sexual behaviors, that is unwanted pregnancy and diseases, and because they need to accomplish their educational profession and possibly develop their life career through education, adolescents were found to hold strong behavior stances and strong negative sexual behavior evaluations. Because of their psychological, social, and physical changes, adolescents find themselves in a stressful position in their social environment where behaviors of sexuality are discouraged yet their bodies are ready for reproduction.

Religious values were insignificant in influencing adolescents' sexual behaviors aged 19–21 who are college students, for all social environment constructs namely family, school, and peers. The form of sexual behaviors that an adolescent engages in depends on a multiple of factors. Its regarded inappropriate in Ugandan culture to engage in intimate sexual behaviors before marriage, even though some adolescents feel sexual desires, hence, adolescents may be restraining their impulses and desires through sexual self-regulation, whereas after they have come to trust each other and establish some degree of intimacy, they may engage in more sexual expression without conflicting with their social environments.

The sample characteristics of the current study might have affected the results in several ways, participants were randomly selected and, thus may or may not be representative of all adolescents in this age group. Adolescents with low levels of sexual self-regulation, strong religious values, and attitudes, may have found this task to be more difficult than adolescents with moderate or high levels of sexual self-regulation. Adolescents experiencing difficulties such as high levels of problem behaviors or poor academic achievement, poor family communication might have been influenced to respond to the questionnaire with bias, hence social desirability; future studies should use more representative samples with different research methodologies.

6. References

Goddard, A. (2015). *Theology and Practice in evangelical Churches, In A. Thatcher (ed.), The Oxford handbook of theology, sexuality, and gender.* In *A.Thatcher(Ed.).*Oxford: Oxford University Press .

Hans, J. K. (2011). Abstinence,sex,and virginity: Do they mean what we think,? *American Journal of Sexuality Education*, 329–342.

Hensel, D.J., Fortenberry, J.D.,& O'Sullivan,L.F., & Orr,D.P. (2011). The developmental association of sexual self-concept with sexual behavior among adolescent women. *Journal of Adolescence*, 675–684.

Hunt, M.E.,& Jung,P.B. (2009). "Goodsex"and religion:A feminist overview. *Journal of sex education*, 156–169.

Iskandar, Z, Setiono, K., Agustiani, H., & Muwaga M. (2013). The influence of the value system and sexual self-regulation toward adolescents' sexuality. *Indian Journal of Positive Psychology*, 315–320.

Lefkowitz,E.S., Gillen,M.M., Shearer, C.L., & Boone,T.L. (2004). Religiosity, sexual behavior, sexual attitudes during emerging adulthood. *The journal of sex research*, 150–159.

Pai, H.C.,Lee, S., & Yen,W.J. (2012). Atest of moderating mechanisms in early adolescent girls. *Journal of Advanced Nursing*, 46–55.

Penhollow,T., Young,M.,& Bailey,W. (2007). Relationship between religiosity and "hooking up. *American Journal of Health Education*, 338–345.

Young, & Vazsonyi. (2011). *Family in the white American Protestant experience.* Beverly Hills: Sage Publication.

Fuad Nashori, Normeilina Sari, Tri Setiani, Putri Dyah Arminingtyas, Raden Rachmy Diana & Iswan Saputro

Subjective Well-Being among Adolescent Bullying Victims: The Role of Forgiveness Therapy

Abstract: This study examined the effectiveness of forgiveness therapy to promote subjective well-being for bullying victims among adolescents. The hypothesis of this study stated that ones receiving a therapy in the intervention group, have a high subjective well-being score compared with those of the control group who did not receive a therapy. Adolescents completed a range of questionnaires to assess changes in their conditions (The Forgiveness Scale, The Satisfaction with Life Scale, and Positive Affect Negative Affect Schedule). Male and female adolescents (12–17 years old), who experienced bullying but did not yet receive any other kind of interventions, participated in this study. The subjects in this study were identified as bullying victims through the bullying scale. The data were analyzed using t-test. Results showed that adolescents in the intervention group reported an increase in life satisfaction and affect scores compared to those of the control group.

Keywords: Forgiveness Therapy, Subjective Well-being, Life Satisfaction, Affect.

1. Introduction

Adolescents are one of the community groups that often experience bullying. The results of a survey conducted by the Ministry of Social Welfare in Indonesia showed that 84 % of adolescents who aged 12 to 17 years old experienced bullying (Laksana, 2017). Individuals who experienced bullying felt uncomfortable, helpless, angry, fearful, ashamed, and socially anxious (Ortega, Elipe, Mora-Merchan, et al., 2012).

The decrease of subjective well-being among bullying victims needs psychological intervention, such as forgiveness as one of the Islamic coping strategies (Achour, Bensaid & Nor, 2016). Individual subjective well-being can be improved through forgiveness therapy. Forgiveness can make an individual receive God's mercy (*rahmat*) and alleviation in life (Qur'an and Their Translation, 2: 178). Some researchers found that forgiveness can also affect individuals' subjective well-being. Forgiveness has a positive correlation with life satisfaction (Yárnoz-Yaben, Garmendia, & Comino, 2016; Macaskill, 2012), resilience (Saputro &

Nashori, 2018), self-esteem (Kim & Lee, 2014), and psychological well-being (Krause & Ellison, 2003).

Forgiveness also increases positive affects (Yárnoz-Yaben, Garmendia, & Comino, 2016) and decreases negative affects, such as stress (Rahmandani, 2015), desire for revenge (Scull, 2015), depressive symptoms (Dezutter, Toussaint & Leijssen, 2016), anger, upset, anxiety, hate (Worthington, van Oyen, Lerner, & Scherer, 2005), and aggression (Qarina & Nashori, 2018). Forgiveness therapy effectively decreases anger, willingness to revenge, and PTSD among women after spousal emotional abuse (Park, Enright, Essex, Zahn-Waxler & Klatt, 2013). Therefore, forgiveness therapy effectively increases the affect among bullying victims. Thus, the aim of this study is to find out whether forgiveness therapy can increase subjective well-being among adolescent bullying victims.

2. Theoretical Review

Research that examined bullying among adolescents and students has been carried out extensively (Egan & Todorov, 2009; Ozkan, & Cifci, 2009; Pertiwi & Nashori, 2011; Nashori, Mayasari, Dewisukma, et al., 2017; Hinduja & Patchin, 2017). However, research that focused on subjective well-being among bullying victims in adolescents has not been conducted much. One of the effects of bullying amongst adolescents is the decline of subjective well-being level. Subjective well-being is a cognitive and affective evaluation carried out by individuals toward their lives. Cognitive evaluation in an individual who feels happy is associated with a high level of life satisfaction, while the results of affects evaluation are in the form of much positive affection and little negative affection (Diener, Suh, Lucas & Smith, 1999).

Forgiveness is an individual act of turning negative emotions into positive ones for people who have made mistakes (Enright, 2002). A forgiveness therapy also is one of the interventions in Islamic psychology. According to Nashori, Diana, and Hidayat (2020), there are two approaches to develop an intervention, namely the original Islamic psychology approach and the integrative Islamic psychology approach. In the Islamic psychology approach, ideas are derived entirely from the Qur'an and hadiths as the basic principle of the intervention. Meanwhile, the integrative Islamic psychology approach is carried out by integrating (1) the ideas, research, and conventionally applied psychology developed in the Western tradition and (2) the ideas, research, and applied original Islamic psychology.

This study uses an integrative Islamic psychology approach with integrating the forgiveness theory in mainstream psychology (Enright, 2002) and the forgiveness theory in the Islamic psychology (Nashori, 2011). Forgiveness is one of the most important commands in Islam, and it is written thirty-four times in the Qur'an. Then, after forgiving a person, praying for the good of the transgressor is also one of the important elements in forgiveness (Nashori, 2011).

3. Method

3.1 Research Design

This research was conducted using an experimental method. The design of this research adopted the randomized matched two-group design (Seniati, Yulianto, & Setiadi, 2011). Matching was intended to make two groups of participants equal. After obtaining two equal groups, randomization was conducted to determine which group was positioned as the intervention group, and which one was categorized as the control group. Measurements were made three times by means of pretest, first posttest, and second posttest conducted two weeks after the completion of the forgiveness therapy.

3.2 Participants

This study involved 8 males and 8 females who aged from 12 to 17 years. They had experienced bullying but did not yet receive any other kind of interventions in Yogyakarta, Indonesia. The participants in this study were identified as bullying victims resting upon the bullying scale before the intervention began. The participants were divided into two groups namely the intervention group (4 males and 4 females) and the control group (4 males and 4 females).

3.3 Measurement Tools

The measurement tools in this study were the Satisfaction with Life Scale (SWLS) and Positive Affect and Negative Affect Schedule (PANAS) to measure subjective well-being and Forgiveness Scale to measure forgiveness.

3.3.1 The Satisfaction with Life Scale (SWLS)

SWLS was developed by Pavot and Diener (1993) to measure individuals' life satisfaction. This scale was adapted for Indonesian people by Takwin, Singgih and Panggabean (2012), and it already had Cronbach's alpha of 0.87.

3.3.2 Positive Affect and Negative Affect Schedule (PANAS)

Participants' positive affects and negative affects were measured using PANAS that had been developed by Watson, Clark, and Tellegen (1988). This scale was adapted for Indonesian people by Takwin, Singgih and Panggabean (2012), and the scale already had Cronbach's alpha of 0.86 for the positive affect scale and 0.87 for the negative affect scale.

3.3.3 Forgiveness Scale

Forgiveness scale was used to measure participants' forgiveness developed by Nashori (2012). This scale consisted of 14 items with the Cronbachs' alpha of 0.93.

3.3.4 Bullying

The measurements of bullying victims were undertaken with measuring bullying victimization, perpetration, and bystander scale constructed by Wolke, Woods, Bloomfield, and Karstadt (2000). This scale consisted of 35 items to identify the victims of bullying, and it already had Cronbach's alpha of 0.94.

3.4 Forgiveness Therapy

The forgiveness therapy was prepared based upon forgiveness stages as proposed by Enright (2002) which encompassed some phases, namely uncovering, decision, work, deepening, and forgiveness. The therapy was also formulated using the Islamic values based on the Qur'an and hadiths of Prophet Muhammad (Nashori, 2011). The Qur'an also has an important message to keep sending prayers for the transgressors. The forgiveness therapy was conducted for five meetings with twenty-eight sessions, and the therapy took two hours for each meeting.

3.5 Data Analysis Method

The data analysis method used in this study was the parametric test with Independent Sample T-Test analysis to see the difference in the subjective well-being levels among the participants before and after the intervention in the form of forgiveness therapy in the intervention group and control group. Data analysis was carried out using the Statistical Program for Social Science (SPSS) program 22.0 for Windows.

4. Results

The result of hypothesis testing by using the Independent Sample t-Test analysis showed a significant difference in life satisfaction of adolescent bullying victims after they received the forgiveness therapy in comparison with those of the control group (Table 1). The first hypothesis was accepted with t = 2.141 and $p = 0.050$. Furthermore, a significant difference in life satisfaction was also found in the 2-week measurement after the therapy (second posttest) was carried out with the t = 2.275 and $p = 0.039$. In the affect score, there was no significant difference found between ones in the intervention group and those of the control group after the provision of forgiveness therapy, with t = 3.175 and $p = 0.070$. However, there was a significant difference in the affect score on the 2-week follow-up measurement after the therapy was given to adolescents in the intervention group compared to those of the control group, with t = 4.085 and $p = 0.010$. The second hypothesis was accepted, or in other words, there was a significant difference in the affects of adolescent bullying victims after they received the forgiveness therapy in comparison with those of the control group.

Table 1. Test on the differences of SWLS and PANAS in the intervention group and the control group in each measurement

	Measurement	t	*p*
SWLS	Posttest 1	2.141	0.050
	Posttest 2	2.275	0.039
PANAS	Posttest 1	3.175	0.070
	Posttest 2	4.085	0.010

The Mann-Whitney analysis was used because the distribution of forgiveness data did not meet the criteria of normal distribution and/or not homogeneous. The result showed that there was a significant difference in forgiveness scores of adolescent bullying victims after receiving the forgiveness therapy compared with those of the control group on the first posttest measurement ($Z = -2.741$; $p = 0.006$) and second posttest or two-week after the provision of forgiveness therapy measurement ($Z = -2.059$; $p = 0.038$) (see Table 2).

Table 2. Test on the differences of forgiveness in the intervention group and the control group in each measurement

	Measurement	Z	p
Forgiveness	Posttest 1	-2.741	0.006
	Posttest 2	-2.059	0.038

5. Conclusion

The results of the present study showed that there was a significant difference in subjective well-being levels between the bullying victims in the intervention group after receiving the forgiveness therapy compared with those of the control group. In other words, forgiveness therapy could increase subjective well-being among adolescent bullying victims. These results are supported by previous research that also exhibited a positive correlation between forgiveness and life satisfaction (Macaskill, 2012; Yárnoz-Yaben, Garmendia, & Comino, 2016). When the bullying victims decided to forgive, they were able to accept the realities they faced. They perceived that through forgiveness, the experiences of bullying as a negative condition could turn into an experience leading them to maturity.

The forgiveness therapy could also increase positive affects and decrease negative affects. The foregoing result occurred because during the therapeutic process, there was a disclosure of negative emotions, acceptance of suffering due to interactions with transgressors, and knowing alongside practicing how to manage negative emotions. Also, during the therapy process, participants were trained to give empathy to the transgressors; they were invited to feel the benefit of forgiveness; and they were asked to write hopes and practice praying for transgressors. Fincham, Hall, and Beach (2006) found that forgiveness therapy can increase emotional well-being and a healthy intimate relationship. The result of the current study was also supported by Egan and Todorov (2009) stating that a high forgiveness level has experienced a low level of negative emotion. This showed that forgiveness could be a cure among adolescent bullying victims after they experienced bullying, and it could strengthen individuals' positive affects.

Drawing upon the data of the present study, it can be concluded that the forgiveness therapy is effective to increase subjective well-being among adolescent bullying victims, in terms of both life satisfaction and affects. Thus, the results of this study strengthen the theory that a high level of forgiveness will be followed by a high degree of subjective well-being.

6. References

Achour, M., Bensaid, B. & Nor, M. R. B. M. (2016). An islamic perspective on coping with life stressors. Applied Research in Quality of Life, *11*(3), 663–685.

Dezutter J., Toussaint L. & Leijssen M. (2016). Forgiveness, ego-Integrity, and depressive symptoms in community dwelling and residential elderly adults. *Journals of Gerontology B, Psychological Sciences and Social Sciences, 71*(5), 786–797.

Diener E, Suh, E. M., Lucas R. E. & Smith H. (1999). Subjective well-being: Three decades of progress. *Psychological Bulletin, 125*(2), 276–302.

Egan, L. A., & Todorov, N. (2009). Forgiveness as a coping strategy to allow school students to deal with the effects of being bullied: Theoretical and empirical discussion. *Journal of Social and Clinical Psychology, 28*(2), 198.

Enright, R. D. (2002). *Forgiveness is a choice: A step by step process for resolving anger and restoring hope*. Washington: United Book Press.

Fincham, F. D., Hall, J. & Beach, S. R. H. (2006). Forgiveness in marriage: Current status and future directions. *Family Relation, 55,* 415–427.

Hinduja, S. & Patchin, J.W. (2017). Cultivating youth resilience to prevent bullying and cyberbullying victimization. Child Abuse & Neglect, *73*, 51–62.

Kim, H. K. & Lee, M. (2014). Effectiveness of forgiveness therapy on resilience, self-esteem, and spirituality of wives of alcoholics. *Journal of Korean Academy of Nursing, 44*(3), 237–247

Krause, N. & Ellison, C. G. (2003). Forgiveness by God, forgiveness of others, and psychological well-being in late life. *Journal for the Scientific Study of Religion, 42*(1), 77–93. doi.org/10.1111/1468-5906.00162

Laksana, B. A. (2020, January 5). Mensos: 84% anak usia 12–17 tahun mengalami bullying [Mensos: 84% of 12–17 year olds experience bullying]. Retrieved from https://news.detik.com/berita/d-3568407/mensos-84-anak-usia-12-17-tahun-mengalami-bullying

Macaskill (2012). The mental health of university students in the United Kingdom. *Sheffield Hallam University. Research Archive. https://shura.shu.ac.uk/6449/1/*

Nashori, H. F., Diana, R. R. & Hidayat, B. (2020). The trends in Islamic psychology intervention in Indonesia. In Ralph W. Wood Jr and Sariya Cheruvallil-Contractor (eds.), *Research in social scientific study of religion* (pp 162–180). UK: Brill NV.

Nashori, H.F. (2011). Meningkatkan kualitas hidup dengan pemaafan [Improve the quality of life with forgiveness]. *Jurnal Unisia, 33*(75), 214–226.

Nashori, H.F., Mayasari, G., Dewisukma, G., Iskandar, D., Wicaksono, K., Prehastamto, C., & Andriansyah, Y. (2017). The model of bullying behavior in senior High School: A case study in Indonesia. *Psychology and Education Journal*, *54*(1–2).

Nashori. F. (2012). Pemaafan pada etnis Jawa [Forgiveness of Javanese ethnicity]. *Disertasi*. Bandung: Program Doktor Psikologi Program Pascasarjana Universitas Padjadjaran.

Ortega, R., Elipe, P., Mora-Merchán, J. A., Genta, M. L., Brighi, A., Guarini, A., & Tippett, N. (2012). The emotional impact of bullying and cyberbullying on victims: a European cross-national study. *Aggressive behavior*, *38*(5), 342–356.

Ozkan, Y., & Cifci, G. (2009). The effect of empathy level on peer bullying in schools humanity & social. *Sciences Journal*, *4*(1), 31–38.

Park, J. H., Enright, R. D., Essex, M. J., Zahn-Waxler, C., & Klatt, J. S. (2013). Forgiveness intervention for female South Korean adolescent aggressive victims. *Journal of Applied Developmental Psychology*, *34*(6), 268–276.

Pavot, W. & Diener, E. (1993). Review of the satisfaction with life scale. *Psychological Assessment*, *5*(2), 164–172.

Pertiwi, S.V. & Nashori, F. (2011). Kecenderungan bullying pada siswa Sekolah Menengah Pertama [The tendency of bullying in junior high school students]. *Jurnal Psikologi*, *7*(1).

Qarina, S. & Nashori, H.F. (2018). Pemaafan dan perilaku agresi Siswa [Student forgiveness and aggression behavior]. *Jurnal Unisia*, *38*(84).

Rahmandani, A. (2015). Pemaafan dan aspek kognitif dari stres pada mahasiswi jurusan kebidanan tingkat dua [Forgiveness and cognitive aspects of stress in second-year midwifery students]. *Jurnal Psikologi Undip*, *14*(2),118–128.

Saputro, I. & Nashori, H.F. (2018). Resiliensi mahasiswa ditinjau dari pemaafan dan sifat kepribadian agreeableness [Student resilience viewed from forgiveness and agreeableness personality traits]. *Jurnal Psikologi Islam*, *4*(2).

Scull, N. C. (2015). Forgiveness, revenge, and adherence to Islam as moderators for psychological wellbeing and depression among survivors of the 1990 Iraqi invasion of Kuwait. *Journal of Muslim Mental Health*, *9*(1). doi:10.3998/jmmh.10381607.0009.103.

Seniati, L., Yulianto, A. & Setiadi, B. N. (2011). *Psikologi eksperimen (The Psychology of Experiment)*. Jakarta:Indeks.

Takwin, B., Singgih, E. E., & Panggabean, S. K. (2012). The role of self management in increasing the subjective well-being of DKI Jakarta's citizens. *Makara: Sosial Humaniora*, *16*(1), 1–8.

The Qur'an and Their Translation (T.M. Hasbi Ashshiddiqi, Bustami A. Gani, Mochtar Jahja, A. Toha Jahja Umar, A. Mukti Ali, Kamal Mochtar, Gozali

Taib, A. Musaddad, Ali Maksum, & Busjairi Madjidi). (2015). Kementerian Agama RI.

Watson, D., Clark, L. A. & Tellegen, A. (1988). Development and validation of brief measures of positive and negative affect: The PANAS scale. *Journal of Personality and Social Psychology, 54*(6), 1063–1070.

Wolke, D., Woods, S., Bloomfield, L. & Karstadt, L. (2000). The association between direct and relational bullying and behaviour problems among primary school children. *The Journal of Child Psychology and Psychiatry and Allied Disciplines, 41*(8), 989–1002.

Worthington Jr, E. L., van Oyen, W. C., Lerner, A. J. & Scherer, M. (2005). Forgiveness in health research and medical practice. *Explore, 1*(3), 169–176.

Yárnoz-Yaben, S., Garmendia, A. & Comino, P. (2016). Looking at the bright side: Forgiveness and subjective well-being in divorced Spanish parents. Journal of Happiness Studies, 17(5), 1905–1919.

Rosleny Marliani, Ila Nurlaila Hidayat, Edi Komarudin & Zulmi Ramdani

Testing of Patience Measurement: Convergent Validity of the Patience Scale

Abstract: Validity is one of the most important elements on a psychological scale. Validity refers to the feasibility of an instrument with the theory it uses. The development of Islamic psychology today has created various measurements of aspects of psychology which are also widely discussed in religious contexts, one of which is the Patience Scale. Convergent validity is part of testing construct validity that is multitrait-multimethod, where the same construct when measured by different instruments, will produce a correlation between the two as well as vice versa. This study aims to look at the convergent validity of the patience scale. The two types of the scale used are Patience Scale A Likert Scale version and the other Patience Scale B scale version that focuses on the subject. The results of the study of 300 subjects involved in the study proved that the two scales used had a high correlation, thus providing information that the two scales had good convergent properties so that either Scale A or B could be used as measurement instruments for Patience constructs.

Keywords: Convergent Validity, Islamic Construct, Multi-Method Approach, Patience Scale.

1. Introduction

The current development of Islamic Psychology is characterized by many psychological measurements that try to carry out operations on the characteristics or teachings given in a religious context (Ramdani, Supriyatin, & Susanti, 2018). To see aspects of personality in the context of Islam, Othman, Hamzah and Hashim (2014) trying to develop an Islamic personality model compared to the Big Five Factor personality model. Personality in Islam is also developed through quantitative and qualitative approaches to gain an understanding of the constructs of an appropriate Islamic personality (Khir et al., 2016). In various other contexts, it is more specific than a lot of research then makes Islamic values the foundation for living life. One of them is the use of Islamic approaches in the treatment and healing of individual psychological disorders (Edriss, Rosales, Nugent, Conrad, & Nugent, 2017; Miryan & Azadboni, 2011).

Research on the development of psychological constructs in the Islamic perspective is also widely practiced in Indonesia. Amaliah, Aspiranti, & Purnamasari (2015) conducted research to investigate the elements of Islam needed in aspects of work that involve practicing divine values. Another study tries to explain the concept of religiosity in an Islamic perspective in depth (Salsabila, Rofifoh, Natanael, & Ramdani, 2019). In addition, other researchers focused on developing models for measuring Islamic psychology such as happiness (Marliani, Ramdani, & Imran, 2019) and the concept of *Tabayyun* (Fathoni, Verina, Rahmah, Paiqotul, & Ramdani, 2019).

Research on Islamic constructs has also been carried out by Subandi (2011) which then further encourages a lot of research to develop measuring instruments based on Islamic values. Research on the constructs of patience has been developed in Indonesia, especially related to various aspects of other life such as patience as a solution in solving problems and stress experienced by individuals (Afriady, 2008; Safitri, 2018). Construction has also been done by measuring patience Ramdani et al., (2018) by carrying out a mix method approach to obtain the definition of patience which results in the understanding that patience is a condition that requires an individual to control himself, accept what happens in him, think rationally about the problem and be able to actively try to solve his problem. So far not many Islamic psychology researchers have tried to do an in-depth study of the psychometric aspects of the patience scale, even though one of the advantages that might strengthen this concept is to use a more comprehensive psychometric approach. Research on the construct of patience has not been fully carried out using strong psychometric analysis, so that in this study psychometric analysis will be conducted focusing on the convergence test of patience measuring instruments.

2. Method

This study uses a quantitative correlation approach, namely by observing the convergence between the two scales tested. This convergence test is included in the testing of construct validity which focuses on the multi-method approach. Two different measuring instruments will significantly produce a correlation when measuring the same construct (Campbell & Fiske, 1959).

2.1 Sample

The participants involved in this study were 345 people divided into three groups. The first group was 9 people who served as an expert judgment in providing validation regarding the measuring instruments used. The second group amounted to 36 people who were used as a pilot study group to see the different power items. The third group is the final participants of 300 people who will be given a set of measuring instruments that aim to see the reliability and convergent validity of the scale used.

2.2 Measurement Tools

This research was conducted by correlating two measuring instruments that are in the same construct even though the method in the measurements taken is different. The instrument was based on the process of modifying the measuring instrument where the existing theories and dimensions were applied in this study (Ramdani, 2018). Patience has four dimensions, namely being patient in carrying out the commands of Allah, being patient in accepting Allah's calamities, being patient in avoiding Allah's prohibitions, and being patient in carrying out the blessings of Allah (Ramdani et al., 2018).

2.2.1 Questionnaire 1

The first measuring instrument is the scale of measurement version A made using a Likert scale approach consisting of 20 items with five answer choices ranging from very appropriate to very inappropriate. The scale is made by considering the proportionality of items per dimension, which is five items.

2.2.2 Questionnaire 2

The second measuring instrument is a type of scale that is based on a scaling method that focuses on the subject, where each dimension is represented by three items so that there are a total of 12 items in the B scale measurement scale. Each item consists of a certain condition that describes a situation where a person must be patient, then three answer choices must be chosen, only one that describes the most ideal and appropriate answers that must be done by the subject when faced with the problem of patience. The total number of items in this study is 32 items which are then sorted from number 1 to number 32. The first 20 items are items in scale version A format, while the rest are items on the scale of version B.

The study was conducted by distributing online questionnaires to student respondents who were selected by purposive sampling technique. Respondents were selected according to their characteristics, namely those who are Muslim and willing to participate in all research activities. Respondents agreed to fill in the informed consent provided by the researcher. The data were processed using the SPSS program and interpreted according to the analytical procedure in convergent validity.

3. Results

This research was carried out gradually and procedurally to obtain maximum results. The following presentation is the result of the content validity test conducted by 9 experts who have a background in both the fields of psychometric and psychological measurement.

Table 1. Results of content validity

Aiken's Validity Criteria							
Item	**Score**	**Item**	**Score**	**Item**	**Score**	**Item**	**Score**
1	.75	9	.83	17	.88	25	.83
2	.86	10	.75	18	.77	26	.83
3	.75	11	.94	19	.77	27	.75
4	.64	12	.92	20	.83	28	.94
5	.58	13	.86	21	.86	29	.92
6	.75	14	.92	22	.81	30	.88
7	.94	15	.94	23	.81	31	.86
8	.86	16	.88	24	.75	32	.83

Notes. The limit of the item that passes is > .72 (Sig.05)

The results in the content validation test illustrate that two items do not meet the Aiken validation graduation standard because they have a validation value below 0.72, namely item number 4 and item number 5. Therefore, the two items were procedurally discarded in this study. Then a trial is carried out to see the different power values of each item that will be tested.

Table 2. Results of discrimination power

Item Discrimination							
Item	**Score**	**Item**	**Score**	**Item**	**Score**	**Item**	**Score**
1	.079	9	.508	17	.531	25	.159
2	.476	10	.530	18	.598	26	.665
3	.499	11	.532	19	.494	27	.442
4	-	12	.494	20	.592	28	.429
5	-	13	.482	21	.093	29	.627
6	.201	14	.437	22	.374	30	.419
7	.199	15	.577	23	.598	31	.461
8	.589	16	.338	24	.780	32	.537

Notes. The limit of the item that passes is > .3 (Azwar, 2015), (-) the item is lost

The results in the different power tests indicate that four items have fallen at this stage. These items are item number 1, 6,7,21 and 25. So that the total items to be tested on the final scale are as many as 25 items, with details of 15 items to scale version A and 10 items for scale B version.

Table 3. Correlation between scale A and scale B

	Correlation among Variables					
				Scale A		
	Aspects	**Commands**	**Prohibition**	**Disaster**	**Enjoyment**	**Scale A**
Scale of B	Commands	.347	.224	.256	.312	.357
	Prohibition	.164	.108	.083	.174	.166
	Enjoyment	.084	.067	.166	.156	.150
	Enjoyment	.130	.141	.169	.166	.189
	Scale of B	.250	.187	.238	.285	.301

Notes. A good correlation limit is above .3 (Azwar, 2015)

Table 4. Reliability coefficient of scale

	Scale	
	A	**B**
Reliability Coefficient	.863	.617
N (Sample)	300	300

Notes. A good correlation limit is above .3 (Azwar, 2015)

The results of the correlation between scale A and scale B show a moderate correlation coefficient, although not so large. The correlation coefficient is indicated by a score of 0.301, so it can be concluded that there is convergence in the two measuring instruments. Patient constructs which are then developed in the two measuring instruments above provide important information related to the right way to build a reliable measuring instrument. Multi-method validity testing has been carried out in various life contexts where most of these studies are to prove theoretically that the scale we use in any form measures the aspects to be measured (Campbell & Fiske, 1959).

At least in this study, there are several assumptions put forward by researchers related to the results obtained, which include the clarity of the measured construct, the methodology built-in making measuring instruments, and the appropriate administrative measures of measuring. Measuring instruments that are built with a clear construct will produce a good correlation if measured in any form because this is related to the theoretical consistency it has (Flett, 2018). Also, the construct of patience built in this study is also able to comprehend phenomena comprehensively so that the relevance of the information obtained reinforces the results of validity (Schmittmann et al., 2013). Other things related to the results of the validation are also very much determined by the methodology used. A structured methodology involving a variety of analyzes and tests that are consistent will result in effective control of the measuring instruments made (Demuth & Mey, 2015; Silva, Silva, & Machado, 2018; Heng, Wagner, Barnes, & Guarana, 2018). The process of administration of measuring instruments and accuracy in presenting measuring instruments to the subject also makes the measuring instruments tested produce increasingly good validity (Ramdani, 2018).

4. Conclusion

This study states that there is an appropriate convergence, this is indicated by a high correlation coefficient between two different measuring instruments and measuring the same construct. Also, the scale in this study can be an alternative for future researchers to develop methodologies and constructs in Islamic Psychology. Future research must use a lot of stronger psychometric analysis with more subjects of the course and by validating criteria with other variables outside the construct of patience.

5. References

Afriady, D. (2008). Hubungan antara kesabaran dengan kemampuan pemecahan masalah pada karyawan [The relationship between patience and problem-solving abilities in employees]. *Naskah Publikasi Fakultas Psikologi Dan Sosial Humaniora UII Yogyakarta.*

Amaliah, I., Aspiranti, T., & Purnamasari, P. (2015). The Impact of the values of islamic religiosity to islamic job satisfaction in Tasikmalaya West Java, Indonesia. *Procedia - Social and Behavioral Sciences*, *211*(September), 984–991. November, 14. https://doi.org/10.1016/j.sbspro.2015.11.131

Azwar, S. (2015). *Validitas dan reliabilitas.* Yogyakarta: Pustaka Belajar.

Campbell, D. T., & Fiske, D. W. (1959). Convergent and discriminant validation by multitrait-multimethod matrix. *Psychological Bulletin*, *56*(2), 81–105. https://doi.org/10.1037/h0046016

Demuth, C., & Mey, G. (2015). Qualitative methodology in developmental psychology. *International Encyclopedia of the Social & Behavioral Sciences: Second Edition, 19*, 668–675. https://doi.org/10.1016/B978-0-08-097086-8.23156-5

Edriss, H., Rosales, B. N., Nugent, C., Conrad, C., & Nugent, K. (2017). Islamic medicine in the Middle Ages. *American Journal of the Medical Sciences, 354*(3), 223–229. https://doi.org/10.1016/j.amjms.2017.03.021

Fathoni, A. B., Verina, A., Rahmah, B., Paiqotul, N., & Ramdani, Z. (2019). Defining Tabayyun as a Psychological Attribute: Study of Thematical Exploration. *International Summit on Science Technology and Humanity (ISETH2019)* (pp. 3–17). Solo: Universitas Muhammadiyah Solo.

Flett, G. L. (2018). Mattering as a psychological construct. *The Psychology of Mattering*, (1999), 51–74. https://doi.org/10.1016/B978-0-12-809 415-0.00004-9

Heng, Y. T., Wagner, D. T., Barnes, C. M., & Guarana, C. L. (2018). Archival research: Expanding the methodological toolkit in social psychology. *Journal of Experimental Social Psychology, 78*(August 2017), 14–22. https://doi.org/10.1016/j.jesp.2018.04.012

Khir, M. M., Othman, A. K., Hamzah, M. I., Demong, N. A. R., Omar, E. N., & Abbas, M. K. M. (2016). Islamic personality model: A conceptual framework. *Procedia Economics and Finance, 37*(16), 137–144. https://doi.org/10.1016/S2212-5671(16)30104-6

Marliani, R., Ramdani, Z., & Imran, M. H. (2019). Validation of happiness scale convergence in santri. *Psikohumaniora: Jurnal Penelitian Psikologi*, 143–156.

Miryan, S. A., & Azadboni, R. M. (2011). How to treat psychological disorder: Islamic perspective. *Procedia – Social and Behavioral Sciences, 3.* 2507–2509. https://doi.org/10.1016/j.sbspro.2011.10.489

Othman, A. K., Hamzah, M. I., & Hashim, N. (2014). Conceptualizing the islamic personality model. *Procedia – Social and Behavioral Sciences, 13.* 114–119. https://doi.org/10.1016/j.sbspro.2014.04.014

Ramdani, Z. (2018). Construction of academic integrity scale. *International Journal of Research Studies in Psychology, 7*, 87–97. https://doi.org/10.5861/ijrsp.2018.3003

Ramdani, Z., Supriyatin, T., & Susanti, S. (2018). Perumusan dan pengujian instrumen alat ukur kesabaran sebagai bentuk coping strategy [Formulation and testing of instruments for measuring patience as a form of coping strategy]. *Jurnal Psikologi Islam Dan Budaya, 1*(2), 97–106.

Safitri, A. (2018). Hubungan antara kesabaran dengan stres menghadapi ujian pada mahasiswa [The relationship between patience and stress in facing exams in students]. *Jurnal ISLAMIKA, 0*(01), 34–40.

Salsabila, D. F., Rofifoh, R., Natanael, Y., & Ramdani, Z. (2019). Uji Validitas Konstruk Indonesian-Psychological Measurement of Islamic Religiousness (I-PMIR). *JPIB: Jurnal Psikologi Islam dan Budaya*, 77–86.

Schmittmann, V. D., Cramer, A. O. J., Waldorp, L. J., Epskamp, S., Kievit, R. A., & Borsboom, D. (2013). Deconstructing the construct: A network perspective on psychological phenomena. *New Ideas in Psychology*, *31*(1), 43–53. https://doi.org/10.1016/j.newideapsych.2011.02.007

Silva, K. M., Silva, F. J., & Machado, A. (2018). The evolution of the behavior systems framework and its connection to interbehavioral psychology. *Behavioural Processes*. https://doi.org/10.1016/j.beproc.2018.11.001

Subandi. (2011). Sabar: Sebuah konsep psikologi [Patience: A psychological concept]. *Jurnal Psikologi*, *38*(2), 215–227.

Shukran Abd. Rahman

Islamic Psychology in Organization Context: An Overview

Abstract: This paper provides basic exposures on the discipline of Industrial and Organisational Psychology; and relates it with the input on Islamic Psychology. The discussion requires a good understanding of the concept of Psychology from Islamic Perspectives. Literature which scrutinises the approaches to attain knowledge in the field of Psychology, the notions covered in the field, and the underlying values of the field have been consulted. The discussion includes the scopes covered by the subject, the approaches to source the knowledge, and the underlying or governing values of organisational practices. It highlights the areas of organisational practices which could be based on the application of Islamic principles and knowledge. The findings shed light on the importance of referring to two major sources (the Quran and Hadith) of information pertaining to human characteristics, and the ways the sources have shaped the principles and knowledge on human nature which are applicable in organisation settings.

1. Introduction

The study on the nature and reality of human characteristics started as early as when human beings were created. Scholars had used different approaches when discussing this subject, due to the different era or zeitgeist they belong to, and the ideology or religion they subscribed (Schultz & Schultz 2016). This led to the emergence of a distinct field, identified as Psychology which has been accepted as a field of knowledge which studies and explains the nature of humans. Its scopes of studies range from mental processes to human behaviours, standing on various bases of information about human nature.

The different subject matter discussed in the field is the result of different approaches used by scholars or the underlying values, ideologies, orientations, or belief systems they subscribed to. They have put remarkable efforts to substantiate the facts, principles, and explanation about human characters; or uphold certain philosophy when describing human nature. The history of Psychology has documented the work of early scholars who described the nature of humans by observing the functions of machines, the attributes of trees, animals, and environment. Instead of relying on an objective approach, they used personal imagination, opinion, evaluation and judgment. Hence, the ontology or the scopes they studied are within their limited thinking or reach, neglecting the invisible scope which are not attained through human investigation (Shukran, 2020).

Known as general psychology, there have been a wide extent of facts, principles, laws of human behaviors and mental processes adopted by students and researchers in the field of Psychology (Koch & Leary, 1985). Psychology scholars in western countries defined many concepts in Psychology by conducting scientific studies on individual behaviour and mental processes. The study of individuals, in many instances, refers to the study of individuals who may be independent of each other, have autonomous capabilities, and are self-reliant. This may depict the individualistic-orientated nature of a person, instead of the collectivistic–oriented outlook of men, as in the case of many individuals in non-western countries. In studying human behaviours and mental processes, psychologist use theories which are regarded as culture-bound, value laden, but with limited validity, generalizability, and applicability, as in the case of General Psychology which is characterized by decontextualized, mechanical, and universal principles of psychological theories which they regard as are universal (Koch & Leary, 1985). It also excludes the subjective aspects of human functioning (consciousness, agency, meaning and goals) (Kim, Yang, & Hwang, 2006). In other words, General Psychology has appeared to provide objective, but out of context theories of human behaviours, using western society when explaining psychological theories and principles.

The collectivistic–orientated nature of men considers individuals as members of society who are related to each other, whose behaviours and mental processes depend on that of others in the context (Kim, Yang, & Hwang, 2006). In this regard, scholars and practitioners have questioned the universality of psychological theories or general psychology, for many of them have not been empirically justified as applicable in the settings which culture are different from that of the place where the theories were developed. The internal and external validity of general psychology have been questioned because many of them originated and reflected the values, goals, and issues in the United States (Kim & Berry, 1993). These make them inappropriate to be generalized to other societies, and hence, necessitating efforts to improve the understanding of non-western culture when studying individuals in their settings, by using non-western lenses.

Scientific approaches have been used to understand phenomena that take place in this world, and in turn shape the way people manage or control the environment. Indigenous psychologists have been attempting to extend the scope and ideas of general psychology into its use in several settings, aimed at explaining human behaviours in such context, improving the ways they do things, changing their undesirable behaviours or developing news behaviours.

Over time, psychologists too have sought to leverage on local knowledge to construct theories which could be used to explain the roles of psychological principles in changing, developing or improving human life and livelihood across different cultures (Hwang, 2005). This initiative emerged as a reaction to the existing general or mainstream psychology which aimed to reflect the social, political, religious, and cultural aspects of people in the world.

The above paragraphs highlight the scopes of subject matter covered in General Psychology; and the approaches it adopted is acquiring knowledge on human nature. This article discusses the fundamental principles in the field of Industrial and Organisational Psychology, from Islamic perspectives. It also discusses the approaches which could be used to study the principles from Islamic perspectives, and highlights some of the subjects covered in the field. The discussion is expected to shed light on the importance of referring to two major sources of information pertaining to human characteristics, and the ways the sources have shaped the principles and knowledge on human nature which are applicable in organisation settings

2. Method

Source of Information: Translation of relevant verses of the Quran, work of early scholars, and contemporary literature which discuss the nature of human and work or organisation context have been consulted.

Analysis: A Thematic Analysis has been used to analyse the pattern of ideas derived from the Quranic verses and hadith, in relation to the approaches to attain knowledge in the field of Psychology; and the principles concerning organization.

3. Findings

3.1 Fundamentals of Islamic Perspectives

Islam provides fundamental knowledge on the nature of human existence and their way of life. The teaching of Islam has laid the foundations to study of human characteristics in that they spell out essential aspects of human nature. The Islamic perspectives of Psychology have also underscored the fundamental values (axiology) to be upheld when studying human beings, the ultimate one being the need to attain truth about the nature of man. Such truth is achievable by studying men in empirical manner, and by referring to divine information (Shukran, 2020). That said, the ways to source knowledge in Psychology, or its epistemology, requires scholars to subscribe to both approaches, without denying or negating one another. Such fundamentals inform the approaches to study humans, and the scopes to be covered in the studies of humans (Shukran, 2020). Hence, in understanding the nature of man, it is also fundamental to understand the principles to acquire knowledge; and the information about human beings which are provided in the Quran and the Prophet's tradition (hadith). The two sources have comprehensively described humans (the ontology of human reality), as well as the ways to acquire information about human characters.

The fundamental axiological notions to be upheld when studying human are the concept of Iman (belief), Islam (the way of life); and Ihsan (excellence or perfection). Iman, the inward actions of being Muslim entails the belief in Allah, His Angels, His Books, His Messengers and all the scriptures which He sent down to Prophet Muhammad (peace be upon him) and all prophets before him (Peace Be Upon Them). The pillar of Iman also includes the belief that in Allah's providence, in that He is capable of creating anything He wants, and the belief in the Last Day which is the Judgment Day and Herefater (Aisyah, 2016).

The term Islam does only not refer to the name of a religion but a comprehensive way, process, and outcome of life. The word Islam refers to the notion of accepting the fact that there is no God but Allah; and that Muhammad (Peace Be Upon Him) is the messenger of Allah. A person who accepts Islam acknowledges that the message of Allah is revealed to humans through the Prophet Muhammad (Peace Be Upon Him). He or she is to observe the other obligations – performing the five daily prayers, observing fasting in Ramadan, paying zakat, and performing pilgrimage (Hajj) at the House of Allah in Makkah, if one is capable of doing so.

Ihsan is a concept which is associated with a state when an individual attains a thinking and feeling that his or her actions are seen by Allah. Jamal Ahmed Badi (2019) states that Ihsan denotes the act of doing somethings in a sincere, complete, nice and right manner. The state of Ihsan has been described in a Prophet's tradition to refer to a condition when an individual performs a task or carries out activities before Allah in that he could see Him. The concept states that if one cannot see Him, he, however, accepts the fact that Allah sees his or her. A person who upholds *Ihsan* or a *Muhsen* is an individual who is responsible for all the things he or she does; is sure that Allah is seeing him/her in everything he/she says or does in his life; and performs work in good manner. A *Muhsin* also would perform to the best of his or her abilities in all undertakings, including at work. He or she would do or say what pleases Allah and conforms to His commands. The concept of *Ihsan* is not only confined to *ibadah khusus* (specific rituals) such as prayer or fasting but covers all aspects of life. The value of *Ihsan* would govern an individual's performance or regulate his or her behaviour in all settings, including at the workplace. *Ihsan* drives individuals to work with passion and diligence. The Prophet Muhammad (peace be upon him) has emphasised the value of *Ihsan,* encouraging us to perform work to the utmost of our abilities (Aini, 2020).

3.2 Understanding the Notion of Islamic Perspective in the Context of Organisation

As stated above, Islam is a religion which provides a complete way of life, guiding human on all aspects of activities e.g., socio-economic system (Khraim, 2010). This article dwells into the teachings of Islam on the relationship between people in collective setting such as organisation, family, and society. It covers several principles that guide the way individuals should interact with others, discussed under several concepts that pertain to organisational context.

What does a psychologist do in an organization? Areas under the purview of a psychologist who serves an organisation may include the tasks that involve managing personnel selection; enhancing job satisfaction, designing and conducting training, conducting performance appraisal and many more. An I/O Psychologist would help organizations to understand human behaviors, and in turn, recommend strategies to enhance employee's job satisfaction, improving employer's ability to manage employees, and designing intervention for change, improvement, or development in the organisation. These tasks are performed based on information gathered by examining specific aspects of employees (e.g their attitudes and behavior), organization (e.g companies' strengths, weaknesses, opportunities and challenges), the work itself (e.g., job description, work design), and their combination. The readily available information about human characteristics or the ways to deal with them could be sourced from the Quran and Hadith. In the Quran, Allah said "We assuredly established you in the earth and arranged for your livelihood in it. Little do you give thanks"Al-A'raf':10, (Abul Ala Maududi, 2020) The verse highlights the facts that Allah has created men and provided capacity to deal with livelihood on this earth. He has established for men various ways and guidance for them to manage their life on this earth, providing rich input for Psychologists to inform the approaches on managing people in organisation.

In short, a psychologist working in or for an organisation applies psychological principles and Islamic teaching in helping the organisation to bring about positive change and development for individuals, groups, work processes, products, and services in the organizations; hence making the organization a good workplace for employees. In fact, there are a broad range of scopes which could be linked with the notions found in the principles of Islam, Iman, and Ihsan.

Scopes/topics of Psychology in Organization Context

Psychology is a science of human characteristics, encompassing all aspects of human nature and covering a broad range of aspects, beyond individual behaviors and mental processes. It includes many different areas that can be combined with it such as education, religion, anthropology, and even the workplace as well as business. Organisational Psychology is a science which is concerned with the behavior of working people and with the behavior of people who function in organizations (Earley & Erez, 1997). While the former suggests that Organisational Psychology is about the characteristics of people who work in employing organisation; and their after-office behaviours; the latter could concern the characteristics of people who are associated with any types of organisations, including family institution, non-governmental organisations, and any informal group which are characterised by the presence of interacting individuals who work on meeting certain goals. The link between the notions of Islam, Iman, Ihsan in the context of organization is outlined in the following table.

Table 1. Notions of Islam, Iman, Ihsan vis a vis Scopes of Organization

	Notions of Islam, Iman, Ihsan	Domains of Organization Scopes
Fundamental Principles	1. Message of Allah Almighty is revealed to humanity (Islam) 2. Prophet Muhammad (SAW) carried the message and lead people. 3. Belief in Allah, His Angels, His Books, His Messengers, before (Iman), His Providence, and Hereafter (Aisyah, 2016). 4. Ihsan, to worship Allah as if you see Him, and if you do not see Him, He sees you (Ihsan)	1. Document of Rules, Guidance, Culture etc which guide human behaviours, including in social settings. 2. Leader's quality and leadership styles 3. Relationship between Man and others (Rahmatan Lil Alamin)-group vs individual ecosystem 4. Values that regulate men 5. God consciousness 6. Attitudes towards activities, people and others
Ways to study organization	1. The Quran 2. Hadis 3. Observation (as encouraged in the concept of Iqra')	1. Method of acquiring knowledge 2. Revelation as sources of knowledge 3. Observation as sources of knowledge 4. The need to link knowledge with context necessitating various thinking patterns
Scopes of subjects that requires address	1. Pillars of Islam (Basic obligations of Muslims) 2. Pillars of Iman (The Belief System) 3. The concept of Ihsan (The Concept of Excellence)	1. Relationship and Responsibilities with (a) Creator; (b)Self; (c) Others 2. Needs, Goals and Drives in Life/ organisation 3. Value System 4. Reward and Punishment 5. Organisation and Unity (saff)

Industrial-organizational psychology is a scientific study of organization which applies the rigor and methods of psychology to address issues of critical relevance to business, such as talent management, coaching, assessment, selection, training, organizational development, performance, and work-life balance. The principles of I/O are also applicable to other settings, including the ones mentioned above. This specialization of Psychology applies psychological theories and principles to support organizational development (i.e to set mission, goal, objectives of organizations); and develop individuals in organization (i.e to increase workplace productivity; to address organization related issues -such as the physical and mental well being of employees). To deliberate, this paper focuses on two levels of scopes which could be developed, changed, or improved through the application of psychological principles and knowledge, namely the individual and social levels which scopes are discussed below.

Individual Levels

The individual level refers to the scopes in organization which focus on the quality of individuals independent of other people and organization. The following are some of the scopes to be highlighted.

3.3 Individual Differences

In organization, due attention should be given in understanding individual differences as it has significant bearing on the type and quality of job an individual is able to accomplish. Factually, individuals differ in their traits and hence their behaviours, leading to the presence of employees with diverse backgrounds in an organization. Allah has created men to have a set of components namely biological, social, cultural, economic, psychological, psychical, spiritual and transcendental aspects (Muhammad Tahir-ul-Qadri, 2006), though the level of such components in an individual varies from one another depending on various factors. It is the differences that make an individual different from one another, causing multifold patterns of personality, and in effect different types of capacity. In organization, knowledge on individual differences is important to make strategic decisions with regard to personnel decisions and organization development matters.

3.4 Informed Personnel and Organisational Decisions

With regard to individual differences, Psychologists help organizations even before new employees are admitted as employees, in that only individual who have the right specification be selected to join the organization. For instance, psychologists had conducted selection and placement of military personnel in World War I and World War II. Learning from a Hadith of the Prophet: there is a need to assign a task only onto individuals who have the right specification, failing which the tasks will not be successfully accomplished and could even lead to its detrimental effects. Imam Bukhari reported that it has been narrated by Abu Huraira that Prophet Muhammad (Peace Be Upon Him) said: When honesty is lost, then wait for the Hour. It was asked, how will honesty be lost? The Prophet replied: When tasks or authority are given to those who do not deserve them or do not have the competencies to handle them, then wait for the Hour. The term hour here has been referred to by scholars as detrimental effects of giving the tasks or authority to individuals who do not fit to hold it (Yuksel Cayuroglu, 2019). In this regard, the field of personnel psychology is an essential application of psychology to the process of selecting the most capable individuals. A verse in Chapter An-Nisa underscores the need to have a meritorious selection process, based on specific criteria which could be accomplished through proper screening; interview; or testing. *"Indeed, Allah commands you to render trust to whom they are due and when you judge between people, judge them with justice. Excellent is what Allah instructs you. Indeed, Allah is ever hearing and seeing", from Chapter an Nisa: verse 58 (*Abul Ala Maududi, n.d*)*

3.5 Personal Development

The current world of work requires employees to be flexible in their competencies, being aware of the increasingly changing technology and lifestyle. As such, this scope underscores the need to establish avenues for people to learn or be trained when given a task to perform. An organisation should not only function as a place to do business or make profit by making the employees deliver products or serve clients. Organisations have the responsibilities to develop their employees, enhancing the competencies so that they can accomplish their tasks. In this relation, information about employees' personality, aptitude, and job performances are useful to design competency development programmes to enhance their abilities in carrying out their job descriptions. Organisations should also take care of employees' welfare and wellbeing, giving attention to the efforts of developing their spiritual, educational, and social aspects. Ibn 'Umar has reported that he heard from the Prophet (Peace be upon him) that "All of you are shepherds and each of you is responsible (*mas'ul*) for his flock. An Imam is a shepherd, and he is responsible for those in his care. A man is a shepherd in respect of his family and is responsible for those under his care. The woman is a shepherd in respect of her husband's house and is responsible for those under her care. The servant is a shepherd in respect of his master's property and is responsible for what is in his care. All of you are shepherds and each of you is responsible for his flock." (Sahih Al-Bukhari). The term "*mas'ul*" in this hadith has been defined by scholars as responsibility (Aini, 2020).

Hence, In Islam, employees' personal development, career development and well-being should be placed under the responsibility of leaders or employers, in that they are accountable of their subordinates' personal and professional development.

3.6 Work Design

The focus on employee or personnel management necessitates organisations to assign people with the tasks, duties, and responsibilities that they can deliver. Once an individual has been found to have specific competencies or suitable characteristics to perform a job, he or she should be empowered to take up the job. They should be given a clear set of work design failing which may risk or hamper the delivery of the assigned job. Prophet Muhammad (Peace Be Upon Him) said"*Whoever believes in God and the Day of judgement should not employ a worker until he/she knows what he is going* to receive" (Sahih Muslim 5/66). In fact, in the Quran, it is learnt that meeting certain specifications is important before an individual is assigned a task as Allah depicted in the case of Prophet Shuaib's daughter who told her father "O my father, hire him. Indeed, the best one you can hire is the strong and the trustworthy"' -Surah al-Qasas, verse 26 (Abul Ala Maududi, n.d)

3.6.1 Group Levels

The group level refers to the scopes in organization which involve interaction between an individual with others, as well as with their job and organization. The following are some of the scopes to be highlighted.

3.7 Leadership

As a leader, the key objective of the Prophet's mission was to improve and change the inner nature of human beings so that they would be able to succeed in the present world and hereafter. In this regard, the focus of organizational leadership should focus on setting clear mission, goal, objectives of organization and that of the organization's members. Learning from the Prophet, it is important to create awareness among organisation members that they should assert the need of relating their work with the act of worshiping the Creator or Ibadah (Baqutayan, 2011). Members in organisations should be inspired on the actual reasons for working and the right way to accomplish work. They should be educated on the values that could steer them to the path of the Creator and subsequently attain perpetual well-being, both in the current time and hereafter. In other words, leaders in an organisation are not only responsible to inspire employees in doing good to the organisation but to themselves as well.

3.8 Participative and Consultative Work Culture

Consultation or *shura* is a concept which should be adopted by organisations, providing rooms for leaders to form a positive work culture and in turn productive work processes. Organisation may be able to set strategic directions by accumulating ideas and feedback from members. It would enable organisations to nurture heightened commitment among members. Learning from the Quran and Hadith, there were many key decisions in the past which were made through consultations despite the personal intellectual ability that a leader has. In Chapter Ali-Imran, verse 159, Allah emphasizes the importance of consulting others when accomplishing any duties or carrying out responsibilities. "Take counsel from them in matters of importance. And when you are resolved on a course of action, place your trust in Allah; surely Allah loves those who put their trust (in Him)" (Abul Ala Maududi, 2020). The verse was meant for the Prophet Muhammad (Peace be upon him) who was ordained by Allah to consult his circle of people, a manner to be emulated when leading people and managing their affairs. Through consultation, a leader could leverage on the unique capabilities of his or her followers or acquire their critical and creative thinking to achieve the desired goal of the organization.

3.9 Solidified Team

Islam emphasises good and beneficial relationship with other people for their presence would better ones' life condition. It emphasizes the essentiality of strengthening solidarity through the spirit of brotherhood; and solidifying the ties of mutual relationship between people. Learning from the Quran, employees or members in organization should be led to hold the idea that they need each other when accomplishing their tasks, or to attain satisfaction when being at work place. In Chapter Al-Saff, Allah emphasizes the essentiality of having a solidified team when accomplishing tasks. "Indeed, Allah loves those who fight in His cause in a row as though they are a [single] structure joined firmly" (Fakhri, Adelzadeh, & Ghanimat, 2012). Islam teaches that brotherhood between the people transcends all racial and tribal barriers, as it is upheld by their common faith of Islam. In the Prophet's (Peace Be Upon Him) leadership, he has managed to establish a strong and sustainable society in Madinah, making each member to be responsible toward each other and assume an all-embracing responsibility to care for each other. In short, good interpersonal skills and social skills among team members are important enablers for them to fare well at work and attain the organizational goals; and in turn achieve satisfaction from it. A strong work team would be able to work collaboratively, uphold workplace harmony, as well as generate collective ideas and understanding. In effect, they will be motivated to provide high impact performance to their organization. This, in turn, enhances the organizational productivity and increases the likelihood for employees to attain job satisfaction.

3.10 Work Motivation

Motivation is a force that energises, directs, and maintains behaviours, attributed to employees' intrinsic as well as extrinsic motivation. The former could be the function of an individual's subscription to the belief system discussed above (Iman, Islam, and Ihsan) while the latter could also be provided by organization as reinforcement system. Both types of motivation would result in a desire in employees to accomplish impactful performance. In extrinsic motivation, employees could be driven by providing stimulus that could enhance the likelihood for employees to behave in certain ways. This could be done by providing external reward. The Prophet's way to motivate does not always involve tangible rewards but a set of efforts to recognize unique or distinct job performance of his *sahabah* (companions); appreciate their talents, recognize their strengths, acknowledge their unique characters; or grant special trait-term or identity to his companions. An important idea in the concept of motivation is that intrinsic motivation is viewed by scholars as the authentic motivation. It is the drive from within an individual which is not linked to any tangible rewards or external pleasure. In Chapter Ali- Amran, (3:200), Allah says "Believers, be steadfast, and vie in steadfastness, stand firm in your faith, and hold Allah in fear that you may attain true success" (Abul Ala Maududi, 2020).

4. Conclusion

Organisational Psychology applies psychological theories and principles in developing people, group, work processes, products, services as well as employee and customer satisfaction. Aimed at contributing to organizational development and improving individuals' well-being in organization, psychologists should be able to apply relevant behavioral sciences principles and Islamic knowledge to increase workplace productivity. Psychologists must be competent to address organization related issues -such as the physical and mental well being of employees. Emulating Prophet Muhammad (Peace Be Upon Him), psychologist serving organisations must empower organization to uphold good balance between task-performances, relationship amongst organization members, and their Creator.

5. References

Abul Ala Maududi (n.d). Translation of Chapter Al-A'raf 7:10, *The Noble Quran*. retrieved September 5, 2020, from https://quran.com/7, September, 2.

Aini Maznina A. Manaf (2020). Upholding the Right Work Ethic when Working From Home During COVID-19 Pandemic, *Emotional and Psychological Support*, retrieved September 5, 2020 from https://flagship.iium.edu.my/eps/upholding-the-right-work-ethic-when-working-from-home-during-covid-19-pandemic/?fbclid=IwAR3HnoRCTz-sy8AtAd2q4sbzu5cpR9inHnqvd1ld Ri9Zf0aIrkliwWDzJZ4

Aisyah, M. (2016). Measuring The Hablumminallah in Muslim Consumers' Religious Behavior Model. In *2016 Global Conference on Business, Management and Entrepreneurship*. Atlantis Press.

Baqutayan, S. M. S. (2011). The importance of religious orientation in managing stress. *International Journal of Psychological Studies*, *3*(1), 113

Cayuroglu, Y. (2019). Islam and Good Governance, retrieved August 15, 2020 from https://www.politurco.com/importance-of-assigning-adept-people-according-to-islam.html

Earley, P. C., & Erez, M. (Eds.). (1997). *The New Lexington Press management and organization sciences series and New Lexington Press social and behavioral sciences series.New perspectives on international industrial/ organizational psychology.*The New Lexington Press/Jossey-Bass Publishers.

Fakhri, K. P., Adelzadeh, P., & Ghanimat, P. (2012). Studying the statue of organization in Holy Quran. Journal of Applied Environmental and Biological Sciences, *2*, 162–7.

Hwang, KK. (2005). The third wave of cultural psychology-The indigenous movement. *The Psychologist, 18*(2), 80–83.

Jamal Ahmed Badi (2019). Hadith 17: The Concept of Ihsan, retrieved September 4, 2020 from https://muslimjapan.com/hadith_english/hadith-17-the-concept-of-ihsan/

Khraim, H. (2010). Measuring religiosity in consumer research from Islamic perspective. *International Journal of Marketing Studies*, *2*(2), 166

Kim U., Yang KS., Hwang KK. (2006) Contributions to Indigenous and Cultural Psychology. In: Kim U., Yang KS., Hwang KK. (eds) Indigenous and Cultural Psychology. International and Cultural Psychology. Springer, Boston, MA . https://doi.org/10.1007/0-387-28662-4_1

Kim, U. E., & Berry, J. W. (1993). *Indigenous psychologies: Research and experience in cultural context*. Sage Publications, Inc

Koch, S., & Leary, D. E. (1985). *A century of psychology as science.* New York: McGraw Hill

Muhammad Tahir-ul-Qadri (2006). Islam on Human Personality, Minhaj-ul-Quran International, . retrieved September 5, 2020 from https://www.minhaj.org/english/index.html

Schultz, D. P., Schultz, S. E. (2016). *A history of modern psychology.* (11th Edition). Canada: Cengage Learning

Shukran A. R. (2020). The Epistemology, Ontology and Axiology of Psychology from Islamic Perspectives (Imam Nursi As A Model). *The Journal of Risale-I Nur Studies, 5* (8), retrieved August 14, 2020 from http://thejrns.org/the-epistemology-ontology-and-axiology-of-psychology-from-islamic-perspectives-imam-nursi-as-a-model/

Bintang Ilham Avicena & Ratna Syifa'a Rachmahana

The Relationship between Religiosity and the Dark Triad of Personality among Indonesian Muslim College Students

Abstract: This study aims to determine the relationship between religiosity and the dark triad of personality among Indonesian islamic university students. The hypothesis of this study is that religiosity has a negative correlation with the dark triad of personality. To test this hypothesis, research is conducted using the translated form of Short Dark Triad (SD3) by Jones and Paulhus (2014) and Religiosity Scale by El-Menouar (2014). The subjects of this study were 115 university students in Indonesian islamic universities, in which most of them are citizens of Yogyakarta. A *Spearman's Rho* analysis was conducted in this study, the result showed that there is negative correlation in every dimension of religiosity with Machiavellianism and Psychopathy ($p < 0.05$, $r = -0.172$ - -0.374), but only Orthopraxis and Religious Knowledge have negative correlation towards Narcissism. This result is in line with research formerly done by Lowicki and Zajenkowski (2015) which suspects that religiosity in general correlated negatively with psychopathy and machiavellianism but is inconclusive in narcissism. Ghorbani, et al (2017) proposed that religiosity does not directly correlate with the dark triad of personality or any personality traits, but in an indirect sense as religious attitudes such as empathy or *ikhlas* may correlate strongly with personality constructs. Further studies that inspect the relationship between religiosity, religious attitudes, and the dark triad of personality are required to better understand the dynamics between religiosity and the dark triad of personality.

Keywords: religiosity, dark triad of personality, muslim, students

1. Introduction

College-level education is mostly considered to be one of the pillars of advanced society. College students are expected to be the future of a country, even more so in developing countries. College students as agents of change are hoped to be able to solve problems and become solutions for the world. In Islamic-based universities, the students are also given islamic norms or what we call as *akhlak*, with the hope of not only that the students are highly educated but also possess *akhlakul karimah*, or moral excellence, in order to become the next islamic leaders. But apparently, it has not appeared to be so. Such norms and values were not internalized as there were still behaviors that are not in line with islamic values, or even general rule. In academic settings, cheating on exams and plagiarism are quite common (kompasiana.com, 2013). Mass protests are also quite often ended up in a riot, done by islamic-based university students (regional.kompas.com, 2012). Furthermore, there was a misfortune in one of Islamic universities in Indonesia in which there are three deceased students after a hazing and persecution incident during an orientation program (tempo.co, 2017).

We did a preliminary study to confirm whether such behaviors happened in islamic-based universities on 15–20 March 2017 with 97 participants in islamic universities. We found that 55,67 % have cheated on their exams, 71.13 % have cheated on academic tasks, 49,48 % have plagiarized papers or thesis. In a non-academic setting, we found that 72.16 % of students have skipped class without acceptable reason, 26.8 % have elaborately violated university's written rule. In interpersonal relationships, 35 % have called names towards university's lecturers/employees, 39 % have openly mocked other students, 29,89 % have physically abused other students deliberately. In the organizational context, 4.12 % did mark-up on an organization budget, and 5.15 % used their organizational influence for personal gains. In romantic relationships, 16.49 % have cheated on their partner, 17.52 % have done physical/verbal/both abuse to their partner. Based on this study, we decided to continue our research to better understand what drives these students to act as such.

One of the huge factors of such socially aversive behaviors is personality. Although no single definition is acceptable, we can all agree that personality is a pattern of relatively permanent traits and unique characteristics that give both consistency and individuality to a person's behavior (Feist & Feist, 2008). Furthermore, Paulhus and Williams (2002) explained that among personalities that are averse to society, there are three concepts that are regarded as dominant in antisocial behaviors: Narcissism, Machiavellianism, and Psychopathy. These concepts are associated with aggression (Jones & Paulhus, 2010), racism (Hodson, Hogg, MacInnis, 2009), and bullying (Chabrol, Van Leeuwen, Rodgers, & Sejourne, 2009). Paulhus and Williams (2002) conceptualized these three constructs in a subclinical domain, which means that the three may appear in an offensive but non-pathological manner in normal populations.

One of the constructs that conceptually has a negative relationship towards the dark triad of personality, or its manifested behaviors, is religiosity. This conclusion is inferred from the close relations between religion and morality. In a religious culture, supernatural agent representations should promote moral behaviors (Norenzayan & Shariff, 2008). God is seen as a superior being who observes behaviors and punishes moral violations (Norenzayan, 2014). Shafranske and Maloney (in Paraschiva and Nicoleta, 2011) stated that religiosity means representation of devotion towards beliefs and practices in a religious institution. In an islamic-based university, there have been multiple trainings that are based on the Quran to prevent such behaviors from ever manifested. In QS: Al Muthafiffin 1–6, "Woe to those that deal in fraud, those who, when they must receive by measure from men, exact full measure, but when they have to give by measure or weight to men, give less than due. Do they not think that they will be called to account on a Mighty Day, a day when mankind will stand before the Lord of The Worlds?" it is explicitly stated that fraud/cheating behavior is strictly forbidden in Islam.

Religiosity has been formerly correlated with adaptive personality construct, such as high level of Agreeableness and Conscientiousness according to Big Five Personality (Saroglou, 2002) and low level of Psychoticism according to Eysenck Personality Questionnaire (White, Joseph, and Neil, 1995). Furthermore, those who have religiosity-based training are proven to avoid cheating behaviors, one of the manifestations of the dark triad of personality (Bloodgood, Turnley, and Mudrack, 2008).

Based on these findings, we believed that religiosity has a negative correlation with the dark triad of personality, in which we tried to prove this hypothesis with research between the two concepts, especially in Muslim college students in Indonesia

2. Theoretical Review

2.1 Dark Triad of Personality

Dark triad of personality is a constellation of three conceptually distinct personality but empirically overlapping variables. The three concepts, Machiavellianism, narcissism, and subclinical psychopathy, often correlates with one another but with common core of callous manipulation (Furnham, Richards, and Paulhus, 2013). Paulhus and Williams (2002) were the first ones who conceptualize this construct as a follow-up to the study conducted by Kowalski (2001).

The narcissism construct is based on the theory by Raskin and Hall (1981) that defines narcissism as an extreme positive view towards self that has adaptive and maladaptive features and correlates strongly with one's self esteem. Meanwhile, machiavellianism is based on Christie and Geis (1970) theory that defines people with machiavellianism personality as individuals who may not have emotional connection, therefore able to release themselves from conventional morality and are able to manipulate others. Psychopathy is based on Hare (2001) that explicitly stated that this individual has an affect disorder which in turn make one's unable to experience fear, unable to hold long term relationships, extreme courage, and sometimes correlated with high level of intelligence

2.2 Religiosity

Religiosity in this study is defined as the level of religious conception in individuals and his commitment towards his religion (Glock and Stark, in El-Menouar, 2014). In her study, El-Menouar argued that conceptualizing Islamic religiosity needs to be specific, as some indicators from Western conception of religiosity did not translate quite accurately in Islam (e.g.: church attendance is a good indicator of piety in Christian religiosity, while *masjid* attendance is not). Conception is defined as how far someone understands his or her religion while commitment is how strong does someone believe and devote himself/herself towards his or her religion. According to El-Menouar (2014) Religiosity has five different but related dimensions: basic religiosity (*aqidah*), central religiosity tasks (*ibadah/* five pillars of Islam), religious experience, religious knowledge, and orthopraxis.

Generally, religiosity has been linked to the construct of morality since the dawn of civilization. According to McKay and Whitehouse (2015) the feeling of being watched by divine power can make someone more inclined to exercise prosocial behavior such as donation to humanitarian foundations. Shariff and Norenzayan (2007) also showed in their experiment that subjects allocated more money to anonymous strangers when the feeling of being watched by God is activated. The feeling of being watched by God is one part of the dimension of religious experience, where the subject feels that God is always with them. Feeling God in every aspect of someone's life should make them more hesitant of doing socially aversive behaviors as observable indicators of their personality.

Having core belief in higher power (e.g., God) should make someone think twice before acting out of the norms. Similar results should also be expected when someone does practice the commands of God on a daily basis. Further examination is necessary to find the relationship between having the knowledge of the religion and callous manipulation as knowledge can be employed as duplicitous tactics for personal gain.

3. Method

3.1 Sample

The sample of this study is Islamic-based university students in Indonesia that is currently actively enrolled (e.g., taking classes, doing thesis, etc) and have received training regarding basic values of Islam from their respective universities aged between 18–25 years old. The participants must be at least 18 years old, as it is agreed upon among social scientists as an age at which personality has matured. The participants of this study are 115 participants, which consists of 73 female participants and 42 male participants. Ethical considerations in this study include an informed consent form attached in the questionnaire, stating that they: are older than 18 years old, are currently enrolled in Islamic based universities, understand that participation is voluntary, understand that their data is private and will not be used to identify themselves.

3.2 Measurement Tools

All samples were acquired online using Google Forms, and to ensure the validity and reliability of the scales, both scales have been used in preliminary studies with 42 respondents and each subscale was validated with convergent validity.

3.2.1 Short Dark Triad Scale

This study utilized Short Dark Triad (Jones & Paulhus, 2014) that were translated and reconfigured to match Indonesian culture and conditions. Each subscale was correlated with ATCS (Attitude towards cheating scale) by Gardner and Melvin (1988). Machiavellian subscale has Cronbach's alpha of 0.793, narcissism has Cronbach's alpha of 0.751, lastly psychopathy subscale has 0,751 in Cronbach's alpha. The correlation coefficients with ATCS ranged between -0,524 up to -0,733.

3.2.2 Religiosity Scale

Religiosity was conducted with a translated version of religiosity scale by El-Menouar (2014). The approach to religiosity in this study is multidimensional and consists of five different dimensions: basic religiosity, central religious tasks, religious knowledge, religious experience, and orthopraxis. The cronbach's alpha coefficients for each subscale is ranging from 0,651 to 0,909, each subscale then correlated with single dimensional religiosity scale, with r (coefficient correlation) ranging from 0,517 to 0,801.

4. Results

All respondents who agreed to participate in this study were Muslims and were enrolled in Islamic-based universities or similar higher education learning. All participants' answers were recorded anonymously to protect the identity of respondents while also preventing socially desirable answers. As identification, each participant was given a unique code that consisted of letters and numbers of personal information. Detailed sociodemographic characteristics of participants are as follows:

Table 1. Sociodemographic Characteristics of Participants

Sociodemographic factors	**Sample**	
	n	**%**
Gender		
Female	73	63.5
Male	42	36.5
Science grouping		
Humanities and Social Sciences	81	70.43
Natural Sciences and Technology	34	29.51
Student Level		
Second Year	19	16.52
Third Year	21	18.26
Fourth Year	75	65.21

Note. N = 115.

After the data were collected, a Spearman's Rho correlation analysis was conducted. This analysis was chosen because the data failed to pass the normality and linearity tests.

Table 2. Correlation Table of Religiosity and The Dark Triad of Personality (N = 115)

Variable	M	SD	1	2	3	4	5	6	7	8
1. Basic Religiosity[a]	25.391	5,14	-							
2. Central Religious Tasks[a]	16.069	3,53	.564**	-						
3. Religious Knowledge[a]	5.139	1,69	.413**	.438**	-					
4. Religious Experience[a]	7.747	2,12	.302*	.158	.198*	-				
5. Orthopraxis[a]	8.982	2,81	.219*	.453**	.330**	.250**	-			
6. Psychopathy[b]	14.669	4,65	-.271**	-.374**	-.167	-.061	-.275**	-		
7. Narcissism[b]	24.443	5,05	-.062	-.142	-.177	-.097	-.170	.502**	-	
8. Machiavellianism[b]	25.217	6,08	-.172	-.232*	-.256**	-.058	-.289**	.713**	.449**	-

[a]Dimensions of Religiosity

[b]Individual construct of The Dark Triad of Personality
**p* .05. ***p* < .01.

5. Conclusion

Based on the correlation analysis with Spearman's Rho, we found that in general our hypothesis was confirmed; religiosity has a negative correlation with dark triad of personality. However, in a more detailed sense, we found a few additional intriguing findings. Religious experience, as one of the five dimensions of religiosity, does not correlate with any of the three constructs in the dark triad of personality (p = 0.152 – 0.269, r = -0.097 – -0.058). In addition to that, narcissism had no significant correlation with basic religiosity and central religious tasks (respectively, p = 0,255 r = -0,062; p = 0,065 r = -0,142). We also found that the strongest correlations are central religious tasks and psychopathy (p = 0,000, r = -0,374).

The result of this study is in line with Lowicki dan Zajenkowski (2015) which stated that religiosity in general is negatively associated with psychopathy and machiavellianism, but the result with narcissism is inconclusive. Kammerle et al., (2014) even stated that narcissism has a positive correlation with few sub dimensions of religious/spiritual well-being. In this study, the strength of the correlations can be considered as weak correlations (r = -0,167 – -0,289). It might be possible because religiosity does not directly correlate with antisocial personalities, but there are variables that moderate the relationship between the two. Lowicki and Zajenkowski (2015) formulated that empathy moderates the relationship between religiosity and the dark triad of personality. Meanwhile Ghorbani et al., (2017) stated that religiosity does not directly correlate with dark triad of personality but the attitude (*akhlak*) of a muslim and his tendency to protect harmonious relationship that correlates negatively with the dark triad of personality. Therefore, it can be concluded that religiosity does not correlate directly with aversive personalities constructs, but more in the sense of manifestation of religious attitudes.

According to descriptive data that we have collected, in general, our subjects in this study have a high level of religiosity. This shows that our subjects' religiosity is above average and are already religious, in which we believe that basic religious training that has already been arranged by islamic universities in Indonesia is beneficial to improve religiosity among university students. Religiosity has been associated with positive outputs such as low levels of aggression (Huesmann, Dubow, & Boxer, 2011) and high subjective well-being (Ellison, 1991). But in terms of antisocial personalities, religious training or debriefings should be more focused towards manifestations of religious attitudes such as empathy, loving and caring, and the tendency to be more harmonious. These attitudes are manifestations of *akhlaqul karimah* that may be a pillar towards Islam as *rahmatan lil'alamin*.

Meanwhile in the dark triad of personality constellations, in machiavellianism and narcissism we found out that our subjects have medium levels, and low levels of psychopathy. This result should be a discourse material for our islamic universities leaders, that there are moderate amounts of aversive personalities among their students. The dark triad of personality is often associated with negative attitudes towards social life such as high levels of aggression, tendency to malicious intents, even promotes radicalism in terrorism groups if paired with everyday sadism (Paulhus and Jones, 2011). In our tryout research, we found that the three constructs of the dark triad of personality correlates strongly with attitudes towards cheating, in which the higher the dark triad of personality's score, the more tolerant one is towards cheating.

This study has limitations, in which the most profound limitation is the inadequate subject pool. In Indonesia, college students who attend islamic based universities are a very large population, even though a huge portion of all college students. Other limitations such as lack of control variables that were present in the measurements trial may make the participants answer based on socially desirable answers, also other demographic factors such as socioeconomic status, ethnicities, allowance, among other things, were not included in this study.

6. References

Bloodgood, J. M., Turnley, W.H., & Mudrack, P. (2008). The Influence of Ethics Instruction, Religiosity, and Intelligence on Cheating Behavior. *Journal of Business Ethics*, *82*(3), 557–571

Chabrol H., Van Leeuwen, N., Rodgers R., & Séjourné, S. (2009). Contributions of Psychopathic, Narcissistic, Machiavellian, and Sadistic Personality traits to Juvenile Delinquency. *Personality and Individual Differences*. *47*(7), 734–739. doi: 10.1016/j.paid.2009.06.020

Christie, R. & Geis, F. (1970). *Studies In Machiavellianism.*: New York:Academic Press Inc

Cipto, H. (2012, 27 Maret) College Students Riots are Widespread in Makassar. *Kompas*. Accesed on 07 Maret 2017 in http://regional.kompas.com/read/2012/03/27/18133040/Rusuh.Demo.Mahasiswa.Tersebar.di.Makassar

Ellison, C. G. (1991). Religious Involvement and Subjective Well-Being. *Journal of Health and Social Behavior*, *32*(1), 80–99

El-Menouar, Y. (2014). The Five Dimensions of Muslim Religiosity: Results of An Empirical Study. *Journal of Methods, Data, and Analyses*, *8*(1), 53–78.

Feist, J. & Gregory J. Feist. (2008). *Theories of Personality*. New York: McGraw-Hill

Furnham, A., Richards, S. C., & Paulhus, D. L. (2013). The Dark Triad of personality: A 10 year review. *Social and personality psychology compass, 7*(3), 199–216.

Gardner, W. M., & Melvin, K. B. (1988). A scale for measuring attitude toward cheating. *Bulletin of the Psychonomic Society, 26*(5), 429–432.

Ghorbani, N., Watson, P., Zarei, A., & Chen, Z. (2017). Muslim attitudes and spirituality: relationships with Dark Triad and Harmony Control in Iranian teachers. *Mental Health, Religion & Culture*. 1–11. doi: 10.1080/13674676.2017.1320367.

Hare, R. D. (2001). *Violence and Psychopathy*. New York: Springer Science+ Business Media

Hodson G. M., Hogg, S. M., & MacInnis, C. C. (2009). The Role of "Dark Personalities" (Narcissism, Machiavellianism, Psychopathy), Big Five Personality Factors, and Ideology in Explaining Prejudice. *Journal of Research in Personality*. 43, 686–690. doi: 10.1016/j.jrp.2009.02.005

Huesmann, L. R., Dubow, E. F., & Boxer, P. (2011). The Effect of Religious Participation on Aggression Over One's Lifetime and Across Generations. In J. P. Forgas, A. W, Kruglanski, & K. D. Williams (Eds), *The Sydney Symposium of Social Psychology: Vol 13. The psychology of social conflict and aggression* (301–322). New York: Psychology Press.

Jones, D. & Paulhus, D. (2010). Different Provocations Trigger Aggression in Narcissists and Psychopaths. *Social Psychological and Personality Science. 1*. 12–18. 10.1177/1948550609347591.

Jones, D. N. & Paulhus, D. L. (2014). Introducing the Short Dark Triad (SD3): A brief measure of Dark Personality Traits. *Journal of Assessment. 21*(1), 28–41

Kämmerle, M., Unterrainer, H. F., Dahmen-Wassenberg, P., Fink, A., & Kapfhammer, H. P. (2014). Dimensions of religious/spiritual well-being and the dark triad of personality. *Psychopathology, 47*(5), 297–302.

Kowalski, R. M. (2001). *Behaving badly: Aversive behaviors in interpersonal relationships*. American Psychological Association.

Latifah, S.N. (2013, 22 Agustus). Writing and Plagiarism among College Students. Kompasiana.com. accessed on 07 Maret 2017 in http://www.kompasiana.com/sitilatifah/menulis-dan-plagiarism-di-kalangan-mahasiswa_5529d09df17e61282cd623b5

Lowicki, P. & Zajenkowski, M. (2015). No Empathy for People nor for God: The Relationship between The Dark Triad, Religiosity, and Empathy. *Personality and Individual Differences*.

McKay, R., & Whitehouse, H. (2015). Religion and morality. *Psychological bulletin, 141*(2), 447.

Norenzayan, A. (2014). Does religion make people moral?. *Behaviour, 151*(2–3), 365–384.

Norenzayan, A., & Shariff, A. F. (2008). The origin and evolution of religious prosociality. *science, 322*(5898), 58–62.

Paraschiva, P. & Nicoleta, M. (2011). Ways of Approaching Religiosity in Psychological Research. *The Journal of International Social Research. 4*(11), 352–362.

Paulhus, D. L. & Williams, K. M. (2002). The Dark Triad of Personality: Narcissism, Machiavellianism, and Psychopathy. *Journal of Research in Personality.* 36, 556–563.

Raskin, R., & Hall, C. S. (1981). The Narcissistic Personality Inventory: Alternative form reliability and further evidence of construct validity. *Journal of personality assessment, 45*(2), 159–162.

Rudiana, P. A. (2017, 28 Januari). 3 Dead Students in UII, Committee to Reveal Preparation Procedures. m.tempo.co. accessed on 20 April 2017 in https://m.tempo.co/read/news/2017/01/28/063840738/3-mahasiswa-uii-tewas-panitia-ungkap-prosedur-persiapannya

Saroglou, V. (2002). Religion and Five Factors of Personality: A meta-analytic review. *Personality and Individual Differences.* 32. 15–25

Shariff, A. F., & Norenzayan, A. (2007). God is watching you: Priming God concepts increases prosocial behavior in an anonymous economic game. *Psychological science, 18*(9), 803–809.

White, J., Joseph, S., & Neil, A. (1995). Religiosity, Psychoticism, and Schizotypal Traits. *Personality and Individual Differences, 19*(6). 847–851

Talitha Quratu Aini & Mira Aliza Rachmawati

Peer Social Support and Emotional Intelligence as Predictors in the Self-Adjustment of Non-Native High School Freshmen in Yogyakarta

Abstract: During adolescence development, a person experiences change not only in his/her cognitive, biological, and socio-emotional aspects, but also in school life. Transition in school life requires him/her to be able to perform good self-adjustment in a new school setting. This research examines the relationship between peer social support, emotional intelligence, and self-adjustment among non-native high school freshmen in Yogyakarta. Research respondents are 101 non-native high school freshmen in Yogyakarta, which comprise 61 male students and 40 female students. Research results indicate that both peer social support and emotional intelligence can act as predictors in the self-adjustment of non-native high school freshmen in Yogyakarta ($R = 0.500$, $R^2 = 0.250$, $p < 0.05$).

Keywords: peer social support, emotional intelligence, self-adjustment, students living away from homeland

1. Introduction

Adolescence is an important phase in a lifetime development, because in this period, an individual experiences transition from childhood to early adulthood. When entering adolescence, one will experience change in his/her biological, cognitive, and socio-emotional aspect, including in his/her school life. This notion is explicated by Santrock (2016), that an individual will experience transition at all educational levels, starting from elementary school, middle school, high school, to university, and ultimately at employment. When experiencing transition in middle school, an individual will experience more complex demands from the surroundings. Teenagers will interact more with their teachers and peers and join more communities and extracurricular activities.

Countless changes experienced by high school students require them to adjust to such conditions. Self-adjustment is defined as a mental and behavioral response in an individual to balance out needs and demands from the surroundings. Individual capability to adjust him/herself to the surroundings will help reduce pressure and personal frustration (Schneider, 1964).

Self-adjustment needs to be performed not only by students who stay in the same city to continue their study, but also by those who move to another city. As a matter of fact, countless freshmen who live away from their homeland experience difficulty in adjusting to their new surroundings, because they, who previously lived with their families, must move to another city to continue their study (Sitorus & Wiryosutomo, 2013). Devinta, Hidayah and Hendrastomo (2015) added that a person living away from his/her homeland will initially experience inconvenience towards the new surroundings, which may affect his/her physical and emotional state. This is a reaction to living in new surroundings, particularly where the culture is different.

Self-adjustment performed by high school freshmen is closely related to internal and external factors of the students, i.e., emotional intelligence and peer social support. Prior research by Cohen and Wilss (Kase, Endo & Oishi, 2016) indicated that stress among students in new surroundings can be relieved by the presence of peer social support. Research by Sasmitha and Rustika (2015) indicated that peer social support, particularly informational support, plays an important role in an individual's self-adjustment. The research found that informational support and discussion groups help college students to easily adjust themselves to campus environments.

Salovey (Salavera, et al., 2017) added that emotional skill is considered as capable of predicting whether a person can face daily life better and have better well-being. A study by Aritzeta, Balluerka, Gorostiaga, Arbiol, Haranburu and Gartzia (2016) indicated that in academic context, an individual's emotional intelligence is related to better psychological condition, social adaptation, and performance at school.

Thus, emotional intelligence and peer social support are expected to help students to achieve good self-adjustment at school. Based on the explanation above, the researcher will examine the relationship between peer social support, emotional intelligence, and self-adjustment among non-native high school freshmen in Yogyakarta.

2. Theoretical Review

Self-adjustment comprises adaptation behavior and capability to adjust oneself to the prevailing norms in the society and one's capability to manage his/her surroundings. Individual needs self-adjustment to meet personal necessities and to overcome tension, frustration, conflict, and demand from the surroundings (Schneider, 1964). There are seven aspects of self-adjustment by Schneider (1964), namely (a) control over excessive emotion, (b) minimum mechanism of self-defense, (c) low personal frustration, (d) rational reasoning and capability to self-direct, (e) learning capability, (f) capability to utilize the past, (g) being realistic and objective.

Self-adjustment may be influenced by internal and external factors. Schneider (1964) specified several internal factors influencing self-adjustment, namely: (a) individual's physical condition, (b) personal development and maturity, (c) psychological condition (past experience, learning result, self-determination, frustration condition and problem faced by an individual). Adeyemo (2005) added emotional intelligence as an internal factor also influencing self-adjustment. Low and Nelson (Ishak, Jdaitawi, Ibrahim & Mustafa, 2011) described that emotional intelligence is an important predictor of a student's self-adjustment during a transition period in school life. On the other hand, external factors influencing self-adjustment include: (a) family surroundings (Fatimah, 2006), (b) family surroundings (Ali & Asrori, 2010) and (c) society (Ali & Asrori, 2010).

Sarafino and Smith (2011) described peer social support as a support, which includes physical and psychological comfort, provided by a peer group to an individual. In adolescence, students are likely to interact more with their peers than with their family members. Hence, during the school transition period, support will be needed and received more from their peers than from family members (Papalia, Olds & Feldman, 2008). The presence of social support will help an individual to lessen the effect of stress and pressure he/she experiences. There are four aspects of peer social support according to Sarafino and Smith (2011), namely (a) instrumental support, (b) emotional support, (c) informational support and (d) appreciation support.

Emotional intelligence is defined by Mayer and Salovey (Salovey & Sluyter, 1997) as an individual's capability to feel and understand experienced emotions, as well as to manage and employ such emotions as the basis for daily behavior and reasoning. Individual capability to acknowledge feeling and manage emotion will lead him/her to understand others' emotion and help solving others' problems. There are four aspects of emotional intelligence according to Mayer and Salovey (Salovey & Sluyter, 1997), namely (a) self-awareness, (b) emotion regulation, (c) social skills, and (d) empathy.

3. Method

3.1 Research Subjects

This research involves high school freshmen who are non-native of the Province of Special Region of Yogyakarta (living away from their homelands). There are 101 subjects of this research, with 61 male students and 40 female students, in the age group of 15–17 years.

3.2 Measuring Instruments

3.2.1 Questionnaire 1

In this research, the scale of self-adjustment applied by the researchers is a scale constructed based on Schneider's theory (1964), comprising 29 items with reliability α= 0.864. This scale consists of 6 answer alternatives, ranging from "does not resemble me at all" to "greatly resembles me".

3.2.2 Questionnaire 2

In this research, the scale of peer social support applied by the researchers is a scale constructed based on Sarafino and Smith's theory (2011), comprising 11 items with reliability α= 0.830. This scale consists of 6 answer alternatives, ranging from "never" to "always".

3.2.3 Questionnaire 3

In this research, the scale of emotional intelligence applied by the researchers is a scale adapted from the emotional intelligence scale by Schutte (Schutte, et al., 1998). Aspects of the scale are based on emotional intelligence theory stated by (Mayer & Salovey, 1997). Emotional intelligence scale in this research consists of 27 items with reliability α= 0.935. This scale consists of 5 answer alternatives, ranging from "strongly agree" to "strongly disagree".

4. Results

This research is aimed at examining the variables of emotional intelligence and peer social support towards self-adjustment of non-native high school freshmen in Yogyakarta. Researchers are applying regression analysis based on the previous assumption test to examine the hypothesis of this research.

Table 1. Descriptive statistics and Correlations Among Study Variables

Variable	**n**	*M*	*SD*	**1**	**2**	**3**
1. Self-Adjustment	101	129.16	14.437	1		
2. Emotional Intelligence	101	105.07	8.629	.476*	1	
3. Peer Support	101	50.76	7.264	.199***	.098	1

* $p < .05$
*** $p < .001$

Table 2. Result of Regression Analysis

Variable	F	p	R	R^2
Emotional Intelligence, Peer support – Self Adjustment	16.331	0.000	.500	.250

Descriptive statistics comprises the number of research respondents, mean, deviation standard, and correlation among research variables in Table 1. Further, Table 2 indicates that both peer social support and emotional intelligence not only act as predictors of self-adjustment, but also effectively contribute 25 % to it.

5. Conclusion

This research result is in accordance with the research conducted by Salami (2011) that self-esteem, emotional intelligence, and stress contribute to self-adjustment in college freshmen. In addition, social factors, such as social support, contribute to self-adjustment in college freshmen. Students experiencing pressure will resolve academic, social, and emotional issues easier in the new surroundings with social support he/she received, both from parents and peers. Emotional intelligence also acts as a predictor in self-adjustment because one's ability to recognize, understand, express, and regulate emotions indicates the development of his/her emotion and intellect (Salami, 2011).

Students with good emotional intelligence have the capability required in self-adjustment in a new environment, such as self-acceptance, positive relationship with others, independence, ability to manage the surroundings, goal maturity, and self-growth (Adeyemo, 2005). Good emotional intelligence will help a person to build good relationships with others, because emotional intelligence includes the ability to identify and understand others' emotions (Mayer & Salovey, 1997). A research study conducted by Shashono and Slone (Putri, 2016) on early adolescents at the ages of 12–13 years in Israel concluded that the power of positive characters within individuals, such as the degree of gratefulness, emotional intelligence, optimism, and hope can influence self-adjustment. Such a factor is strengthened by interaction and social support received by the students.

It can be concluded from this research result that emotional intelligence and peer social support can act as predictors of self-adjustment success. This result is in accordance with the research by Nikooyeh, Zarani and Fathabadi (2017), that self-adjustment of students at school can be developed from their emotional intelligence. Good relationships with their teachers or peers can be built by means of their emotional intelligence, because such intelligence allows them to understand themselves better and to improve their emotion management. In addition, they can gain better social skills, which can prevent them from committing crime or other deviations. Hence, they will have good self-adjustment in their emotional, social, and academic aspects. The school can help the students in improving their self-adjustment capability by providing lessons of social-emotional skills, such as the capability to express emotion and to be empathetic to their peers and teachers, as well as interpersonal communication. The school can also develop a peer counseling program in order that the students provide support to each other, in forms of both informational and emotional support. It is expected from the program that they will become better students and be accepted in their social surroundings and the society.

In conducting this research, researchers acknowledge that there are several weaknesses in conducting this research. One of them is the lack of approach and supervision in data collection, causing some students to fill out the questionnaire carelessly. Furthermore, some statements in emotional intelligence scale are difficult to be understood, thus neutral answers are most likely to be selected by the students. Respondents' limitation in this research is also one of the weaknesses in this research.

A suggestion for succeeding researchers interested in self-adjustment variables is to consider other external factors affecting students' self-adjustment, such as family and school surroundings. In addition, it is suggested to include more respondents and schools, to have more diverse respondents. Prior to distributing the questionnaire, it is suggested that researchers conduct rapport building to the respondents. The researcher is also required to supervise and guide the respondents to avoid mistakes in filling out the questionnaire.

6. References

Adeyemo, D. A. (2005). The buffering effect of emotional intelligence on the adjustment of secondary school students in transition. *Electronic Journal of Research in Educational Psychology, 3*(2), 79–90.

Ali, M & Asrori, M. (2010). *Psikologi Remaja Perkembangan Peserta Didik.* Jakarta: Bumi Aksara.

Aritzeta, A., Balluerka, N., Gorostiaga, A., Arbiol, I. A., Haranburu, M. & Gartzia, L., (2016). Classroom emotional intelligence and its relationship with school performance. *European Journal of Education and Psychology,* 9, 1–8.

Devinta, M., Hidayah, N., & Hendrastomo, G. (2015). Fenomena *culture shock (gegar budaya)* pada mahasiswa perantauan di Yogyakarta. *Jurnal Pendidikan Sosiologi,* 1–16.

Fatimah, E. (2006). *Psikologi Perkembangan (Perkembangan Peserta Didik).* Bandung: CV. Pustaka Setia.

Ishak, N.A., Jdaitawi, M.T., Ibrahim, Y.S., & Mustafa, F.T. (2011). Moderating effect of gender and age on the relationship between emotional intelligence with social and academic adjustment among first year university students. *International Journal of Psychological Studies, 3*(1), 78–89.

Kase, T., Endo, S., & Oishi, K. (2016). Process linking social support to mental health through a sense of coherence in Japanese university students. *Mental Health & Prevention,* 1–6.

Mayer, J. D., & Salovey, P. (1997). What is emotional intelligence. *Emotional development and emotional intelligence: Educational implications, 3,* 31.

Nikooyeh, E., Zarani, F. & Fathabadi, J. (2017). The mediating role of social skills and sensation seeking in the relationship between trait emotional intelligence and school adjustment in adolescents. Journal of Adolescence 59, 45–50. November, 05, 2021. http://dx.doi.org/10.1016/j.adolescence.2017.05.012

Papalia, D. E., Olds, S. W. & Feldman, R.D. (2008). *Human Development: Perkembangan Manusia* (10th ed.). Jakarta: Salemba Humanika.

Putri, D. R. (2016). Peran dukungan sosial dan kecerdasan emosi terhadap kesejahteraan subjektif pada remaja awal [The role of social support and emotional intelligence on subjective well-being in early adolescence]. *Jurnal Indigenous, 1*(1), 12–22.

Salami, S. O. (2011). Psychosocial predictors of adjustment among first year college of education students. *US-China Education Review, 8*(2), 239–248.

Salavera, C., Usan, P., Chaverri, I., Gracia. N., Aure, P., & Delpueyo, M. (2017). Emotional intelligence and creativity in first- and second-year primary school children. *Procedia: Social and Behavioral Sciences*, 237, 1179–1183. doi: 10.1016/j.sbspro.2017.02.176.

Salovey, P & Sluyter, D. J. (1997). *Emotional development and emotional intelligence: educational implication.* USA: BasicBooks.

Santrock, J. W. (2016). *Adolescence* (16th ed.). New York: McGraw Hill.

Sarafino, E. P & Smith, T. W. (2011). *Health Psychology: Biopsychosocial Interactions* (7th ed). USA: John Wiley & Sons, Inc.

Sasmitha, I.A.G.H.D., & Rustika, I.M. (2015). Peran Efikasi Diri dan Dukungan Sosial Teman Sebaya Terhadap Penyesuaian Diri Mahasiswa Tahun Pertama Program Studi Pendidikan Dokter Fakultas Kedokteran Universitas Udayana [The Role of Self-Efficacy and Peer Social Support on the Adjustment of First

Year Students of the Medical Education Study Program, Faculty of Medicine, Udayana University]. *Jurnal Psikologi Udayana, 2*(2), 280–289.

Schneider, A, A. (1964). *Personal adjustment and mental health.* New York: Rinechart and Winston.

Schutte, N. S., Malouff, J.M., Hall, L. E., Haggert, D. J., Cooper, J. T., Golden, C. J., & Dornheim, L. (1998). Development and validation of measures of emotional intelligence. Personality and Individual Differences, 25, 167–177

Sitorus, L.I.S & Wiryosutomo, H. W. (2013). Perbedaan tingkat kemandirian dan penyesuaian diri mahasiswa perantauan suku Batak ditinjau dari jenis kelamin [Differences in the level of independence and adjustment of overseas Batak students in terms of gender]. *Character: Jurnal Penelitian Psikologi, 1*(2), 1–6.

www.ingramcontent.com/pod-product-compliance
Ingram Content Group UK Ltd.
Pitfield, Milton Keynes, MK11 3LW, UK
UKHW020713071026
15590UKWH00011B/591

9 783631 876039